Christianity and National Integration in Northeast India

Christian Heritage Rediscovered

The Series, as the name suggests, is meant to focus on Christian Faith & Living vis-à-vis topics like Literature & Poetry, Indigenous Philosophizing, Ethical response towards Agriculture, Health & Healing, Science & Technology, Eco-feminist Theology, Sociological approach towards Human Rights, Law & Politics, Arts, History of Ideas, Ancient Civilizations, Cultural Contiguity, Religious Cosmologies & Mysticism, Footsteps of famous Theologians, World Peace & Harmony, Global Capitalism, Network Marketing, Cybertheology, Population & Demographics, Epigraphic Studies, Contextualized Education, and many others. We welcome a Mss. on any topic/s mentioned, whether they are original works, scholarly monographs, collections of conference papers, revised dissertations, or translations of historical documents. Through the Series we, the Publishers, are striving to put forward published works that may help Institutions, Academic Bodies, Researchers, Scholars and the World at large in furthering their respective knowledge and understanding on the concerned subject. We welcome your comments on our efforts and further suggestions on how we can foster the upcoming thought provoking theologically grounded books.

Christian Heritage Rediscovered - 62

Christianity and National Integration in Northeast India

Its Role Among Tribes & Communities for Contributing Towards Cultural, Educational, Humanitarian and Peace Initiatives

O. L. Snaitang

Foreword by
David R. Syiemlieh
Chairman, UPSC, New Delhi

CWI
Christian World Imprints™

First Published in 2018 by

Christian World Imprints™
Christian Publishing & Books from India
H-12 Bali Nagar, **New Delhi-110015**
info@christianworldimprints.com
www.ChristianWorldImprints.com
Phone: +91 11 25465925

ISBN: 978-93-5148-260-4 (HB) ISBN: 978-93-5148-261-1 (PB)

Cataloging in Publication Data--DK
Courtesy: D.K. Agencies (P) Ltd. <docinfo@dkagencies.com>

Snaitang, O. L., 1952- **author.**
Christianity and national integration in Northeast India : its role among tribes & communities for contributing towards cultural, educational, humanitarian and peace initiatives / O.L. Snaitang ; foreword by David R. Syiemlieh.
pages cm. -- (Christian heritage rediscovered ; 62)
Includes bibliographical references.
ISBN 9789351482604 (HB)
ISBN 9789351482611 (PB)

1. Christianity--Social aspects--India, Northeastern. 2. Christianity and politics--India, Northeastern. 3. Missions--India, Northeastern. 4. India, Northeastern--Church history. 5. Tribes--India, Northeastern--Religion. I. Title. II. Series: Christian heritage rediscovered ; 62.

LCC BR1156.I4S63 2018 | DDC 275.41 23

Printed in India

Dedicated to my students, past and present, who after listening to my teachings on the History of Christianity of India have always put up a thought-provoking question, "What's about the history of Christianity in Northeast India?"

Contents

Foreword

I am honoured to have been requested by my teacher friend and scholar, Dr. O. L. Snaitang, to write this foreword for **Christianity and National Integration in Northeast India**.

Studies on Christian missions in North East India and their work among the numerous tribes and communities in the region has become a popular theme for social scientist. Historians in particular have worked on this study for long. The first studies were authored by missionaries themselves and largely published for their own supporters, benefactors and agencies. Historians continue to depend on such mission accounts. A theme that has been attracting the attention of scholars in recent years is the extent those tribes and communities that have accepted and pursue the Christian faith have integrated with the larger populace. Standing out as distinct tribal groups, several were involved is asserting their distinct tribal and political positions. The result was conflict, which happily is on the wane. And because these tribes are Christians, their aspirations have been critiqued as counter to the narrative on integration. There were many other smaller groups which have had much more smooth transition. Their histories require be told and brought into the larger histories of the region. Over these years and more so after independence to refer to a date, the churches have grown.

Christianity has become the preferred faith, a desire that should not be grudged by them.

The research of Dr. O.L. Snaitang is an effort to understand the role of Christianity in national integration and nation building. Whereas Christianity is a faith observed by large numbers in India, it was and continues in some sense to be looked upon in the region from the perspective of western Christianity. Snaitang's study traces the beginnings of this history from the earliest efforts of Christian missionaries, the peoples' response, and brings this narrative to more recent times. Incorporated in the text are the contributions made by the churches to education and literature, medical service, other humanitarian services and peace initiatives. The role played by the indigenous leaders in the continued grown of the churches in what may be considered the second phase of this development is another focus. Backed by impressive primary and secondary sources, the scholarship and interpretation of the author, **Christianity and National Integration in Northeast India** will add to our understanding of North East India.

David R. Syiemlieh

18 June 2017 New Delhi

Acknowledgement

Ever since I began my quest on the status and role of Christianity among the tribes in the country I found that Christianity being a universal religion is an integral part of India's history. Northeast India being a region on the extreme corner of India is a complex and complicated region for the presence of numerous fragmented groups of people with diverse cultural aspects, uncommon religious traditions, unintelligible languages and dialects, independent kingdoms and different ways of life. However, it was somehow brought together to a common sharing of political identity with the larger Indian union. Though outside agencies of change and people's interests had contributed to the evolution of a modern Northeast India it is my vision, passion and compassion to look at the role that Christianity had made in shaping the destiny of the region. Engaging oneself in such a gigantic task is not that easy. The farsighted academic vision and magnanimous spirit of the Indian Council of Historical Research, New Delhi that had extended its helping hand on those that deserved not to get even a glimpse of recognition but granted a Senior Fellowship award in the pursuit of this project remained historic in that sense and a boon to the integrity of an inclusive and broad based research in the country. But for its help in this respect, I would not have expected to have seen such academic inquiry in completion.

Therefore, I do hereby acknowledge my deep sense of thanks and gratitude to the Indian Council of Historical Research (ICHR), New Delhi for the needed financial assistance in pursuing the Project. Although the ICHR was the main funding agency for this research project, it is nevertheless not responsible for the views or opinions expressed in the book. I alone am responsible for opinions, statements and expressions and for any observation in it.

The work would not have been a success but for Dr. C. J. Thomas, Associate Director, ICSSR – NERC, NEHU Campus, Shillong, Prof. Dr. L. S. Gassah, its Honorary Director who have accepted my request to have its Centre as an institution of affiliation. Though their help have contributed to the completion of the project they too take no responsibility for my statements, arguments and conclusions expressed in it.

Prof. Dr. David R. Syiemlieh, a world renowned historian and an acclaimed authority on a Northeast India subject, has been the main source of encouragement right from the beginning of my research till the completion of the work. Given his busy schedule in his alma mater the North Eastern Hill University in both academic and administrative leadership, then as Vice-Chancellor, Rajiv Gandhi University, Arunachal Pradesh later and currently the Chairman, UPSC, New Delhi he was still able to spare his precious time, patiently attended to my work and helped me in almost every stage of my writing. I am greatly indebted to him for all his academic guidance, assistance and more importantly for his well conceived Foreword. Under no circumstances, however, should Prof. Syiemlieh be responsible for the style, expressions, views and statements made by me in the book.

My acknowledgement will not be complete unless I place on record my thanks to the following for granting me permission to publish my articles that have already been published in their publications as under:

First, my article titled "Christian Medical Mission in North-East India" published in **Man and Society: A Journal of North-East Studies**, Vol. VII, Winter 2010, pp. 71 – 85 is reproduced in this book with the permission from the ICSSR – NERC, Shillong.

Second, another write up "An Exploration of Dimensional Perspectives of Devils and Evil Designs among the Khasi-Jaintia People of Meghalaya" originally published in **Construction of Evil in North East India: Myth, Narrative and Discourse**, Copyright 2012 © Prasenjit Biswas & C. Joshua Thomas, pp. 157 – 171, All rights reserved, has been reproduced with the permission of the Copyright holders and the publishers, Sage Publications Pvt. Ltd., New Delhi.

I record my deep sense of gratitude to the Manager of the Christian World Imprints, New Delhi for accepting my request to publish the book in the larger interests of the reading public in the country, scholars and researchers, social workers and those who share responsibility in building the country.

Last but not the least, my thanks go to my wife and children who have stood by me despite my being away from them during periods of my research and writing of the book. My God who has given me the strength even in the midst of trials, despair and discouragement is always my guiding force for what is best, beautiful and constructive for the general welfare of humankind in Northeast India and the nation at large.

My thanks and gratitude go to all those who have helped me in all the stages of the preparation of the project and although I was trying to name each one by name in my acknowledgement note I found that the list is too long. I beg your indulgence.

Comments and suggestions are welcomed so that improvement might well be taken up for its next edition.

Kench's Trace
Shillong 793004
12th June, 2017

Dr. O. L. Snaitang
olsnaitangrevdr@yahoo.in

Chapter 1

Introduction

I. Aim and Rationale

Northeast India is an integral part of India and the larger history of Christianity in India too is traced to the arrival of St. Thomas in the first century itself. Christianity is a Middle East Asian religion but has come and worked in Northeast India through the services of Western Missions and missionaries for over two centuries. It has secured its foothold in Mizoram, Nagaland, Meghalaya and Manipur. Its presence in Tripura, Assam and Arunachal Pradesh is rather negligible. Christianity has contributed to the people in the region through the introduction of standard language in communities that witnessed dialectical fragmentation, indigenous literature, education, medical service, humanitarian works and church planting. These activities although carried with far evangelistic objectives have in the process contributed to a sense of tribal unity and national consciousness. The objective of this study is to trace the extent into which Christianity has played in national integration and nation building in Northeast India in the nineteenth and twentieth centuries. Some of the reasons why this investigation is proposed may well be explained as under.

In view of the fact that there has been a large concentration of Christianity in most hill areas and that these are within the constitutional enclosure of India, it is important and necessary to examine it in-depth for clearer understanding of its presence and role in relation to the nation and it may in turn bring about self-awareness and realization. The study may also serve as a corrective measure to any wrong conception. This subject has, however, not received sufficient scholarly attention. For long historians of Christianity and other social scholars have centered their studies on the several missions and churches and that even to the neglect of their being an integral part of India's cultural history.

Those who have attempted to study on Christianity in Northeast India have mostly left out the question of national integration and nation building – the subject that is intended to be studied. For instance Frederick S. Downs' books **Christianity in North East India: Historical Perspectives** (1983) and **History of Christianity in India: Vol. V Part 5: North East India in the Nineteenth and Twentieth Centuries**

(1992), J. Puthenpurakal's **Baptist Missions in Nagaland** (1984), K. I. Aier's **The Growth of the Baptist Churches in Meghalaya** (1978) and many others are at least products of scholarly research. They have given detailed information on the beginnings, growth and development of Christianity in the region and may have served as important sources of study about its history and activities in Northeast India. However, while the above publications might have presented comprehensive descriptions at least on the positive role of Christianity among the people in North East India, their passing over on the question of Indian national integration and nation building in the nineteenth and twentieth centuries has left a chasm that requires fresh academic attention. Why have most previous studies on a Northeast India Christian subject not given serious attention to national relations and concern? While a study on this aspect is in the process, I assume that external indoctrination or lack of wider academic exposure could have contributed toward creating this lacuna.

My proposed study is, therefore, related to the importance of national unity and development and Christianity is fused in union with the nation. In this attempt one has to adopt a new methodological paradigm reversing the traditional mindset of studying Christianity in the region from the perspective of Western Christianity. Its starting point will be from the perspective of the people and inclusive national consciousness. Northeast Indian people were originally active participants in the larger process of India's national development and the change in the modern period becomes an important subject for serious academic inquiry.

II. Nature and Scope

An explanation of the nature and scope of the proposed research is necessary and important. The first will be in reference to the definition of the terms 'Christianity', 'National Integration' and 'National Building.' The term 'Christianity' is used here to mean a religion of Western origin that sought following through preaching the faith in Jesus Christ and starting of several development activities. It represents churches of Catholic and Protestant persuasions and includes both Western missionaries and native converts.

'National Integration' is a loaded term but will be used in this study in a flexible way. It pertains to developing a sense of belonging, commitment, acceptance and participation in strengthening the country for peace and communal harmony. It also refers to espousing a spirit of respect and coexistence. 'Nation Building' is closely related to the term national integration but has reference to active involvement and service to the people irrespective of caste, creed or color for unity, liberty and equality.

This study is therefore a search for understanding of the role that Christianity has made in relation to national consciousness and development. The framework in which this project is going to be written will be in the context of India's history. It will therefore cover a long period beginning with the pre-colonial period up to the present. I will choose to set the subject in the national context primarily because of its being an integral part in it. Since hill tribal Christians were Indians before they change their faith to Christianity and as the development that led to the introduction of Christianity was of recent past, the proposed research will begin first with a chapter on a Northeast India in the pre-British colonial history. Secondly, the examination will be on the cultural consequences following the arrival of British colonialism and the third stage will look into the origin, growth and development of Christianity and its impact on the people and their perception on India's national unity and integrity. An examination on Christianity and National Integration will be taken up as a fourth dimension. In these chapters, the main thrusts will be towards an integrative national history and may well be elaborated further as follows:-

1. Northeast India in the Pre-Nineteenth Century: Further explanation in regard to the question why I propose to look at the subject from the national historical background is also relevant. Formerly known as Assam, Northeast India is an integral part of India. As of today, the region includes the seven sister states of Assam, Nagaland, Meghalaya, Mizoram, Manipur, Tripura, Arunachal Pradesh and a newly added sibling Sikkim. It is a region of natural beauty that remained isolated for a long period of time. Neighboring countries like Nepal, Tibet, Bhutan, China, Myanmar and Bangladesh encircle the entire geographical region except a narrow land passage through Srirampur pass on the west. Its international boundary line starts from the west of Sikkim and encompasses the region until it touches a portion of land that connects Assam and West Bengal. While Nepal and Tibet share most of the boundary line on the northwest, China and Myanmar cover the entire northern and eastern border. Bangladesh bounds the southern portion and part of the region's northwest. The Srirampur doorway is the only life line by road and rail connecting pass in the region with the rest of the country.

2. British Administration and Its Impact on the People: Though Northeast Indian people were before the advent of the British in the early 19th century passed through periods of isolation, illiteracy, fragmentation and lack of communication, they were nevertheless people who were advanced in their own world. They could survive even in the midst of hardships. They were people who knew how to engage in agriculture, farming, handicrafts and care of the mother earth. Their social system based on clan code and kinship relations was by no means backward. Tribal political structure opened ways for people's collective participation and carried significant democratic elements in administration.

The British came at the time when it had already established its position and rule in the larger Indian union. Their nearest station was Sylhet in the present day Bangladesh. Their entry into the Northeastern region was in response to an invitation from the people who wanted to force out the dominant and unpleasant rule by the Burmese in most parts of the region. The British, who after annexing the region, extended its rule and brought the hill and plain areas under its control under the unified India. Their presence brought significant change upon the culture of the people and had affected mostly on their communication, polity, modern administrative set up and in their life style.

3. Development of Christianity in Northeast India: Given the examination of this aspect from a comprehensive approach, this part will touch upon history of Christianity in three perspectives, viz., the early presence and contact of Christianity, Western Christian Missions and Indigenous Christianity. These ecclesiastical changes are treated in the light of their historical development. The first Christian contact with the people in Northeast India was historically significant but remained temporary. Their main presence was in terms of employment under Mughal imperial rule and they were not missionaries.

Permanent Christian missions that have come and worked in the region began with the coming of the American Baptist Mission in 1836. Others that have followed included the Welsh Calvinistic Methodist Foreign Mission (1841), Anglican Mission (1876), the Catholic Mission (1890) and Baptist Missionary Society (1894). These missions have contributed to the region through language and literature, education, medical service and other humanitarian works but their differences appeared to have divided the people on denominational line.

Indigenous Churches that have come up from the native converts have added to the complexity of Christian churches especially in hill areas. Though these indigenous groups have carried out the work in almost similar fashion with the established Western churches they too added further divisive elements in the community. It is these divisions that tended to shatter people's integrative mind.

4. Christianity and National Integration: This stage will examine the role of Christianity in national integration and nation building. This dimension will be understood only when an in-depth study is made on the contribution of language and literature, educational institutions, healthcare and humanitarian activities, ecclesiastical structures, change in worldview and life style.

Although one could go on explaining the positive impact and contribution of Christianity to the people in Northeast India, however that attempt will by no means complete unless the negative aspect of Christianity is given adequate attention. This fourth perspective is therefore advanced with appropriate survey of the drawbacks of Christian presence and role among the people especially in the hill areas.

III. Previous Research: An Annotated Bibliographical Note

Given the availability of a variety of government and non-government sources, the growing rise of relevant publications on a Northeast India subject may be classified and noted as under:

1. Studies from a Western Mission Perspective: Most early publications on the region were product of studies that had come from a Western mission perspective. John Hughes Morris, **The History of the Welsh Calvinistic**

Methodist Foreign Mission to the End of the Year 1904 (1910); C. Becker, **History of the Catholic Mission in Northeast India 1890-1915** (1923); Victor H. Sword, **Baptist in Assam: A Century of Missionary Services 1836-1936** (1935) and others are examples of such studies. They were histories of denominational missions and written from the perspectives of their particular mission interests and for a western readership in their mission constituencies. The drawbacks of such works were such that hardly did they show positive concerns for India's national interests.

2. Positive Impact of Christianity: There are several publications that came out highly in favour of the positive contribution of Christianity to the people. Some of such included Nalini Natarajan, **The Missionary among the Khasis** (1977); Frederick S. Downs, **Christianity in North East India: Historical Perspectives** (1983) and others. While there could have been certain elements of truth in their positive conclusions, their works however lacked addresses to the importance of adhering to India's national identity and integrity.

3. Studies from National Perspectives: Some scholars who have carefully studied Christian movements in India in general and the Northeast in particular from the people's cultural background appeared to have shown dissatisfaction with the way that Christian Missions have played among the hill people in the region. For instance, H. L. Deb Roy, **A Tribe in Transition: The Jaintias of Meghalaya** (1981); B. P. Sukhla, **What Ails India's Northeast?** (1980); Arun Shourie, **Missionaries in India** (1994) and others who because of their commitment to the nation and indigenous culture, tended to discover that Christianity has ignored encouraging national feeling and interest among its native converts. Though such conclusions are important they however required further investigation through rereading of the sources and evaluating the people in whom Christianity has strongly secured its foothold.

4. Regional Political Studies: Many outstanding scholars have carried out serious studies and researches on the political history in Northeast India. Some of such included H. K. Barpujari, et al., eds., **Political History of Assam 1826-1919** Vol. I (1977); K. K. Bhattacharjee, **Northeast India: Political and Administrative History** (1983); S. Chaube**, Hill Politics in Northeast India** (1973); V. Venkata Rao, **A Century of Tribal Politics in North East India 1874-1974** (1976); David R. Syiemlieh, **British Administration in Meghalaya: Policy and Pattern** (1989); B. Datta Ray & S. P. Agarwal, eds., **Reorganization of North East India Since 1947** (1996), etc. These and several other studies have given serious study to various aspects of political histories and changes but they appeared to have not touched upon the role and participation of Christianity in the process.

IV. Integration of Structure

An understanding of the presence and role of Christianity in Northeast India would not be complete unless there is a survey of several aspects of its historical and cultural background and the interaction with the British Administration in the early 19th century. Chapter Two brings out a broad and comprehensive description of the region's geographical situation, people's groups, aspects of social discrimination and the presence of numerous languages and dialects that hindered people's communication and unity.

The arrival of the British Administration in the early 19th century is well regarded historic for it being an agency that brought about significant major change among the peoples in the region and this is taken up in Chapter Three. One of the major cultural consequences that had happened among the different groups of people in both the hills and plain areas was that the new political power was able to bring all these different groups, kingdoms and areas under a single political and administrative authority. Changes brought about by the British in the early 19th century had contributed to ushering of a modern period in the history of Northeast India.

Chapter Four traces the early Christian contacts with the people from 1627 to 1838. Though early missionaries and mission society had made initial visits and attempts to spread the faith among the people in the region but with an exception of the Catholic settlement at Mariamnagar in Tripura, the rest did not survive in the field except in some recorded human memory.

Western Christian Missions like the American Baptist Mission (1836), the Welsh Presbyterian Mission (1841), the Anglican Mission (1876), the Catholic Mission (1890) and the Baptist Missionary Society (1894) that have come and entered upon periods of stability and permanence are treated in Chapter Five. It provided comprehensive historical information of their origins and growth among the people in the region.

A separate treatment on the rise of independent Christian movements and churches – being the outgrowth of Western Christian Missions and Christianity has been mentioned and described in Chapter Six. Most of these indigenous movements have come up and appeared productive mainly in Mizoram, Manipur, Nagaland and Meghalaya.

Chapter Seven devotes to the contribution of Christianity to nation building and national integration. This Chapter included two major sections. First, it deals with the areas of Christian contribution and the second section makes a critical assessment of Christian presence and role among the people in Northeast India.

Chapter 2

Northeast India in Traditional Historical Perspectives

I. Introduction to Geographical Identity of States

Northeast India was originally a fragmented region. Polity, ethnicity, religion and language which should have unified the people together to a single cultural unity have however become determining factors for difference. It was the British power that had brought these disconnected regions and people to a solidified political unity. After subduing most of the resistant movements in the region, the British had placed them under one administrative control. In the absence of a common nomenclature, the new administration had chosen to call it by the name Assam. The policy was more for political administrative convenience and never was it implied stripping off of the indigenous people's political rights in both the hills and plain areas. The new political power made the united Assam an integral part of India. However, after India's independence, the region witnessed the rise of seven sisters, viz., Assam, Nagaland, Mizoram, Arunachal Pradesh, Tripura Meghalaya[1] and one son, i. e., Sikkim.[2] These emerging states in the region are for the present commonly referred to as Northeast India.

Northeast India is the only region that was mostly encircled by foreign imperial powers like Nepal, Bhuttan, China, Myanmar and Bangladesh. Though the region is an integral part of India, its geographical connection with it, however,

[1] For recent and relevant studies on this political development, See H. K. Barpujari, et al., eds., *Political History of Assam 1826-1919* Vol. I (1977); K. K. Bhattacharjee, *Northeast India: Political and Administrative History* (1983); S. Chaube, *Hill Politics in North East India* (1973); V. Venkata Rao, *A Century of Tribal Politics in North East India 1874 – 1974* (1976); David R. Syiemlieh, *British Administration in Meghalaya: Policy and Pattern* (1989); B. Datta Ray & S. P. Agarwal, eds., *Reorganization of North East India Since* 1947 (1996).

[2] Information about the Sikkim and its integration with India, read Basnet, L. B. **Sikkim: A Short Political History** (1974); Kapadia, H. **Across Peaks and Passes in Darjeeling and Sikkim** (2001); Lama, M. P. **Sikkim** (1994); Rao, P. R. **Sikkim: The Story of its Integration with India** (1978).

is through a narrow land opening strip bounded by Bhutan on the northern portion and Bangladesh on the south.

The region may be broadly classified into two divisions, viz, the Assam region and the hill areas.[3]

1. Geographical Identity of Assam: Assam is the main state in the region and serves as a gate way to most of the states in Northeast India. Areas that fall within its administrative jurisdiction are the Brahmaputra valley, Barak valley and the hill regions.[4] The plain areas like the Brahmaputra and Barak are so far the natural rich areas in agricultural products, pastoral and farming, in oil and natural gas resources. While majority of those who have inhabited the Brahmaputra valley are the Assamese, Ahoms, Boros, Mishings, Adivasis, Rabhas and others those who lived in the Barak valley are Khasi-Jaintias, Dimasas, a significant concentration of Bangla speaking community and many others.

The hill districts of Assam included mostly the North Cachar hills and the Karbi Anglong district. The North Cachar hill region is in one way a mini Northeast in a sense that most tribes in the region have lived and settled in it as indigenous peoples.

2. Nature of Geographical Condition of Hill States: The other region comprises of the remaining states like Arunachal Pradesh, Nagaland, Manipur, Mizoram, Tripura, Meghalaya and Sikkim.[5] These states and districts are not fully connected with each other. For instance, though Meghalaya area is connected with Karbi Anglong and North Cachar hills, it is away from Arunachal Pradesh, Nagaland, Manipur and other hill states. These hill areas were once sparsely populated. Natural vegetations, thick forests and grasses covered these areas. There were several rivers, waterfalls, deep gorges, rocky cliffs and precipices beside blue hills and mountains. Hill areas were also habitat of ferocious animals, snakes or pythons, birds and vultures. Malaria infected mosquitoes and insects took

---

[3] Cf. Allen, B. C. **Gazetteer of the Khasi and Jaintia Hills, Garo Hills Lushai Hills** (1905/1980); **North and North-Eastern Frontier Tribes of India** (Reprinted, 1983). Originally published 1907 as Vol. IV of "Frontier and Overseas Expeditions from India"; Pemberton R. **Report on the Eastern Frontier of British India** (1835/1966); Barpujari, H. K. **Problem of the Hill Tribes North East Frontier, 1822-42** (1970), **Problem of the Hill Tribes North East Frontier, 1843-72** (1970); Chakravorty, B. C. **British Relations with the Hill Tribes of Assam since 1858** (1981)., Singh, K. Suresh ed., **Tribal Movements in India**, Vol. I (1982).

[4] For more information, read Allen, B. C. Gait, E. A. Allen, C. G. H. Howard H. F. **Gazetteer of Bengal and North East India** (1905/1979); **Report on the Administration of Assam (1890); Report on the Administration of Assam** (Calcutta, Foreign Department Press, 1890); Acharyya, N. N. **A Brief History of Assam: From Earliest Time to the year 1983** (1987); Barpujari, H. K., S. K. Barpujari, A. C. Bhuyan, eds., **Political History of Assam, 1825-1919,** Vol. I (1977); Bhuyan, A. C. & S. De, eds, **Political History of Assam, 1920-1939**, Vol. 2 (1970); Bhuyan, A. C. & S. De, eds, **Political History of Assam, 1940-47**, Vol. 3 (1980).

[5] Dube, S. C. ed., **Tribal Heritage of India** Vol. 1, **Ethnicity, Identity and Interaction** (1977); Karotemprel, S. ed., **The Tribes of North East India** (1984); Singh, K. Suresh ed., **Tribal Situation in India** (1972).

control of most of the hills and valleys. More importantly was the presence of natural spirits, demons and jungle creatures that stood on the way for unity and communication. When we take all these together, there was no closer connection in the hill areas among numerous tribes and sub – tribes who mostly confined to villages and in the forests.

II. An Overview of People's Composition in Northeast India

We have described the geographical location and condition of the plain and the hill areas. The region witnessed the presence of different people, ethnic groups and their varying composition. We will take up this aspect by looking at the situation in each state and try to provide introductory background information only.

1. Ethnic People's Groups of Assam:[6] Assam inherits the fertile plain areas and is the most productive state in Northeast India. It is also rich in oil production and tea industry. Assamese, Bengalis, Boros, Karbis are the largest communities in the state. Other indigenous communities who inhabit the state include the Mishings, Khasis, Kacharis, Ahoms, Dimasas, Tiwas, Hajongs, Deoris, Adivasis, Rabhas, Garos, Pnars, Rajbongsis, Takams, Nepalis and others. Though Christian Churches have carried out missionary activities in the state since the early part of the nineteenth century, their presence is highly negligible maintaining an almost stagnant average of a little over of 2%. The Assamese who were the main inhabitants of the state belonged to the larger Sanskritic family and linguistically akin to Bengali and Oryia.

The Boro group of the people who belonged to the Tibeto – Burman descent lived mostly in lower Assam and North Bank of the Brahmaputra river.[7] Their ethnic affinity was more with the Rabhas, Garos and Borok or Twipra people. Boro population is found in Kokrajhar, Goalpara, Darrang, Sonitpur, North Lakhimpur, Dhemaji and even in Karbi Anglong district. Though most of them could understand and speak Assamese, they however have their own Boro language. Their life style, social structure, polity and religion were different from the Assamese at least in the past and other tribal groups alike.

Rajbongsi[8] people, who believed to have shared common origin with the Boros, are other significant groups of people in Assam. Their concentration is mainly in lower Assam in Dhubri district and in West Bengal. Many of them

---

[6] See Cunningham, J. R. DPI of Assam, "Letter of dated 2.11.25" 6443/1; Dihingia, Hameshwar **Assam's Struggles against British Rule, 1820-1863,** (1980); Gait, Edward **A History of Assam** (1905/1981); Hunter W. W. **A Statistical Account of Assam**, Vol. 2 (1879/1975); Lahiri, R. M. **The Annexation of Assam, 1824-1854** (1975); Marbaniang, Iscot **Assam in Nutshell** (1970); **Provincial Gazetteer of Assam**, (1906/1983); Pugh, F. M. **Ka History Jong Ka Assam** (1963/ 1975); Robinson, William **A Descriptive Account of Assam** (1841/ 1975).

[7] Cf. Devi, Premalata **Social and Religious Institutions of Bodos** (1998); Sen, Sipra **Tribes and Castes of Assam** (1999), pp. 125-128.

[8] See Sen, Sipra **Tribes and Castes of Assam**, p. 156.

have become sanskritized and gradually were assimilated and absorbed into the faith of Hinduistic persuasion. Though there was blood relation with the Boros, they were nevertheless maintaining a separate identity. That solidified identity was however not strong as in their gradual movement they began to have become diversified into Chhotabhag and Barabhag. These two groups began to develop their own distinctive dialects. The Rajbongsis were in most instances also known as Koches.

The Takam Mishing[9] people are another significant group of inhabitants and citizens of Assam. Though these people might have originally come from the eastern side of the country but after settling down in Assam they developed their own cultural ways of life and practices and became bonafide indigenous inhabitants. Though one could trace and observe certain elements of cultural difference but their common language and social norms have unified them to a common sense of identity. Though they were progressive in terms of occupation, agriculture, farming and economic dealings they were less exposed to higher education and so illiteracy was one of their problems at least in the recent past. The Takam Mishing group is concentrated in Upper Assam but spread over North Lakhimpur, Dhemaji, Tinsukia, Dibrugargh, Sonitpur, Sibsagar, Jorhat, Golaghat districts and Majuli area.

Another prominent people's group of Assam is the Karbis.[10] Originally these people were one but the exigencies of work and exposure have led to some form of separate identities. Most of them inhabited the present Karbi Anglong district. Though it is believed that they might have migrated from China and passed through Myanmar, they were nevertheless the first inhabitants in their present settled area. The Karbis too have their own dialects and language and maintained their own traditional democratic way of administration.

The other group known as Amri Karbi who because of their settlement in the plain areas of Kamrup and Nagaon districts and by a mere insignificant difference in language and way of life, tended to see themselves as distinctively away from the larger Karbi community and identified as Amri Karbi. Like the Karbi in Karbi Anglong, the Amri Karbis too were greatly influenced by Hinduism. Like most tribal groups in the region, Karbi people though are unified people but were susceptible to any ethnic differentiation.

The Deori group of people who are residing in scattered places over North Lakhimpur, Darrang, Dibrugargh, Dhemaji, Tinsukia and Sibsagar are other communities of Assam. Originally hailed from Lohit district of Arunachal Pradesh, the Deoris preferred to be called Gemasaya. The four main sub – groups, viz. Tengapaniya, Borgonya, Dibongiya and Patorgonya contributed to the composite

---

[9] For information about the Mishings- their history and culture, Cf. Kuli, J. J. ed., **The Misings: Their History and Culture** (1998); Pegu, Nomal **The Mishings of the Brahmaputra Valley** (1981).

[10] Cf. Sen, Sipra *op. cit.*, p. 140.

Deori or Gemasaya ethnic group. Deori too shares much in common with the Idu Mishmi of Arunachal Pradesh. Their constant contact with the Assamese and people of Sanskritic origins had greatly affected their belief system and way of life. Though they could converse in Assamese language, they however possessed their own language and religion.

Like the Bodos, the Rabhas[11] have successfully developed into a separate group and their settlement in Assam was mainly in Goalpara, Kamrup and Darrang districts. They are also found in Cooch Bihar area and Jalpaiguri district of West Bengal. Though the Rabhas could be traced to the larger Bodo family, they are but a distinct group linguistically, religiously and socially. Most Rabhas appeared to have adopted the culture of their Assamese neighbours including adopting of personal names and clan identities.

The Dimasa Kachari group of people stands among the important list of indigenous communities in the state. They too are generally classified under the larger Bodo group. However, following their adoption of a rather different language from the Bodo family, their distinctive identity was over a period of time well acknowledged. The Dimasa Kachari people are presently confined to Karbi Anglong and North Cachar hills districts of Assam. They were a kind of people who could not resist major influence and cultural pressure from other communities especially those from other Sanskritic dominant groups.

The Lalung group whose settlement is now spread over several parts of Kamrup, Nagaon, Karbi Anglong, Lakhimpur and Sibsagar districts is another ethnic community in Assam. Though the name Lalung was a most commonly known name in the past, the Lalung people did not like it because of being an outside imposition. Their preferred name, which has been officially accepted, is Tiwa.[12] Their ancestry is traced to the Tibeto – Burman group. They too have their own language, religion and maintained a rather flexible social pattern.

The Barak Valley, which is a major and integral part of Assam, witnessed substantive concentration of Bengali population. Most of them appeared to have migrated from Bangladesh. That was not the only area of their settlement. Their spread was well traced in Nagaon, Dhubri, Barpeta and Goalpara districts in addition to Karimganj, Hailakandi and Cachar districts. Though the Bengalis and the Assamese shared much of cultural similarities but the intensity of their difference is deeper than their cultural commonality.

Another formidable group of people that had changed the traditional indigenous demographic population was the arrival of the Santhals, Oroans, Mundaris, Soaras, Kharias and others from Orissa, Bihar and Jharkhand, in the 19th century.[13] They have come as part of the labour force in the introduction of

---

[11] See Raha, Manis Kumar **Matriliny and Patriliny: A Study of the Rabha Society** (1989).

[12] See Sen, Sipra *op. cit.*, pp. 136-140.

[13] Read Karotemprel, S. & B. Dutta Roy, eds., **Tea Garden Labourers of North East India** (1990).

tea gardens, factories and industries in Assam. Their total population is estimated to have been more than 7 million. These people were well verse in Hindi but maintained their own local dialects.

Nepali population is also increasing in Assam. They too have begun to enter into the region mostly during the British period but kept the tempo of coming especially after 1947 for employment and settlement. Their main occupation was in providing the needed labour force in markets in addition to pastoral, farming and agriculture. They also formed an important segment in army and security. Though they do not seem to have concentrated in one location but their presence was scattered in different regions of the state.

2. Nagaland and Naga Ethnic Identities:[14] Nagaland is a state of both the hill and plain areas that has by the recent past witnessed the presence of majority of Christian population. Forests and natural vegetation cover the entire state in addition to the flow of beautiful rivers and waterfalls. There were more than 20 tribes in the state whose cultural differences were evident in political administration, social norms, religion, language and economy. Some of such people's groups included the Ao, Sumi, Angami, Zeliang, Lotha, Konyak, Ringmao, Chakhesang, Sangtam, Chang, Phom, Yimchunger, Khemnungam, Thangkhul and others. These groups, though were similar in their physical features, were, however, different culturally. Each of them is clearly identified by the geographical area of habitation. Areas were marked by boundaries and each maintained one's own territorial idenity intact.

Nagas' traditional administrative polity was sound. However, though their political organizations were strong because of a well coordinated democratic structure but their political democratic strength was nonetheless confined to one's own homogenous group only and mostly at the level of a village. The American Baptist Mission that started its work in Nagaland in the first half of the nineteenth century secured its strong foothold among most of the Naga tribal groups. The Christian population is close to 88% the highest ever in the entire region. Though the state was rife by strife between contending parties, some of whom were on the march demanding complete political independence, there were however, substantive moderates who opposed the secession movement and took active part in building the state within the framework of the Constitution of India.

---

[14] For more information about Nagaland, read Ao, A. Lanunungsang, **From Phizo to Muiva: The Naga National Question in North East India** (2002); Channa, S. M. ed., **Nagaland: A Contemporary Ethnography** (1992); Elwin, Verrier **Nagaland** (1961); Horam, M. **Social and Cultural Life of Nagas: The Tangkhul Nagas** (1977); Horam, M. **Naga Insurgency** (1988); Maitra, K. **Nagaland: A Darling of the North-East** (1991); Penzu, **Ancient Naga Head Hunters: Lives and Tales in Prose and Poetry** (2002); Ramunny, Murkot **The World of Nagas** (1993); Yonuo, Asoso **The Rising Nagas: A Historical and Political Study** (1974); Sanyu, Visier **A History of Nagas & Nagaland: Dynamic of Oral Tradition in Village Formation** (1996); Singh, K. S. ed., **People of India: Nagaland** (1994); Zehol, Lucy ed., **Women in Naga Society** (1998).

Naga people adopted a patriarchal pattern of lineage and inheritance. They did not have common social norms. Each group has one's own distinctive dresses and attires. Normally, an indigenous weaved-shawl gives a clear identity of a particular community. Hardly a group would use shawls of other tribes even if they look good, attractive or warm. Doing so would carry a cultural surrendering implication that would amount to insulting of one's own distinctive identity. There is a deep psychological attachment to it and sanctity. Any violation even if it is done without knowledge would in most cases send a defeating message to the family, a clan or the community.

Another significant social composition was language. Each Naga tribal group had a particular spoken language – a language that could neither be understood nor spoken by others. Dialects gave them a kind of separate category and social compartmentalization. Most of them regarded their own language or dialects as a community's honour and pride. A spirit of help and service also follows on linguistic line. The problem with the Naga people as with other hill people was further compounded by the loss of their alphabets.

Religious belief system and rituals were realized mostly not in the community but in respective villages. Each group had some kind of understanding of the supreme being. He was both a benevolent and malevolent god. His acts upon human beings were mostly related to actions, behaviour and faithfulness of the latter. Villages or clans performed their sacrifices in their own way. All Nagas did not have a common religious belief or practices. Some of such were greatly accompanied with a sense of fear of demons or evil spirits. The only area that appeared to have contributed to a sense of ethnic solidarity is in community's festival. For most of the Naga people, festival remained overly civic rather than religious. It was a symbol of expressed unity. It was also an occasion in which people could come together in their traditional attire to a common arranged location. Symbolic illustrations like spears, headgears, shields and shawls that were demonstrated were also followed by dancing and singing. It was also an occasion for drinking rice beer and participating together in some feasts.

3. Tribal Communities in Arunachal Pradesh:[15] Arunachal Pradesh that lies on the north and part of the east of the region is a state with a minimal contact to the outside world. There are more than twenty independent tribal groups in it. Though they share their physical features much in common, their cultural differences were so deep as to overshadow their similar appearances. This state

[15] Read these sources for more information about land and people's culture and history of Arunachal Pradesh: Bose, M. L. **History of Arunachal Pradesh** (1997); Das, Gurudas **Tribes of Arunachal Pradesh in Transition** (1995); Dutta, P. C. **Arunachal Pradesh: An Overview** (1993); Elwin, Verrier **India's North – East Frontier in the Nineteenth Century** (1959); Gopalakrishnan, R. **Arunachal Pradesh: Land & People** (1994); Grewal, Dalvinder S. **Tribes of Arunachal Pradesh** Vol. II (1997); Mibang, T. **Social Change in Arunachal Pradesh: The Minyongs, 1947-1987** (1994); Osik, N. N. **A Brief History of Arunachal Pradesh** (1996); Rao, V. M. **Tribal Women of Arunachal Pradesh** (2003).

shares most of its international boundary line with Bhuttan, China and Myanmar. Unlike most of the neighbouring states, it has a least population density of 13 per sq. km. that is, its total population of over a million spreads over an area of 83,743 sq. km.

Following the signing of the treaty of Yandabo in 1826, Arunachal Pradesh was placed under the British rule. From 1947 to 1962, the region was made a part of the North East Frontier Agency (NEFA).[16] It was only in 1972 that it became a Union Territory and adopted the name Arunachal Pradesh. As of 20th February, 1982, it was elevated to full statehood with its capital at Itanagar. Most of the people's groups in the state are the Abor or Adi, Monpa, Nishi or Dafla, Apatani, Khamti, Mishmi, Wancho, Tangsa, Tangin, Nocte, Miri, Miji, Hrusso, Sherdukpen, Sulung, Singpho, Lisu or Yobin, Khos, Membas and Khambas, Tangam, Lishpa and Chugpa, Meyor and Zakhring.

The Adi or Abor people who inhabited mainly in Siang district were the main group who constituted the largest in the state. They have their own spoken language, maintained a distinctive social structure, have traditional political institutions, professed a kind of natural religion and lived on agriculture and farming. Like other hill people in Northeast India, the Adis did not appear to have possessed a written culture. Though the Adis or Abors were one people but in course of their history, there began to develop a certain autonomous differentiation that appeared to have become reflected in the presence of sub–clans like Padam, Gallong and Miniyong.

The Monpa people are other tribal groups who settled and lived mainly in the West and East Kameng district. The area is mountainous that stretches the Himalaya ranges and resulted in inaccessible contacts with the outside world. The Monpas are followers of Buddhist religion and largely belonged to the Mahayana Buddhism. The religion that they followed was apparently no longer pure because certain tribal elements appeared to have mingled in it. However, they strongly maintained their belief in Buddhist religion. The Monpas were also able to establish a renowned Tamang Buddhist monastery in the seventeenth century and it has now become not just a centre of their socio-religious life but a national pride and heritage. Monpa people were one but had somewhere in their history developed into two groups, viz., Dirang Monke and Tawang Monke. Different dialects too grew gradually with the ethnic division.

The Nishis, known earlier as Dafla, are other indigenous citizens who settled mostly in Subansiri area. They adhered to their primal religion and are more accessible than most major tribal groups in the state. They too have their own distinctive identity in social structure, traditional administration, economy, occupation and language. Like the Adis and Monpas, the Nishis too formed substantive part in this extensive hilly state.

[16] Cf. **Manorama Year Book '82**, pp. 673f.

The lower Subansiri district also witnessed substantive presence of the Apatani group of people. They called themselves Tanu. Though the Apatanis belonged to a separate ethnic identity group but their community is more flexible and permissible to autonomous diversification. Mura and Mite are the recent sub-ethnic branches that have come up almost independently. Their primal religion was also unsophisticated and not strong enough to bind them to a common sense of identity.

Like the Monpas, the Khamtis belonged to the Mahayana group of Buddhism and formed major part of Arunachal Pradesh state. Their ethnic autonomous composite society further confirmed their difference from others. While Khamtis are strong on their own, their separate distinctive identity did not contribute much to the overall national solidarity both at the level of the state and the country alike.

The Mishmi people who might have migrated from Myanmar in the distant past have added to people's composition in the state. They are indigenous citizens of the state. Their area of settlement and occupation is in Lohit district. Their following of Buddhism is always accompanied with a mixture of primal faith and life. Their linguistic history is rife with growing autonomous strands in line with their emerging sub-clans like Idu, Miju, Taraon or Diagaru. Polygamy is permitted in Mishmi society although only rich ones could afford and survive.

The Wanchos, who lived mainly in Tirap area, though identified themselves with the Nagas, are also an integral part of Arunachal Pradesh region. Their identity is preserved in their living under a single territorial area and who called themselves and by others as Wancho people. Like the Mishmis, others tribal chief and rich people enjoyed the privileged of a polygamous life. Side by side with the Wanchos, there is another group called Nocte whose outside exposure in trade was mainly with the Assamese. Both Wanchos and Noctes are experts in tattooing and they themselves are heavily painted and decorated with tattoos. In most probability, these heavy decorated coverings and tattoos were not just outside expressions of their ethnic identity but cultural protective and preventive mechanisms from outside allurement and influence.

The Miris lived close to the Nishis but kept their separate ethnic unity without any major change. Their religion was exclusive for their own community. They worshipped a number of natural spirits and offered them sacrifices whenever needed. They also practice some magical forms and shamanism. The presence of sub-clans such as Bibi, Biku, Taya, Gocham and others tended to weaken the once single community. Though these sub-ethnic differences appeared to have weakened their strength inside but their outside exposure was marked with significant psycho - cultural unity.

The Sulungs, whose population is far below seven thousand in all, are not progressive. They worship primal deities in their own traditional customs and practices. Most of their earnings were invested in sacrifices and performing rituals.

In most cases at least in the past, they depended on the Nishis for employment and living.

Another less known group of people in Arunachal Pradesh is the Hrussos or the Akas whose habitation in just few villages in Kamung district put them together in close proximity. The Khos people who live among the Hrussos are fewer in numbers but are rife with backwardness, poverty, illiteracy and poor health in the distant past life. Their past problems were further compounded by the encouragement of child marriage and polygamy.

The nature of the Mijis is also typical in a sense that a certain impression of maintaining slavery appeared to have existed among them at least until the recent past. Their community was fragmented into two, Nyuppu and Nyulle. The latter were so dependent on their masters and their services were mostly regarded as slavery or of being under someone's protection for survival and sustainability. The Mijis lived in some twenty five villages in Kameng district of Arunachal Pradesh.

Other groups who maintained their cultural and ethnic differences are the Tagins who might have migrated from Tibet but settled down in areas under Siang district, the Membas, the Khambas, the Sherdukpens, the Lishpa and Chugpa people's groups. Then the Lisu or Yobin people who inhabited on border areas with Myanmar were already Christians and belonged to the Church of Christ. A Bible and a Christian Hymn book were already available in Lisu or Yobin language.

When we examined and made a survey on people's groups in Arunachal Pradesh, we could observe their ethnic identities, cultural diversities, backwardness, primal and diverse social norms and life style. We could also observe the presence of polygamy, child marriage and a certain degree of slavery. There are however, other forms that are significant for information and may be further explained as follows:-

First, **Class System:** Another significant feature that could be observed from at least certain groups of people was the practice of social class hierarchical structure. For instance, the Mijis, the Wanchos and the Singphos. While a description of the Mijis is already done above, the Wanchos maintained a class hierarchy like Wangpon, the lower class and Angsa and Wangsu groups, the upper class. The Singpho people who lived in Lohit district divided themselves according to their social ladder or class into four classes, like Shangai, Mijieng, Lubrung and Mirip. Though each tribal group that maintains its class distinction has every reason to justify one's norms but the reality remains that such is under no circumstances be condoned.

Second, **A Question of Survival:** The population of the groups that have described above was also somewhat reckoning. While larger groups like the Adis might have exceeded one hundred and fifty thousand of their population, others like the Monpas, Wanchos, Noctes, Apatnis, Tangsas, Mishmis, Nishis and Miris – their population ranged between ten thousand plus and fifty thousand. Still other groups like the Khamtis, Sulungs, Mijis, Akas, Sherdukpen, Khos, Lishpa and Changpa, Lisus, Membas and Khambas – their population ranged from at least below ten thousand down to just around one thousand. In all these, however, there are other groups like the Meyors and Zakhrings whose population was approximately some hundreds and the Tangams approximately below six hundred in all. For such as these, their question is just how long could they continue to survive?

4. People's Composition in Tripura:[17] Tripura is a state with almost an insignificant presence of Christian following with just 1.68% by the recent 1991 statistical report. Attained its full fledged statehood in 1972, Tripura is bounded by Assam and Mizoram on parts of the north and the east and Bangladesh encompasses the remaining parts. Hills, plains and valleys contribute to making Tripura geographical identity a perfect combination. The total area is 10, 491, 69 Sq. Km. and its inhabitants numbering more than 3 million. Agartala is the state capital and located in the plain area. It was originally a tribal state but changes in the 20th century that have led to large scale influx from the neighbouring Bangladesh had resulted in their outnumbering of the indigenous population. In at least one source of information, a reporter writes,

> The tribals who outnumbered 'others' in 1921 found themselves swamped by 'others' in 1971. This will be clear from a casual glance at the census figures from 1921 to 1971. In 1921 the tribals outnumbered 'others' by about 38,000. In 1971 the 'others' outnumbered the tribals by as many as 6.55 lakhs.[18]

There are no signs of reduction of the demographic non-tribal population in the subsequent years. Christian Churches that have permanent stations in the state are the British Baptist, the New Zealand Baptist, the Catholic Church, Believers Church India and others.

People's composition in Tripura in their past history could be identified ethnically as under:-

Before the arrival of Bangla people from across the border, Boroks[19] or Twipras were the original inhabitants or indigenous people of the state. They

---

[17] For more information, see Chaudhuri, Gan **Tripura: The Land and Its People** (1980); Chaudhuri, J. Gan **An Anthology of Tripura** (1985); N. R. Roychoudhury, **Tripura through the Ages** (1983); D. Deb Barman, **Treatise on Traditional Social Institutions of the Tripuri Community** (1983); S. B. K. Dev Verman, The **Tribes of Tripura: A Dissertation** (1987); James Long, **Analysis of Rajamala or Chrinicles of Tripura** (1850/1995); N. C. Nath, tr. **Sri Rajmala** Vols. I to IV (1999); E. F. Sandys, comp., **History of Tripura** (1915/1997).

[18] **Monorama Year Book**, 1982, p. 653.

[19] Debbarma, Sunil Kumar "A Study of the Impact of the Gospel for Asia (Believers' Church) Ministry on the Borok People of Tripura" (Unpublished B. D. Thesis, Thiruvalla, 2002), Chap. Two-'Historical Background of Borok People.'

were also known as Tripuri or Debberma in the past but now they preferred to be known as Twipra. The rulers or Maharajas belong to this community. It was they who opened the doors for the gradual coming of people of Bangla root. One of the reasons for the Maharajah's complacent attitude to the Bangla people was because of receiving satisfactorily services in the office, economy and in the palace. The Boroks could establish a strong society and community through their common spoken language, social set up and for a certain period of time through political administration.

The Reangs[20] though have some affinity with Borok speaking people, are nevertheless different groups of people. Their ethnic identity is well preserved. Though Reangs are migratory in nature but their settlement in Tripura was in many aspects stable and permanent. Through their contacts with elements of Hinduism, their primal faith tended to become mixed and syncretistic in outlook. Like the Boroks, the Reangs too formed a major part as indigenous people of the state.

The Chakmas[21] though were originally migrants to Tripura but insofar as there had been long and deeply rooted in their minds, beliefs systems and already developed a sense of belonging and ownership, their long years of settlement in the state may no longer be in doubt. Most Chakmas are followers of Buddhism.

Jamatia[22] people were other major people's groups of the state. Majority of Jamatias lived in the southern part. It was reported that in the time of the Maharajahs, the Jamatias who got the royal confidence had been inducted to the army defense as soldiers. Following a change in the political administration, the Jamatias devoted to agriculture especially in paddy cultivation and farming. Like the Twipra, Reangs and Chakmas the Jamatias too are in most instances standing on the ground of economic and political dependence.

Other smaller communities that settled down in Tripura are Noatias, Kaihpengs, Mosoms and others. Though these groups have been there over a long period of time, they have however not become progressive in their business except of maintaining their economic livelihood in agriculture in rural areas and lived mostly in isolation. Following the large scale intrusion of people across the border, the state witnessed significant major changes in demographic population, political administration, economy and communication.

5. Tribes of Matrilineal Origins in Meghalaya: Meghalaya is another state in Northeast India.[23] It is a unique state not only in India but in the whole world

---

[20] See Niyogi, Tushar K. **Folktales and Myths of Riang and Tripuri Communities** (1983); S. B. K. Dev Verman, **The Tribes of Tripura: A Dissertation** (1987), pp. 18-21; Dutta, S. K. **Uprooted Reangs: Strangers in their Motherland** (2005).

[21] For further information, read Talukdar, S. P. **The Chakmas: Life and Struggle** (1988).

[22] See S. B. K. Dev Verman, *op. cit.*, pp. 22f.

[23] Further information about the Khasi – Jaintia people of Meghalaya, cf. Bareh, Hamlet **The History and Culture of the Khasi People** (1967/1985); Barpujari, H. K. **Problem of the**

for it being a home to Khasi-Jaintia and Garo[24] people of matrilineal descent. They are the only surviving matrilineal tribes in India. Other people's groups who settle in the state are Marwaris, Nepalis, Bengalis, Biharis, Tibetans, Bhutias, Punjabis and several other groups. Though most Khasi-Jaintias and Garos have changed their faith to Christianity, there are yet more than 35% of the people who still remain in their own traditional religious traditions. Christian missions and churches that have come and worked in Meghalaya included the Presbyterians, the Anglicans, the Catholics and numerous churches of indigenous origins.

Though these indigenous people share much in common in terms of matrilineal lineage they are however different in most cultural aspects. These

Hill Tribes North East Frontier, 1822-42 (1970); Cantlie, Keith **Notes on Khasi Law** (1934); Chattopadhyaya, S. K. ed., **Tribal Institutions of Meghalaya** (1985); Costa, G. **Ka Riti Jong Ka Ri Laiphew Syiem**, Bynta-I (1936); Costa, G. **Ka Riti Jong Ka Ri Laiphew Syiem**, Bynta-II (1937); Elias, H. **Ki Khanatang U Barim** (1972); Gurdon, Major P. R. T. **The Khasis** (1907/1975); **Ka Jingiateh-Jutang Ka Hima Mylliem** (1938); Kharakor, Sr. Philomena **Ka Khasi Kolshor Kumba Ka Paw Ha Ka Khasi Literashor, 1930-1940** (1989); **U Khasi Ha La Ka Rukom Bad Kiwei de Ki Jingthoh** (1976); Khongphai, A. S. **Principles of Khasi Law** (1974); Laloo, Donbok T. **Ka Rongbiria U Hynniewtrep** (1974); Lyngdoh, J. D. S., **I Thymmei Ka Long-Briew** (1979); Lyngdoh, Fr. S. Sngi. **Ki Riti-Khyndew ba la buh u Longshuwa-Manshuwa Jong Ka Ri Bhoi** (1965); Marwein, Phrangbonsen Trevore **Meghalaya Hand Book** (1981); Mathur, P. R. G. **Khasi of Meghalaya: A Study in Tribalism and Religion** (1979); Mawrie, H. Onderson, **Ka Pyrkhat U Khasi** (1973); Mukhim, Rose Mary **Ki Mraw Ka Jingngeitbieit** (1982); Nakane, Chie **Garo and Khasi: A Comparative Study in Matrilineal Systems** (1967); Natarajan, Nalini **The Missionary among the Khasis** (1977); Nonglait, U Homiwell Lyngdoh **Ka Pomblang Nongkrem bad ka Thang Syiem Sohra** (1928); Nonglait, U Homiwell Lyngdoh **Ki Syiem Khasi Bad Synteng** (1938/ 1964); Nonglait, U Homiwell Lyngdoh **Ka Niam Khasi**, (1937/1970); Nongrum, U Kitbor W. **Ki Nongthoh Kot Khasi**, Ka Bynta I (1982); Ondromoney, U. **Ka Geography Khasi**, Part I, (1927); Pakem, B. ed., **Shillong, 1971-1981,** (1984); Rao, V. Venkata, Barrister Pakem and Niru Hazarika, **A Century of Government and Politics in North-East India** Vol. 2. **Meghalaya 1874 to 1983** (1984); Roberts, Mrs. John ed., **Jaintia Folklore and Legends and the History of the Khasi Religion: From the Papers of the Rev. John Roberts D. D.** (n. d.); Roberts, J. H. **Ka Shang Khmih-Pyrthei la Ka Ri Khasi: Ka Diari Naduh Ka Sngi U Blei, Nai Nohprah 14 tarik 1884 Haduh Ka Sngi Saitjain, Nai Kylla Lyngkot 17 tarik 1885**, tr. F. M. Pugh (1964); Rodborne, Trevore, **Ka Niam Jong U Khasi-Pnar** (1946); Roy, U Hipshon ed., **Khasi Heritage: A Collection of Essays on Khasi Religion and Culture** (1979); Roy, U Jeebon, **Ka Kitab Ba Batai Pynshynna Shaphang Uwei U Blei** (1901); Roy, U Jeebon, **Ka Niam Jong Ki Khasi** (1887); Rymbai, R. T. **Ban Pynieng La Ka Rasong bad Kiwei de ki Ese** (1982); Rynjah, Tngensi **Ka History Ka Ri Khasi-Jaintia: Ki Por Barim Bajah** (1983); Shadap, Namita Catherine-Sen **The Origin and Early History of Khasi-Synteng people** (1981); Shullai, L. G. **Ki Hima Khasi** (1975); Singh, Kynpham **A Collection of Writings About Khasi Hills and A Collection of Poems** (Shillong, 1979); Singh, U Rabon **Ka Kitab Niam Khein Ki Khasi** (Probably written 1900/1972).

[24] Relevant data on the Garo people, see Burling, Robins **Rengsanggri: Family and Kinship in a Garo Village** (1997); Gassah, L. S. ed., **Garo Hills Land and the People** (1984); Momin, Mignonette ed., **Readings in History and Culture of the Garos: Essays in Honour of Milton S. Sangma** (2003); Sangma, D. R. **Jadoreng: The Psycho-Physical Culture of the Garos** (1993); Sangma, M. S. **History and Culture of the Garos** (1983); Sangma, M. N. **Unpublished Documents on Garo Affairs** (1993).

cultural differences were evident even in each ethnic group. Language that should have brought each of these tribal groups to a common identity was absent instead there existed significant rise of most unintelligible dialects. Political organizations too contributed much to the rise of sub-ethnic identities. Each state maintained its own territorial integrity, durbar and rule of law and administered by an elected chief. These differences often led to intra-tribal warfare and conflict especially in their ancient history.

Even religion was not a factor for people's sense of oneness in their traditional belief system. Though in a once upon a time period these people, especially the Khasi-Jaintia people, might have experienced a sense of religious oneness but in due course they were fragmented and reduced their religious system mostly to the level of a clan. Each clan performed religious duties, upon the leadership and supervision of a senior uncle. Although their belief in the existence of one God was so strong but the subsequent cropping up of numerous deities tended to weaken people's religion. Myths and superstitions filled people's minds and some of such continued to dominate the people and their daily activities.

The social structure was the only cultural component that places the matrilineal communities on strong position. As already mentioned, though differences among the Khasi-Jaintia people were so strong but the social connection through inter-clan relationships, and kinship solidarity provided the solidified link that cannot be ignored outright. The Khasi-Jaintia people were identified by territorial areas or dialectical identities. Some sub-ethnic identities like Synteng, Maram, Lyngngam or Bhoi were used by our people mostly in a derogatory and negative sense. They were frowned upon and looked down as backward and low. However, clan relationships and kinships codes became persuasive that crossed over these negative religio-political and social hurdles.

6. People's Groups in Mizoram:[25] Like Nagaland and Meghalaya, Mizoram is another hill state with majority of Christian population (about 100% among the Mizo). It is a landlocked state bounded by Myanmar on the east and south and Bangladesh on the west. Mountains, deep gorges and rivers though have added beauty to the state have nevertheless hampered development.

Though Mizo is a unified ethnic community, there are however several sub-ethnic identities like the Lushai, Pawi, Paite, Ralte, Hmar, Kuki, Mara, Lai and other sub-groups. Other communities that have come and settled in Mizoram included the Brus, Chakmas, and other people from the mainline India. While the Presbyterian and Baptist Churches are in some command in the state, there

---

[25] For more stories about Mizoram, read Anderson, H. **Among the Lushais** (1914); Chapman, E & M. Clark, **Mizo Miracle**. Edited by Marjorie Sykes (1968); Dena, Lal **Christian Missions and Colonialism: A Study of Missionary Movement in Northeast India with Particular Reference to Manipur & Lushai Hills, 1894-1947** (1988); Dev, Bimal J & Dilip K. Lahiri, **Lushai Customs and Ceremonies** (1983); Nibedon, Nirmal **Mizoram: The Dagger Brigade** (1980); Ray, A. **Mizoram: Dynamics of Change** (1982); Thanga, L. B. **The Mizos: A Study in Racial Personality** (1978).

are however numerous instituted independent denominations of local origins in addition to the growing influence of the Catholic and the Seventh Day Adventist.

7. Ethnic People's Composition in Manipur: Another vibrant and volatile Northeast Indian state is Manipur.[26] Bounded on the east and south by Myanmar, Manipur lies very much with India. Its neighbouring states are Nagaland on the north, Assam on the west and Mizoram on the south and part of its western portion alike. It has an area of 22,327 sq. km. and a total population of more than 2 million. Formerly a princely state, Manipur acceded to India in 1947. It was made a territory under the administration of a Chief Commissioner in 1949 and a Union Territory in 1969. Following the re-organization of most of the states in the region, Manipur became a full-fledged state of the Indian Union on 21st January, 1972. Whereas most inhabitants belong to the mainline Baptist, Presbyterian or Catholic Churches, there are several others who associate with a member of independent churches. Manipur witnesses the presence of majority of Hindu population especially among the Meitheis in the plains.

8. A Brief Political Profile of Sikkim: Though this study will not cover the recent attached state Sikkim, it is nevertheless not out of place to provide a little information about its political history. Sikkim is a smallest mountain state bounded by Tibet on the north, Bhuttan on the east, West Bengal on the south and Nepal on the west. Its total population of 540,851 spread over an area of 7096 sq. km. and gave an average population density of 76 per sq. km. In response to the resolution of the Sikkim Assembly on 10th April, 1975 that led to the termination of the institution of Chogyal and Sikkim be integrated with India as a state of the Indian Union, the Parliament passed the Thirty Eight Amendment Act 1975 that resulted in making Sikkim the 22nd State of the Indian Union with effect from 26th April, 1975. Its capital Gangtok lies on the east district of the state. Lepchas and Bhutias were the original settlers of Sikkim.

Most probably like the state of Tripura, however, the gradual immigration of some people's groups from neighbouring Nepal kingdom in the 18th and 19th centuries had led to reducing the Lepchas and Bhutias into minorities. Though the work of the Church of North India and the Free Church from Finland appeared to have provided the needed spiritual service to the people besides the rise of several independent and charismatic groups yet the percentage of Christian population is still negligible. Judging by the fact that Lepchas hailed from Assam and their

[26] Read Allen, B. C. **Naga Hills and Manipur** (1981); Dena, Lal **British Policy towards Manipur, 1891-1919** (1984); Dev, Bimal & D. K. Lahiri, **Manipur Culture and Politics** (1985); Hodson, T. C. **The Naga Tribes of Manipur** (1982); Hodson, T. C. **The Meiteis** (1982); Johnstone, J. **Manipur and the Naga Hills** (1983); Jajo, C. **Christian Life in a Tribal Context in Manipur** (1990); Kanti, R. D. **Manipur Tribal Scene: Studies in Society and Change** (1985); Kirti, M. Singh **Religion and Culture of Manipur** (1988); Parrot, S. N. **The Religion of Manipur** (1980); Roy, Jyotirmoy **History of Manipur** (1958); Sen, Sipra **Tribes and Castes of Manipur** (1982); Singh, R. P. **Geography of Manipur** (1982); Tombi, N. Singh **Manipur and the Mainstream** (1975).

physical affinity with the Northeast, the central government had thought it right to tag it together with the already burdened seven sisters of the region, the North Eastern Council.

A Summary: As before and now, Northeast India gets the distinction of being the most backward and under-developed region because of a long period of apathetic attitude, isolation, neglectedness, alienation and lack of energetic vision from local leadership and even from the Centre. The region is endowed with "abundant natural resources in forest, minerals and hydro-power, nevertheless, its economy still remains primitive" and well up to this period it is still depending on central help for survival. In order to help co-ordinate the economics of the region and lead it to the path of economic development, the central government constituted the North Eastern Council in 1972. Its main office is located in Shillong. Though its functioning in running the affairs appeared to have been rife with contradictions, it is nevertheless an inclusive binding body that brings together all 8 states to a common platform. Closely related to it, is the creation of the Department on North Eastern Region (DONER) as a separate ministry under the Government of India. It is another well planned economic mechanism to introduce various ways and means in order to bring about an all round development or otherwise to the region.

III. Traditional People's Discriminatory and Oppressive Social System

Given the presence of different groups of people both in the hills and the plain area, the Indo-Aryan and the Mongoloid roots with differences in religion, political organization and habitats; their social structure was also marked with distinctive degrees of variation. While a description on this aspect is important and necessary but since the focus of the study is on national integration and nation building, it will draw attention only on areas that tended to alienate, oppress or discriminate certain sections in the society.

1. Presence of Caste System:[27] One of the pertinent components in Indian social system is the presence of caste system. This system was introduced in India following the arrival of people of Aryan roots. It functioned on the system of classification. Under this schematic categorization, the Brahmins, the Kshyatriyas and the Vaisyas were regarded as those who stood on the respective social higher hierarchical order. The Sudras belonged to the lower order. Others who did not fall under the said groups were classified as the outcastes or the untouchables. This system which was practiced in Indian society was believed to have received divine sanction and order. In other words, caste system falls under the religious faith and practices.

Caste system in Indian society tended to function in an inhuman way. Those who belong to the higher social order did not appear to have acknowledged the

[27] Cf. Ghurye, G. S. **Caste and Race in India** (1969); Hutton, J. H. **Caste in India** (1986). For the rise of Brahmins in Assam, see Sen, Sipra *op. cit.*, p. 157.

dalits or tribals as full human beings. They regarded them as functional beings. People of low origins faced ill-treatment, oppression, discrimination and social abuse. Inter-marriage with the low caste is unthinkable. The discrimination was apparent even in temples, markets, habitation or dining tables.

The presence of caste system is a clear violation of human rights. Low caste people were not given the freedom to have access to the holy ancient Vedic texts. The system held them in perpetual slavery, poverty and illiteracy. They were barred from attending traditional educational schools. The ancient healthcare system and medicines could not be given to the low caste people.

Therefore, the presence of caste system among certain people's groups in the plain areas was detrimental to the harmony and unity of India's national unity and integrity.

2. Traditional Head Hunting Culture:[28] While caste system prevailed among people of Aryan stock in the plains, head hunting was mostly a social practice among certain people's groups in the hill areas. It was a practice of achieving human heads as trophies and some hill tribal societies not only did they entertain such practices but placed special recognition on the list of heroes. In other words, some traditional hill tribal societies encouraged inhuman culture. The system provided an occasion that women would prefer to marry someone who had claimed many human heads. They felt it as a pride or honour in the community.

3. Practice of Human Sacrifice: Another inhuman social practice in the region was the presence of human sacrifice. Some sections in the plains appeared to have established a shrine that entertained sacrifices of human beings to their gods or goddesses. This was an example that human sacrifice was found present among certain group of people in the region.[29] It is a horrible and most inhuman rituals. Believed to have been the influence of Hinduism, the Raja of Jaintia entertained the rituals of sacrificing human beings. Until the time that the British abolished this practice as early as 1835, the practice of human sacrifice was calculated to have been in action for about 500 years.

Besides, though the Khasi-Jaintia people were not head hunters but some clans who reared the clan deity known as *U Thlen* (a kind of spirit whose appearance could have been in the form of a python, a black cat or a fish)[30] appeared to have clandestinely offered human blood to him. It was a wealth generating deity. This practice encouraged violence, enmity and culture of blood. Though traditional culture could have sanctioned such practices but they were never instruments that build a healthy nation.

---

[28] Penzu, **Ancient Naga Head Hunters: Lives and Tales in Prose and Poetry** (2002); Zaithanga, V. L. **From Head Hunting to Soul Hunting** (1981).

[29] See Giri, Helen **U Khasi Ha Ka Por U Phareng** (n.d. c.2000), p. 6.

[30] Mawrie, H. O. **The Khasi Milieu** (1981), pp. 45-48.

4. Social Victim of Injustices: The other negative social injustice that was prevalent in most of the societies in the region was the discrimination of women.[31] Women were created equally but in the course of human development, that equal status was downgraded to the low level. Even in matrilineal societies where women were regarded significant and precious, their low status became evident in most spheres in the society. They were debarred from taking the leading role in administration, legislation, judiciary or religion. Although most societies in the region witnessed their presence of more than half of the total population in each community, they were nevertheless placed at the secondary level.

The other negative aspect was the practice of slavery.[32] Some families, who have become victims to the cycle of debts, have no other way except to pass through the slavery channels. Though in some Mizo society the presence of the institution of slavery was apparently regarded as protective and preventive mechanisms but on the whole it was unfortunate that such practice that implied taking away of rights, freedom and dignity of human persons was entertained in certain traditional societies in the region.

IV. Dialects and Languages of Northeast India[33]

We have seen that people's composition and political organization have not contributed much to people's cultural unity because their differences were much deeper than the geographical identity. Besides that, languages and dialects have also further bolstered cultural difference.

Northeast India is also a home to numerous languages and dialects. In any community, the role of a common a spoken language is very important for it brings unity and strengthens its culture. But a division of languages in a community always contributes to cultural weakness and remains vulnerable to outside hegemony, conquest and be ruled. Like differences in ethnic composition, languages were also not a factor for unity for the region and even for homogenous group of people. A brief description of languages in the region will enable us to understand its complexity and complication alike.

---

[31] See Imchen, N. ed., **Women's Issues in the 21st Century** (2001); Hnuni, R. L. **Transforming Theology for Empowering Women** (1999). Other informative studies on women in Northeast India, cf. Rao, V. M. **Tribal Women of Arunachal Pradesh** (2003); Zehol, Lucy ed., **Women in Naga Society** (1998); Nakane, Chie **Garo and Khasi: A Comparative Study in Matrilineal Systems** (Paris, Norton & Co., 1967); Downs, F. S. **The Christian Impact on the Status of Women in North East India** (1996); Sen, S. ed., **Women in Meghalaya** (1997); Bhuyan, B. C. **The Tribal Women** (1993).

[32] Some accounts about the presence of slavery in some areas in Northeast India, read Thakur, Amrendra Kumar **Slavery in Arunachal Pradesh** (2003) Also, see Downs, F. S. **History of Christianity in India: Vol. V, Part 5 North East India in the Nineteenth and Twentieth Centuries** (1992), pp. 150-153.

[33] Read Miri, M. ed., **Linguistic Situation in North-East India** (1982/2003).

Arunachal Pradesh witnessed the presence of many languages and dialects. Though important linguistic groups include the Adi, Apatani and Dafla languages, there are several others like Ashing, Bokar, Bori, Adi, Gallong, Milang, Minyong and Miri in addition to Aya, Nisang, Lupa, Nabiim, Aka Lel, Bangmi, Bangro, Nissi and many others. Differences in these languages were such that they could not understand amongst them or be communicated. A similar phenomenon takes place even among people under an umbrella of ethnic homogeneity. Linguistic and dialectical variations contribute to ripping people's social fabric apart.

Assam too has under its fold languages like Assamese, Boro, Kachari, Mishing, Karbi, Garo, Hmar, Dimasa, Tiwa, Khasi and groups of Kuki linguistic family. Later, several Bengali, Santal, Soara, Oraon and Hindi languages have found significant presence in Assam. The presence of different languages means the presence of ethnic identities. These identities though are spreading but their concentrated places are well identified by geographical location, economy, occupation, social structure, traditional polity, arts and by religious systems.

Nagaland was a composite region that became evident in its geographical unity and compactness. Social structure, political organization, religious belief system, dresses and more importantly languages, however, were so different and fragmented that its unity was broken. Some significant languages and dialects prevalent in Nagaland included the Ao, Konyak, Sema, Lotha, Angami, Sangtam, Nruenghnei, Thangkhul besides Yimchungru, Kezhama, Chokri, Rengma, Ntenyi, Mao, Liangmai, Zeme, Mzeme and many others. Each linguistic group concentrates in one geographical location or district and securely assures separate identities. Dialectical difference was also prominent and active in each major linguistic group. For instance, among the Ao in Mokokchung district, there are Chungli and Mongsen dialects. Their unintelligibility was clearly marked in words, pronunciation, phonetic sounds and sub-ethnic history.

Manipur is another region that featured the existence and growth of varying languages and dialects. Meitei or Manipuri was a language spoken by majority of the people. It was previously a language of the plain Meitei people only. Manipur, like Assam and Meghalaya, witnessed the rise and growth of numerous groups. Other linguistic and dialectical groups included Tangkhul, Thado, Vaiphei, Paite, Gangte, Simte, Kom, Anal, Chote/Chothe, Aimol, Koireng, Molsom, Monsang, Moyon, Purum, Mao, Rengma, Meluri, Poumai, Rongmei, Liangmei, Maram, Khoirao, Maring, Thangal and many others. These languages and dialects were deeply embedded in their limited geographical enclosure that their identities were confined to smaller groups and geographical jurisdiction.

Mizoram is a land of the Mizos but like the other states in the region, it represents another significant reality for the presence of numerous languages and dialects. Like Meitheis in Manipur, so also is Mizo language in Mizoram. It was known before as Lushai. Other dialects are Mara, Lai, Reang or Bru, Pawi and others. Again, the presence of linguistic variations did not strengthen people's unity but carried far disintegrative tendencies at least in the past history. The role of Mizo language has however contributed much to the unity and integrity of a strong and vibrant Mizo identity.

Tripura too is not a single linguistic region. Though its ancient solidified language was Kokborok but following the Bangla intrusion that subsequently pushed the Borok to the fringe, there witnessed the rise of Bangla language also. Other languages and dialects are Reang, Darlong, Hrangkhol, Chorei, Langrawng, Bawn and several others.

Meghalaya is a tiny state but has under its roof major languages like Khasi and Garo. Language was however not a unifying factor for their unity. Garo people have many unintelligible dialects and sub- dialects. Khasis also are full with numerous dialects. There are as many as twenty nine dialects in the community. Some of them are Pnar, Amwi, War Pynursla, Nongkrem, Bhoi, Lyngngam, Maram, Langrin, Mairang, Mawphlang, Mawsynram and many many others. Even within the Cherrapunji state, there are at least three dialects, viz., Sohra, Khatarshnong and Khathynriewshnong. The last two are unintelligible dialects among most of the Sohra speaking group on the upland.

The diversity and unintelligibility of these languages and dialects did not send positive signs for their cultural solidarity among themselves and in relation with others. Languages and dialects weaken people's unity. They no doubt assert a certain level of separateness and produce some kind of traditional pride but that separate linguistic recognition does not build the entire community. These distinctive identities produced enmity that mostly resulted in war, violence and territorial encroachment. A sense of community tended to have reduced to a limited dialectical spoken group and a collective consciousness did not get strong root. The difference played its gradual role of cultural disintegration. The difference did not affect just a community or a state it also affects the unity and integrity of a nation.

The other major weakness was the absence of a written script. With an exception of the Assamese, Meitei, Monpa people and others who have their own written scripts, the rest and mostly the hill and plain tribal people were without any written alphabet. Their strong memory and symbolic movements though how important they were but on the course of their movement, these memories tended to have disappeared into oblivion. It became vulnerable once the impact of globalization reaches its peak.

These two realities, unintelligible dialects and scriptless or without written alphabet, have kept the people in backwardness, poverty, illiteracy, socially low and defeat. These in turn affect their social health and well being.

V. Experiences in Polity and Religion[34]

1. Lacuna in Traditional Democracy: Traditional political structure and religion were other areas where one could see discrimination, inequality and partiality. Most hill tribal societies allowed the flow of a democratic system in their administration. There was collective participation of each adult member right from the clan council and village durbar and up to the level of the Chief's durbar. However, the kind of democracy that was applied was incomplete as women were never entertained and the post of chief was restricted only to selective legitimate clans and not on an open forum for all inhabitants. Pride in one's territorial area more often than not resulted in looking down at others and denied their legitimate rights of ownership of land and participation in community's decision making institutions.

2. A Religion that was Not Universal: Religion was also another component that witnessed certain degree of incompleteness. Reservation of priestly duties only to the priestly clan was an indication of religious inequality and discrimination. There was also so much of exclusiveness in it. Tribal religions and gods were exclusive and remained confined only to their communities. In some groups, like the Khasis, religion was basically a clan religion and those who belong to other clans though they may have a part in public worship but were never an integral part of the religious rites and duties.

A Summary: Northeast India witnessed the beauty of multi-cultural society. However, the move that led to violation of human rights was not encouraging. Inequality, partiality, injustice, discrimination and exclusiveness were elements that imprisoned human freedom and some of these so called traditional values did not contribute much neither towards the building of the community nor the nation.

---

[34] Some information about the religions in the region, read Sen, Soumen ed., **Religion in North-East India** (1993); Miri, Sujata ed., **Religion and Society of North–East India** (1980).

Chapter 3

Impact of British Colonialism on People in Northeast India

I. Reasons for British Annexation and Rule of the Region

European colonial powers[1] that have come to India included the Portuguese, the Danish, the French and the English or the British. Of these, it was the English[2] that demonstrated itself different. While the Portuguese,[3] the Danish and the French concentrated their colonial mission masters on controlling of trading coastal regions for their economic profits in India, the English though their primary objective was to have monopoly on economic business, they extended their fight for dominance in politics, land, society, language, literature and rule. As a result, the English penetrated deep into the interior of the country. They invaded the different empires and kingdoms of the country, captured, took control of the administration and pursued their political and economic interests.[4]

Northeast India situation was somewhat different. The English did not want, at the initial period, to extend their administration to the Northeastern region because, among other reasons, of economic non productivity. Though the plains of Brahmaputra and Barak valleys were fertile and could produce excessive paddy and other crops but extending their control over the region, the English masters were in most cases not interested. The hill areas were more expensive in ruling than the plains. In short, the English did not bother much on the people's

---

[1] For information on the advent of European powers to India, read Majumdar, R. C., H. C. Raychaudhuri & Kalikinkar Datta, **An Advanced History of India** (1991), pp. 623-636.

[2] *Ibid.*, pp. 637-756.

[3] The Portuguese traveller Vasco da Gama discovered India by landing at Calicut in 1498. Following this incident, the Portuguese came to India under the leadership of the governor Albuquerque (1509-1515) who captured and took control of Goa from the Sultan of Bijapur in 1510 and made it as the major controlling maritime station in India. It was colonial power that was instrumental for bringing the Latin Catholic faith to India.

[4] Cf. Majumdar, R. C., H. C. Raychaudhuri & Kalikinkar Datta, *op. cit.*, pp. 637ff.

condition in the region. Why then did the British power show interest in the affairs of Northeast India?

1. Assam was Hitherto under the Control and Rule of the Burmese.[5] The Burmese period in Assam was a period of suffering and hardship especially for the Assamese because the colonialists did not rule with a sympathetic or merciful spirit.[6] They unleashed a reign of terror upon the native people even at the cost of violation of human rights. In such political unhealthy situations, the Assamese appeared to have sought help from the British and they in turn willingly complied. In their fight against the Burmese, the British who with the support from the native chiefs[7] could force the Burmese out of Assam and by the Treaty of Yandaboo, 1826,[8] the Burmese vowed not to claim Assam anymore. The year 1826 was therefore regarded as the beginning of a modern period in Northeast Indian history. Hence, the British entered Assam not by invasion but by people's invitation.

2. The Situation in the Hill Areas was Different. Communication was the main problem in the region besides the multiplicity of unintelligible languages, dense jungles, poverty, and illiteracy. Why were the British officers interested in the affairs of the Hills Areas then? There were at least three reasons why the colonialists favoured to capture and rule the Hills.

1). Constructing of Road Communication: After establishing resident officials at Sylhet in Eastern Bengal, Nowgong and Gauhati in Assam Valley, the British wanted to build roads through Khasi and Jaintia Hills in order to connect these two plains areas. The colonial masters then concluded treaty agreements with the Chief of Jaintia state and Chief of Nongkhlaw in Khasi hills because the proposed road communication had to pass through their territories.[9] The interest of the British to extend their occupation and rule of the region was also in relation to the construction of road connectivity between Sylhet and the plains of Brahmaputra valley.

2). Controlling of Tribal Raiding: What was common with most hill people in the region, especially those who lived on border areas with the plains, was raiding? The tribes mostly engaged in attacking people in the plains.[10] Though

---

[5] Acharyya, N. N. **A Brief History of Assam: From Earliest Time to the Year 1983** (1987); Barpujari, H. K., S. K. Barpujari, A. C. Bhuyan, eds., **Political History of Assam, 1825-1919**, Vol. I (1977); Bhattacharjee, K. K. **North East India: Political and Administrative History** (1983); Bhuyan, A. C. & S. De, eds, **Political History of Assam, 1920-1939**, Vol. 2 (1970); Bhuyan, A. C. & S. De, eds, **Political History of Assam, 1940-47**, Vol. 3 (1980); Lahiri, R. M., **The Annexation of Assam, 1824-1854** (1975).

[6] See Lahiri, R. M., *Ibid.*, pp. 2-8.

[7] *Ibid.*, pp. 14-27. Also Gait, E. **A History of Assam** (1905/1981), pp. 280-289.

[8] *Ibid.*, p. 289.

[9] Aitchison, C. U **A Collection of Treaties, Engagements, and Sannads Relating to India and Neighbouring Countries,** Vol. I (1892), pp. 219, 224.

[10] Allen, B. C. et al., **Gazetteer of Bengal and North East India** (1905/1979), 483.

those who did not belong to the community would view such attack as an act of barbarism but the fact remained that the indigenous tribal people attacked these plain areas because other people's groups have not just encroached and occupied these areas in the border areas by force but settled at the cost of displacing the tribal people's right of ownership.

Tribal raiding frequently caused unnecessary law and order and the British did not want to see protest and unrest from the people and so extended their administrative outposts into the hills proper in order to curb and root out the menace of tribal raiding. One of the reasons why the British administration encouraged Christian missionaries working in the hill areas was mainly to help in civilizing the people.[11]

3). Health Resort: After establishing stations in the hills, the British found that the hill areas were healthier than the plains.[12] Then, they started by setting up sanatoria or health resorts in Cherrapunji first and leisurely settled there. Unlike the plains, most hill areas were hardly affected by malaria, cholera and other deadly diseases. As a result, the British who were interested only in controlling the warring tribes, were now interested in building permanent offices, especially in Shillong, Aizawl, Kohima, Imphal and elsewhere in the region.

II. Impact of British Administration on People and Region

The presence of the British colonial power in the region for almost one hundred and twenty five years had tremendously impacted the people and some significant consequences that had come about might well be seen in both positive and negative aspects as under:-

1. Bringing the Entire Region under a Single Administration:[13] As soon as the Burmese presence in Assam was displaced, the British power came in and took control of the region. Before that, Northeast India witnessed political disunity, instability, inter tribal feud and cultural fragmentation. Now, once the British established its stable presence in the region it began to consolidate these divided political territories through signing of agreements, treaties and sannads with native rulers or chiefs. They annexed them and placed under their single administration. There had been no other previous powers that had solidified politically the Northeastern region except the British.

It is no denying the fact that political unity in Northeast India and even in the larger India is a product of colonial achievement. Maharajas, tribal chiefs, village durbars and numerous ethnic groups in the region, that were traditionally autonomous and independent, were either subdued or conquered and brought together under the British rule.

[11] Snaitang, O. L. **Christianity and Social Change in Northeast India** (1993), p. 52.

[12] *Ibid.*, p. 43.

[13] Read Lahiri, R. M., **The Annexation of Assam, 1824-1854** (1975).

Given the fact that the Assamese were the ones who had sought help from the British and most likely as a mark of appreciation, the annexed states like the Khasi State, Manipur, Tripura, Mizoram, Garo hills, Arunachal Pradesh and Nagaland were placed together under the name Assam. Apparently, the British masters did not bother much on the hill areas because among other reasons, their non-producing revenue areas, resistance and difficulties in communication. Tagging these annexed territories to Assam was an award and the British had done so for serving the land-locked hill areas and never did it appear as an act of exploitation of their distinctive cultural identity, autonomy and independence.

The consolidation also facilitated national unity. The consolidated composite Assam was integrated with Indian Union. Colonial rule had contributed much to a sense of national consciousness and unity. The development demonstrated the feeling of being together even in the midst of diversities. Besides that, the hill areas were in fact border areas with China, Myanmar and East Pakistan and their annexation and integration has in most cases prevented outside invasion or encroachment of tribal lands and territories.

2. Impact of New Administrative Policies:[14] After successfully brought autonomous and independent states and kingdoms together under the comprehensive and inclusive name Assam-a name that suited well for British political interests and rule, the colonial rulers began creating some administrative political policies that facilitated convenient ruling of certain territories or states and people alike. A description of the development among the Khasi states is in order. After consolidating the erstwhile fragmented 29 Khasi states, the British made significant administrative provisions for the retention of the traditional democratic ruling system for Khasi States and for the protection of the interests of non-state or British areas under direct British administration.[15] Four Khasi States, like Sutnga, Nongpoh, Muliang and Sohbar states were made non-states.[16] The traditional kingly rule in these states was replaced by the new administrative mechanism. Even a portion of Shillong city known as European ward and Cantonment areas and numerous villages in Khasi hills were converted into British administered areas. Gradually, these converted areas were grouped together under a single administration and called it the Khasi and Jaintia hills District. The Khasi states enclosure was outside the district and regarded differently but under a single political control.

The British did not only introduce new political policies for the territories but created avenues for development and protection. The chief of Sutnga, commonly known to the British and neighbouring areas as Raja of Jaintia, was the most powerful chief but fearing of his insurrection besides non-cooperation, the

[14] Shullai, L. G. **Ki Hima Khasi** (1975).

[15] Cf. Snaitang, O. L. *op.cit.*, p. 46.

[16] *Ibid.*, p. 46.

British changed the kingship and replaced his office in 1835.[17] In the process, they the state received political attention that resulted in changing of the name Sutnga to Jaintia, supported, promoted and encouraged the system or ruling through the dolois (ruling by local chief of subordinate level). History is proof that the once mighty solidified state was well integrated into 12 (twelve) doloiships who were placed under the rule and protection of the British government. Doloiship, therefore, was an indication of the policy of decentralization of political administration in the larger interests of the people in the region. In other words, British policy of decentralizing the Sutnga state appeared to have fallen in line with people's political interest and ambition.

Next to the integrative promotion of doloiship, the British created Sirdarship[18] in other areas and villages. These colonial created chiefs were agents for strengthening British interests and rule in the region and might have enabled them to protect the areas and people from being exploited.

While the plain areas of Assam and the Khasi-Jaintia hills were made open to people without restriction, the British encircled the hills of Arunachal Pradesh and hitherto called North East Frontier Agency (NEFA). It was a protected place and restricted people's movements. Because of its isolation and difficult hilly terrain, the British policy makers who perhaps wanted to make the region untouched by development - a region for tribal sanctuary and because of their convenience did not even set up an office in Arunachal Pradesh proper but in Shillong. Its relocation to Itanagar was done only in the late 1970s.

The renowned policy maker, Verrier Elwin, was of the opinion of a static culture for the people in Arunachal Pradesh.[19] His vision for maintaining people's traditional life style resulted in underdevelopment, slavery of exposure and prevention of modern agencies of change. Though Elwin's vision could have functioned well in ancient set up of people's antiquity but given the growing rise and influence of cross cultural interaction, science and technology and globalization this was a case of preventing tribal growth in wisdom, knowledge and a curb of their opportunities.

The other policy that the new administration had adopted was the policy of declaring certain hill areas like Mizoram, Nagaland and Arunachal Pradesh as inner line areas by the Bengal Eastern Frontier Regulation of 1873.[20] If there is anything to be believed, its implication might well be seen in respect of making strong land laws for the indigenous people, regulating outside economic exploitation, preserving indigenous people's cultural values and protecting the tribes who were in minority and remained vulnerable to immigration and influx

---

[17] *Ibid.*, 45.

[18] Nichols-Roy, J. J. M. "Ka Draft ka Ain Synshar ia ka bynta ka Assam, Kyrteng: Khasi and Jaintia Hills" (Unpublished document in Khasi, 1947), pp. 1, 3.

[19] Elwin, Verrier **Philosophy for NEFA** (1959).

[20] Cf. **The Bengal Eastern Frontier Regulation of 1873.**

of outside people who were already in majority. It was also a preventive regulatory mechanism and control of non – indigenous people's entry into these areas with economic interests.

3. Application of Devised Administrative Policies: The first thing that British officers did at least with tribal chiefs was by asking them to sign treaty agreements - agreements that enabled the new administration gaining controlling powers. Subsequent treaties called sunnads further curbed native leaders' authority.[21] Along with these signed treaty documents, the new administration brought laws and jurisprudences that were framed and passed by Board of Directors or legislation outside the region.[22] Members of these legislating bodies were British and acts were passed mostly in their interests and administrative convenience but the results were also in the larger interests of the tribes.

Office buildings were set up in most district headquarters besides residential quarters. The region witnessed the presence of British officers. But, subordinate clerks that they have appointed were mostly non-local people.[23] This happened not only in district offices in the hill areas but even in offices in the plains of Assam among the Assamese.

The setting up of administrative Secretariat came out with the establishment of Cantonments for military outposts and defence. Military personnel were also non-native and their presence created an environment of fear and trembling among most of the local inhabitants including the chiefs. People's fear was further intensified and compounded by bringing of guns, arms and ammunitions. Blasting of unharmed explosives like crackers caused unnecessary furore not only among the local citizens but among the innocent animals and birds. The psychology of most tribal chiefs was downgraded and for the first time in their long history, the chiefs were subjected to an alien authority-an authority that was more powerful and systematic.

4. Change Brought about by New Administrative Systems:[24] The new administration introduced a system of working through writing. The first thing that they did was in making written treaty agreements with native leaders and filed them for reference. These documents were binding and these illiterate native leaders who depended mostly on their interpreters were at a loss. Official dealings with public were also made through written applications. Records of business transaction, lands and appointments were processed through writings followed by authorized signatures and stamping of appropriate official seals.

---

[21] Cf. Aitchison, C. U **A Collection of Treaties, Engagements, and Sannads Relating to India and Neighbouring Countries,** Vol. I (1892).

[22] Downs, "Christianity as a Tribal Response to Change in North East India" **Missiology: International Review**, VIII. 4 (October 1980), 407-416.

[23] *Ibid.*, pp. 408f.

[24] Snaitang, O. L. *op. cit.*, pp. 46-49.

A written culture also appeared on the area of accounting. It involved financial budget in the form of income and expenditure and officials have to process such in proper order. Besides, the new administration introduced a system of weights and measures in shops and business enterprises. These procedures were also applied on measuring of liquid materials like cooking oil, kerosene, etc.

British officials began preparing Reports, wrote books and published them. A written culture went out side by side with the imposition of English language as a medium of communication in offices. Native inhabitants were exposed to these new developments and made them looking for help in order to enable them to function successfully in the modern social environment.

These new institutional elements contributed to the ushering of a modern British set up. These new developments were also integral parts of the British administration and bound to have major impact on Northeast Indian people's life, thinking and working procedure. Hill people who did not have written alphabet but functioned on unwritten words, agreements and vows were under the British introduced set up in a dilemma. Even communities like the Assamese, Meiteis and others who had written scripts had to pass through an almost similar situation like the hill people because the new regime introduced Roman or Latin alphabet and English in their administration. Natives faced a practical functioning crisis. Their main problem was how to effectively function in a modern British imposed setting. In a region that witnessed the presence of numerous Babel of tongues, the colonial authority imparted their language as the medium of official written and spoken communication.

Introducing of a calculated clock of twenty four hours a day and the scheduled working hours was another system that had affected people's laxity and freedom. Clocks and watches were brought in and people had to learn the fraction of calculation in terms of second, minute, hour, etc. Though these new timing procedures appeared to have applied well in human sphere but insofar as the people in the region were never used to it, the imposition then caused unnecessary problem of adjustment. People were through the modern timing schedules becoming prisoners of the working hours.

The traumatic change was also happening in the introduction of Western counting of days, weeks, months and years. The European calendar year and almanac were made applicable on the people in the region, in India and elsewhere alike. These new calendar years though were made universally worldwide but had greatly affected the traditional counting in hill people's calculation. For instance, the Khasi-Jaintia people and even the neighbours in the plains of Bangladesh normally calculated eight days in a week. Each day was named after the markets, pre-major market day and post-major market day. Though this old system of counting continues to work so even in the modern set up but its usual functioning had to be readjusted with the modern calendar or almanac even with great inconvenience at least in the initial years of imposition.

Tribal people who were practically people with strong work culture - they worked mostly on most needed times, had under the new administration redesigned their working hours and started acknowledging holidays like Sundays and other government designated days. When this new working system was introduced to the people, there was no other option for them save positive concession, submission and adjustment.

5. New Social Elements and People's Culture:[25] The advent of the new colonial power witnessed significant influence on people's social life style. Their coming was seen with the display and use of western dresses, clothing materials, tailoring, cosmetics, shoes and slippers. These fashionable cultures had not just shaped people's mind and money but attracted them even at the cost of replacing traditional dresses especially male dresses.

Shaving materials, shampoos and use of soaps in addition to applying of perfumes, powder and hair oil had enhanced people's life style. In most cases, people were so conscious of their social dignity that they hardly attending big gatherings, Sunday services or meeting officials unless they had dressed up in a good manner. It was mainly for social relationships and dignity that made hill people attracted to Western life style and never for social liberation.

Most hill people were receptive to the colonialists and neighbours. Their occupation soon led to friendly relations and resulted in inter-marriage. This development became evident in the creation of new family names. The loss of most matrilineal clan names in such inter-marital contacts was in most instances irrecoverable especially for those whose settlement was no more in Meghalaya. Besides that, the new system had replaced people's family mode of addresses. The traditional way of calling a husband as father of (Kpa u/ka ...) was through the British imposed way replaced by Mr. & Mrs. A or B. In this new family combined fashion, the family clan of a mother was no more in well acknowledged recognition. Some families whose fathers were highly educated, rich or in high positions tended to have changed their clan name to that of a father. It was intermarriage and salaried system that precipitated nuclear family in the once kinship extended family.

The traditional set up among the hill people and even that of the plains was such that men alone who descending from legitimate ruling or leading clans could take leadership in ruling in areas of legislation, administration, judiciary, executive department and religion. No woman was allowed to become head of these respective functionaries.

The advent of the new dispensation had in most cases turned this traditional pattern upside down, i.e., leadership was no longer determined on descent or muscle power but on qualification at least in governmental offices, educational

---

[25] Downs, F. S. "Faith and Life Style: How Christianity was understood by 19th century Converts in North East India," **Bangalore Theological Forum**, XIV. 1 (January–June 1982), pp. 20-43.

institutions and other scientific institutional areas. Except qualified candidates were appointed as officers, accountants or treasury officers, judges and the appointment was no longer determined on a person's descent, strong muscles or mouth power. The new power had at least brought liberation to women. Such new development was greatly felt in the sub-continent and Asia alike where the position of women was regarded low.

6. Impact on Traditional Economy:[26] Hill people's economic life was simple. Their main products were fruit crops, betel leaves, areca nuts and vegetables. Most of these crops were grown in warm areas. Other agricultural products included sweet potatoes, yam, paddy, maize, millet and others and they were mostly cultivated in the cold climatic region. Other areas of engagements were in producing handicraft materials like winnowing fans, stools, rain shades, cones, head straps, baskets and various materials. Most people also engaged in iron smelting works that produced spades, daos, knives, spears, etc. The other occupation that helped the people made a living was pastoral and included rearing of cattle, chicken, sheep, piggery, goat, horse and a little bit of fishery. Producing of non-intoxicated arrack and drinks was also of some significance.

These products were selling articles in markets. Daily markets were non-existent in hill people's ancient days. The eight days a week witnessed rotation of market days in respective areas of the region. Most markets in areas bordering with Bangla or Assam would see the presence of non-tribal traders. These people came in boats and brought essential commodities like rice, salt, dried fish, eatables, match boxes and other materials like spices and biscuits.

In all these active business dealings both in products and sale, the main economic dealing was carried out through the barter system. Though the circulation of money was done in markets in the plain areas, it was not popular in the ancient life style as notes and coins did not matter much at least for the hill people.

The impact that the British system had been on the people in the region could well be seen in areas as under:-

1). Using of Money in Economic Dealing:[27] Following their occupation and rule, the British introduced use of money as means of economic transaction in markets and society. Its application affected the natives in Northeastern India who were once familiar mainly with the barter system of exchanging goods. Though the people found it difficult to adjust to the new economic system in the early British rule but once they knew it they found it rather beneficial and gaining. There was no economic parity in the traditional exchange of goods. This new economic system became a common denominator that made the people realize the goods' value and the importance of money.

---

[26] Downs, "Christianity as a Tribal Response to Change in North East India" **Missiology: International Review**, *op. cit.*, 408-409.

[27] *Ibid.*

Money did not just determine the value of materials but become so powerful that its voice could touch people's hearts and could even change their minds. Its power was such that the entire barter economy was completely eliminated from the region.

2). Introduction of Weights and Measures:[28] Along with the ushering of money, the new set up brought the system of weights and measures and made applicable in shops, markets and in land deal. This method enabled mutual benefits on both the sellers and buyers. It also helped check malpractices, exploitations, black marketers and cheatings. The setting up of a departmental agency that looked after these aspects had created mass awareness to a little extent. While this dimension is no doubt contributing to the natives but its effectiveness and usefulness remained dependent upon their knowledge. It was at that point that hill people were looking for some agencies to help them learn the new institutional means in the modern world otherwise these new measures would drive their ethnic identity and growth in despair and turmoil.

3). Ration Shops and Essential Commodities:[29] The practice of selling commodities at government controlled prices and through public distributing units was a new introductory economic dealing that reached out to the citizens. Most of these shops began to operate almost daily. Commodities that were sold to the people included rice, salt, sugar, cooking oil, dal, kerosene oil and other materials.

These ration shops contributed to some form of market stability in selling goods in designated towns or district headquarters on regular basis. People began to know what kind of materials or essential commodities that was available in ration shops. However, as the process of urbanization began to evolve, what the government had initiated appeared to have become more effective in the hands of the new arrival business communities.

7. **British Government and Religion:** The other area that the new administration had initiated was religion. The British officials belonged to their official religion, the Church of England or the Anglican Church. As it was in Britain, the Church was a major part of the state. Though the British maintained a strict policy of religious neutrality or non-interference in indigenous religions in India, they however created bishoprics and brought official chaplains to provide spiritual services to the British officials. Their presence soon led to the building of churches and parsonages, setting up of chaplaincy and putting separately a plot of land as a cemetery.

Northeast India was in the eyes of certain British officials a region that was different religiously from the other parts of India and in need of Christianity that could control frequent attacks on the plain people, eliminate illiteracy and humanization. They did not regard hill people's religions as true religion at all

[28] *Ibid.*

[29] *Ibid.*

because most apparently of their fragmented natures, no proper place of worship, no scriptures, creeds or hymn books. So, their interference in this aspect was by no means carrying any implication of inappropriate or illegal violation.

1). Nature of British officials in Northeast India: W. N. Garrett and Matthew Smith:[30] These were British government servants who served as judges resident in Sylhet. They were posted there before 1813. They were Christians with high evangelical convictions. Garrett was a nephew of Robert Raikes, the pioneer of Sunday school movement in England. It was they who might have sent letter of invitation to the Serampore Mission requesting them to send missionaries to Khasi hills. In response to this official invitation, the Serampore Mission sent Rev. Krishna Chandra Pal who reached Pandua, Khasi hills in April or May 1813.

Pal's work was productive because before leaving Pandua for Serampore, there were seven adults who professed their faith in Jesus Christ and sought baptism.[31] Two of them by the name of U Duwan and U Anna were Khasis and they were the first known Christian converts from the community. Unlike in the Anglican tradition that normally performed baptism inside the church, Rev. K. C. Pal who belonged to the Baptist tradition took the baptismal candidates to the open running river. The British officials who took over the sacramental duty from Rev. Pal began to question the converts' faith and confession.[32] It was told that these British officials made public preparation for the baptismal performance and before baptizing them there was a kind of respect and declaration through gun salute.

2). Attitude and Role of David Scott:[33] As mentioned elsewhere, David Scott studied at Fort William College, Kolkata and came under the influence of William Carey. After passing out his examination, he was appointed as a British agent and commissioner for the southern portion of Northeast India. Though his job was for setting up of a successful and stable administration in the region, he was also responsible for promoting Christian missionary works especially in the hills.

Like the British residents in Sylhet, David Scott too was instrumental for encouraging the Serampore missionaries in the region. He was responsible for starting a mission station at Cherrapunji under the supervision of Alexander Lish in 1832 and a school at Guwahati under James Rae.

---

[30] Snaitang, O. L. "William Carey and the Church in Northeast India" in Daniel, J. T. K. & R. E. Hedlund, eds., **Carey's Obligations and India's Renaissance** (1993), p. 92f.

[31] *Ibid.*, p. 91.

[32] *Ibid.*, p. 93.

[33] For a detail study and further story about David Scott, see Barooah, Nirode K. **David Scott in North East India, 1802-1831: A Study in British Paternalism** (1970).

More importantly however, was the introduction of a rather more comprehensive missionary outreach at Singimari in Garo hills.[34] It was comprehensive because the kind of educational school that was set up was representative of a holistic mission. It combined school education with agriculture, animal husbandry and self-employment programmes.

It was under his headship that saw government subsidy of missionary school education. In his opinion, educational activity of Christian missions was secular and so government financial assistance to them would by no means implying violation of the government policy of religious neutrality in the country.[35]

3). Role and Influence of Frances Jenkins:[36] Like David Scott, Jenkins was another British Agent who worked in upper Assam-Nagaland. He was an officer with sympathy on Christian evangelization. It was in such situation that the American Baptist Mission could come in and started work in upper Assam, Nagaland and elsewhere in the region as early as 1836. Prior to that American Baptist year, Jenkins was instrumental for starting a school at Goalpara.[37] Its significance was that it could produce outstanding Garo ecclesiastical leaders like Omed and Ramke whose role among the Garo people contributed greatly in breaking new grounds.[38] So, the Baptist Church in Garo hills was an outcome of an indigenous initiative.

Therefore, though the British colonial authority did not encourage Christian missionary operation in India but its role in inviting Christian missionaries had come from personal interests of some British responsible officers. Christian Missions that worked in the region did not seek help from the British government but the assistance had come from the government initiative. Here, one should understand that the role of individual officers in shaping the destiny of a particular area or people was so crucial.

The American Baptist Mission that had come to the region in response to an invitation from the British government got involved in missionary activities even without help from the government. There was no British colonial control or dictate on the missionaries in the region. The Welsh Mission that had come later had worked on school education even without government grant-in-aid. As a matter of fact, this grant-in-aid system that was given to Christian managed schools was also made applicable to private schools later.

---

[34] Snaitang, O. L. "William Carey and the Church in Northeast India" in Daniel, J. T. K. & R. E. Hedlund, eds., *op. cit.*, p. 92.

[35] *Ibid.*, pp. 93f.

[36] *Ibid.*, 94.

[37] Aier, K. I. **The Growth of Baptist Churches in Meghalaya** (1978), pp. 27-33.

[38] *Ibid.*

Chapter 4

Appeared, Disappeared and Integrated Christian Communities (1627-1838)

Christianity began to gain permanent and stable services only after the arrival of the American Baptist Mission (1836), the Welsh Presbyterian Mission (1841), the Anglican Church (1876), the Catholic Mission (1890) and the British Baptist Missionary Society (1894). There were however contacts and missionary endeavors before 1836 – the Christian communities that in the words of Prof. Syiemlieh, had "disappeared and integrated." This chapter will try to provide detail information about these initial developments since the first contact as early as 1627 till 1838.

I. Early Christian Contacts

The early Christian presence and contacts with people in Northeast India were seen in two different developments. First, it was Catholic missionaries and mercenaries who have come first. In the early seventeenth century, Catholic missionaries happened to pass by Assam and they were the first Christian priests ever landed on the region. Their intention was however not to work in Northeast India but to go to Lhasa, Tibet through Assam. Secondly, the other Catholic Christians who settled in the region were Portuguese and Indo-Portuguese soldiers served under the Mughal powers and Maharajah of Tripura. Their presence was notably recorded at Rangamati–Hossumpur; Bondashil-Baniyachong; Mariamnagar, Kashipur.

Second, besides the Catholic presence, it was missionaries of Serampore Mission who had started missionary works in Khasi Hills in 1813.Though their works were productive and successful but because of the sudden change of the Baptist Missionary Society policy in Serampore, the mission operation in the region was completely withdrawn in 1838

1. Tibet-Bound Missionaries:[1] We have described how Northeast India was in the mind of the larger Catholic vision and ecclesiastical division.[2] The region was initially made a part of the diocese of Mylapore, then Tibet and later of Bengal.[3] Their visions and design before the end of the sixteenth century appeared to have ended in ecclesiastical proceedings and ecclesiastical mapping.

Northeast India remained an isolated region. People lived on their own worldview and style. The 16th century Northeast India world was a world of villages, illiteracy, poverty and superstition. The entire region witnessed the presence of dense forest, agricultural vegetations and thick jungles. There were wild animals, insects and deadly mosquitoes. Besides that there were rivers, waterfalls and streamlets. Heavy floods in monsoon season inundated the plain areas, whereas some places in the hills were enveloped in darkness even in the day time because of thick clouds and fogs. These places were once believed to have been occupied by natural spirits. These perceptions further led to superstitious belief. Again these phenomena did not facilitate easy communication, freedom of movement or penetrability except within a limited area and mostly among homogenous neighbours.

Besides that, the entire sub-continent was also inaccessible. There were no motor, rail or air transportations. Moving from one place to another involved traveling by bullock carts in plain areas or by horses. Majority of travelers walked on foot. People had to face natural hardships by extreme humid climate, rainfall, storms or cold waves in winter. It is therefore not easy for Christian missionaries to travel to this region for evangelization.

Even in the midst of isolation, the region had at least gained a place in the Catholic Church's dreams and ecclesiastical inclusion. Tibet was a land of European Catholic romanticism. It was a religious seat of Buddhism where its spiritual pontiff, Dalai Lama, resided. It was also thought it a missiological strategic centre for wider mission especially to the great Chinese main land empire and other parts under the larger Himalayan region.

In this connection, it is not surprising to know that the first Catholic priest contact with Assam was not for missionary work in Assam but a way through to Tibet. In their thinking going through Assam was more feasible than from any part of India. Fr. George Kottuppallil an ecclesiastical historian, informed us as follows:

> The first recorded contact of the Assamese with the Catholic missionaries was in 1627 when the Tibet Bound Jesuit Missionaries,

---

[1] Kuttuppallil, George "A Historical Survey of the Catholic Church in Northeast India from 1627 to 1969" in S. Katotemprel, ed., **The Catholic Church in Northeast India, 1890-1990** (1993), pp. 31f.

[2] *Ibid.*

[3] *Ibid.*, pp. 32-35.

> Stephen Cacella and John Cabral, visited parts of Goalpara and Kamrup District on their way to Tibet. Tibet the land of mystery was part and parcel of the romantic missionary literature of Europe from the 16th to 19th century, while Assam was hardly known to the outside world except as an unhealthy region that offered a possible passage to Tibet.[4]

This information provided ample evidence that Northeast India was never envisioned as an important place for missionary services.

The Catholic Christians who happened to have settled in Northeast India, especially in Rangamati, Bondashil and Mariamnagar were not interested in missionary outreach but were part of the Portuguese settlements in India. The Portuguese were the first European expansions who had come to Goa, India in the early sixteenth century. Their mercenaries came not as traders like most of Portuguese business agents did, but in search for employment. They were expert in using guns and operating cannons. Most Mughal emperors who were able to possess cannons in their military defence could however not able to find qualified operators from Indian mercenaries except the Portuguese. As a result, most Portuguese mercenaries were appointed in Mughal armies and posted in several places. These foreign soldiers stayed here for a longer period and some of them settled down permanently. There were amongst them who married Indian women and inducted them to the Catholic Church.

Now, these Portuguese Catholic soldiers were appointed and stationed mostly at Rangamati, Bondashil and Mariamnagar.

2. Catholic Presence in Rangamati and Hossompur:[5] It was noted that Rangamati, which referred to the large presence of Catholic Portuguese soldiers, was the one that situated on the side of Brahmaputra in lower Assam. It was an important centre of the Mughal power. Fr. Kottuppallil wrote "Raja Ram Singh, the Mughal army commander, had made this (i.e Rangamati) his centre from 1667 to 1687."[6] Bengal was then the mission field of the Augustinian Order and had its centre at Bandel, West Bengal. It was from there that records of the presence of about 7000 of Catholic Christians at Rangamati was maintained, i.e, in the later half of the seventeenth century.[7] These Christians, both Portuguese and Indo-Portuguese, in the opinion of a famous Jesuit scholar N. Hosten, might have been employed under Mir Jumla and accompanied him in his Assam expedition (1661-1663) and stationed at Rangamati.[8]

---

[4] *Ibid.*, p. 31.

[5] Syiemlieh, David R. **Disappeared and Integrated: The Indo Portuguese in North East India** (2007), pp. 3f.

[6] Kottuppallil, George, *op. cit.*, p. 31.

[7] Syiemlieh, David R. *op. cit.*, p. 3.

[8] *Ibid.*

Another adjacent place that the Portuguese Catholic soldiers had settled was Hossampur.[9] It was told that an Augustinian friar, Fr. Frey Sicardo who visited the Catholic soldiers for spiritual ministry at Rangamati, reported of the existence of another military station at Hossampur, an outpost close to Rangamati. It appeared that the Catholic Christians at Hossampur were more dedicated and religious as they were able to build a church dedicated to St. Nicholas de Tolentino.

These two Portuguese Catholic settlements did not last as by a century later both sites and the Catholic mercenaries had disappeared.

Though there was no evidence for the disappearance of such a sizable Christian population especially from Rangamati, there could have been at least two reasons. First, Rangamati was a place located at a bend of the river Brahmaputra. As the land surface in lower Assam was soft, the place could have been eroded by heavy floods and inundation during monsoon. As a result, the Catholic Christians at Rangamati might have left the place and settled elsewhere. Second, it was told that the powerful influence of the Mughal had declined since the early 18th century and the mercenaries could have been laid off from services in the imperial army. Such incident could have made the Indo-Portuguese soldiers to relocate their settlement from Rangamati and Hossumpur and moved elsewhere.

3. Catholic Settlements at Bondashil and Baniyachong: Bondashil is a village located on the bank of the river Barak near Badarpur in Cachar district. While it is difficult to ascertain the presence of the Portuguese soldiers at Bondashil, at least one related information writes:

> The tradition still prevalent among the people is that their ancestor had earlier served the principality of Sardhana near Meerut under the dashing German adventurer Walter Reinhardt and his charming wife Begum Sumru. Sardhana's army of 5000 men was at one point put under the disposal of the Mughal emperor. When the Mughal Emperor collapsed, a group of these soldiers may have left to secure military service as mercenaries in Sylhet and with the Cachar Raja.[10]

The reason that Portuguese Catholic mercenaries had landed in Sylhet for further employment with the British and the Raja of Cachar was in most probability realistic.

Then the Burmese who flexed its political muscles by extending its power and rule over Assam had unleashed a reign of terror. It also planned to expand its rule on Bengal through the Cachar territory. The Cachar Raja, Shri Govinda Chandra, who spotted the Burmese political design, sought immediate help and protection from the British East India Company. In response to the Cachar Raja's

---

[9] *Ibid.*, p. 4.

[10] *Ibid.*, p. 5.

appeal, the British power in Bengal deputed the Portuguese mercenaries from Sylhet in 1823/24 to help the Raja in fighting against the Burmese.[11]

The Portuguese soldiers stationed at Bardarpur and built a fort. Their presence was successful and that the intending Burmese expansionistic plan was thwarted from further advances. The Cachar Raja, who had lost his power, was restored by the British through help of the Portuguese mercenaries. As a mark of respect to the British and the soldiers, the Cachar Raja granted the Portuguese Catholic a land at Baniyachong in Sylhet for their settlement.[12] In this way, the new rewarded site became a settlement of the Portuguese Catholic mercenaries. While moving to Baniyachong majority of the Christian soldiers stayed on at Bondashil.

The Bondashil Catholic community received occasional pastoral visit.[13] Fr. Freycinon who visited the Portuguese Christians settled at Bondashil in 1844 was well acknowledged as the first priest who had landed there. The Cachar Sylhet area was then brought under the ecclesiastical jurisdiction of the Holy Cross Congregation. Fr. Benoit Adolphe Mercier, who was recently ordained to the ministry under the Holy Cross Order, looked after the Bondashil Portuguese church and made frequent pastoral visits. There were three memorable recorded visits. First, Fr. Mercier visited Bondashil in 1860 from Dhaka. He took advantage of this visit to go to Cherrapunjee, Shillong and Guahati. It was a long journey but with a pastoral mission.

Secondly, Fr. Mercier visited the Bondashil church in 1861. This second visit was historic because of the accompanying of the Rt. Rev. Dafal, Bishop of East Bengal. That was the first visit of a Bishop to Bondashil and even to the whole of Assam or Northeast India. During this historic pastoral visit some converts were admitted to the church.

Fr. Mercier's third visit took place in 1864. This time he performed the sacrament of holy matrimony of Maria Filghera to John Anton on 23rd July 1864. Again this was the first ever official church's marriage that took place in the region.

In 1870, Fr. Aime Marrie Fourmoud, Fr. Marcier confrere, stayed at Bondashil as a permanent resident priest.

4. Mariamnagar and Kashipur Catholic Settlements:[14] Though the Mariamnagar Catholic community composed of the Indo – Portuguese soldiers, it did not appear to have any connection with the Rangamati and Bondashil communities. Tripura was a Princely state. Its peaceful existence was shattered by threats from the Mughs of Arakkan and the Chittagong hills. While the Tripura military defence was weak to fight the impending attacks and intrusion

---

[11] *Ibid.*

[12] *Ibid.*, p. 6.

[13] Syiemlieh, David R. "Portuguese Settlements in Northeast India" in Fernandez, F. & J. Varickasseril, eds., **Mission: A Service of Love** (1998), p. 303.

[14] *Ibid.*, 304.

of the neighbouring enemies, King Amar Manikya of Tripura then inducted the Portuguese soldiers of Noakhali and Chittagong army. The objective of their employment was to chase out the neighbouring Mughs and to maintain security to the King's kingdom and its capital Udaipur.

The kingdom's capital at Udaipur was in due course shifted to Agartala in around 1760. The king rewarded the Portuguese mercenaries by giving them a rent free land for settlement. It was a fertile land for agriculture, rearing cattle and farming. The Portuguese Catholic soldiers named their location Mariamnagar.[15] Besides that, some mercenaries settled down at Kashipur, a village not very far from Mariamnagar.

Catholic priests in Indian union were few and located mostly in capital cities and it was difficult for them to attend to their scattered communities especially in Northeast India. However, Fr. Ignatius Gomes was able to visit the Catholic Christians at Mariamnagar in 1683. Though the visit could have strengthened the community, he however could no longer visit them again. Another priest who visited Mariamnagar in 1843 was Fr. Barbe of Chittagong. He had a good impression of Catholic Christians there because even in the long absence of priestly visit among them, they were nevertheless upholding their faith in tact. They also maintained cleanliness in the village, comfortable habitation and clean dresses. He served to their spiritual needs, like performing baptism and marriages also.

The Catholic mercenaries at Mariamnagar who were conscious of their faith and movements continued to retain their Catholic faith even if priests could not turn up to attend to their spiritual needs regularly. While doing so religiously, The Mariamnagar Catholic Christians were accommodative to their neighbouring Bengali culture. In the words of Dr. David R. Syiemlieh,

> They (Indo – Portuguese Catholic Christian) spoke Bengali, sang Bengali songs, use musical instruments of the dominant community, dressed like them and also acquired their food habits, though with preference for pork on special occasions."[16]

A Summary: The Portuguese and Indo Portuguese soldiers who settled at Rangamati and Hossumpur, Bondashil and Baniyachong, Mariamnagar and Kashipur were Christians of Catholic tradition. Their presence in sizable number was well acknowledged. The Church could not provide continuity because these Catholic Christians were mercenaries but not missionaries. Their main work was fighting the enemies under the Mughal imperial power and not evangelizing the natives. Therefore, the Catholic mission had to start its missionary work in

---

[15] *Ibid.*

[16] Syiemlieh, David R. **Disappeared and Integrated**, p. 11.

Northeast India afresh and they could do so only before the end of the nineteenth century.

II. Serampore Missionary Work in Northeast India (1813–1837/8)[17]

Another Western Mission that had started work in the region but could not provide continuity was the Serampore Mission. It began its missionary work in Khasi hills in 1813 but closed down for good in 1838.

It was difficult for Western mission societies to start any missionary work in British administered India because of its policy of religious neutrality. The only areas that Western Christian missionaries could set up their missionary activities were areas under the control of Danish colonial government, like Tranquebar in Tamilnadu and Serampore in West Bengal. While the Royal Danish-Halle Lutheran mission worked at Tranquebar and Tanjore area,[18] William Carey and his colleagues of the Baptist Missionary Society could set up their activities at Serampore.[19]

1. Background: William Carey[20] deserved the credit and honour for stirring up missionary interests in UK and elsewhere in the Western world. His pamphlet entitled the **Enquiry** (1792)[21] was so influential and it resulted in the formation of the Baptist Missionary Society on 2nd October, 1792. The Society sent William Carey, his family and Dr. John Thomas as missionaries to West Bengal, India. They landed Calcutta on 11th November, 1793. Difficulties loomed large on William Carey from different frontiers. First, the British government opposition to the BMS missionaries[22] was so intense that William Carey could not carry out his missionary work in Kolkata. Secondly, poverty, sickness and even death that had passed by the missionaries were enormous that made Dorothy Carey mentally deranged. Later, William Carey had to accept appointment to the Indigo factory

[17] For information about the history and activities of the Serampore Mission, see Potts, D. E. **British Baptist Missionaries in India, 1793-1837: The History of Serampore Missions** (1967). Also see Daniel, J. T. K & R. E Hedlund, **Carey's Obligation and India's Renaissance** (1993).

[18] See Lehmann, E. A. **It Began at Tranquebar** (1956).

[19] Cf. Wenger, E. L. "The Serampore Mission and Its Founders" in **The Story of Serampore and Its College** (n. d. Published in c. 1993), pp. 2-5.

[20] For a rather authoritative and comprehensive biography on William Carey, cf. Carey, S. Pearce **William Carey** (1934).

[21] Its full title is **The Enquiry into the Obligations of Christians to use Means for the Conversion of Heathens**.

[22] By the time of William Carey's arrival in Kolkata in 1793, the British government in India maintained its policy of religious neutrality. In other words, no Christian missionaries were allowed to carry out missionary activities under British administered-India. However, through the influence of the Company's Board members, like Charles Grant and Chaplains, like David Brown, Claudius Buchanan and others, who were Christians of evangelical interests, they could bring about tremendous change in the standing policy of non – interference in native religions by the time of the renewal of the Company's Charter in 1813.

at Madnabati, Malda District, North Bengal. His service with the factory had however not put off his missionary zeal and interests. His translation of the Bible into Bengali went out in full swing. He had also started school education and initiated printing processes in Madnabati as well.

2. An Introduction of Serampore Mission: It was in 1799 that witnessed the beginning of the Serampore Mission following the arrival of the BMS new recruited missionaries, viz., Joshua Marshmann, William Ward, William Grant and Daniel Brunsdon. The latter two missionaries, Grant and Brunsdon, could not survive long. They died barely two years of their missionary services at Serampore. Realizing obstacles and hostility in British India, the new recruits went straight to Serampore and placed themselves to the protection and care of Col. Bie, the then Danish Governor in Serampore.[23]

William Carey had tried hard to get these new arrived missionaries joined his service at Madnabati and strengthened his missionary activities then but was unsuccessful. Later he had to relinquish his service at Madnabati Indigo factory, abandoned his mission works, moved to Serampore and reached there on 10th January, 1800. That was the beginning of Serampore Mission that witnessed the exemplary works of these three gifted missionaries that turned over Serampore into the title of "the cradle of Modern Missions."

The missionary works of the Serampore Mission were seen in Bible translations, promotion of popular indigenous literatures, educational activities, medical services, humanitarian works, Church planting, agri-horticultural society, botanical garden, printing and more importantly in the establishment of a theological university.

The Serampore trio believed in holistic mission and their integrative and comprehensive ministries were testimonies of their totally holistic mission involvement.

3. Serampore Mission and Northeast India:[24] The Serampore Mission did not plan to expand its missionary operation to Northeastern India. Finance and short of manpower could have been the main reasons for not favouring missionary expansion. It however sent Rev. Krishna Chandra Pal, a Bengali convert, to start mission work in the region. Rev. Pal came to Pandua, Khasi hills in 1813. Why did the Serampore trio expand their missionary works to Northeast India?

1). Christian Mission and Colonialism: It is no denying the fact that there was closer connection between Serampore Mission and British colonialism in the region. It was British officers resident at Sylhet who invited the Serampore Mission to start missionary work in Northeast India. As the government found it difficult to control and stop the warring Khasi-Jaintia and Garo people from frequent raiding of people in the plains, they thought it proper to hand over the

---

[23] See Firth, C. B. **An Introduction to Indian Church History** (1961/1983), p. 148.

[24] Snaitang, O. L. "William Carey and the Church in Northeast India" in Daniel J. T. K. & R. E Hedlund, eds., *op. cit.*, pp. 89-95.

primal people to the care and influence of Christian missionaries. At the same time, their vision was that the Christian missionaries could help in bringing about development and humanization.

Given the fact that the British Government adopted the policy of non-interference in religion, the officers in the region did not see any problem in encouraging Christian work among the primal people. The nature of these officers also contributed to this development. One of the reasons for promoting Christian missionary works in the region was that W. N. Garrett and Matthew Smith[25] who were British Officers posted in Sylhet were Christian with deep evangelical conviction and commitment. Garrett served in the capacity of a judge and was a nephew of Robert Raikes, the pioneer of the Sunday School movement in Britian. It was he who invited William Carey to start missionary work in the region. Matthew Smith, a colleague of W. N. Garrett, was a friend of William Carey and shared the evangelical faith in common.

William Carey sent Rev. Krishna Chandra Pal, a Bengali convert to Pandua who reached Pandua, a marketing centre in April or May 1813. Through his labours, there were seven adult men who were convinced by the new faith and received baptism in accordance with the Baptist tradition. Two of the baptized persons were Khasis, U Duwan and U Anna. The officers who did not want to see that the mission worked independently, they took control of the baptismal proceedings like questioning the candidates' confession of faith and fixing the venue for the ceremony. Rev. Pal's duty was only in performing the baptismal rite.

As a reiteration, David Scott[26] was the first Agent to the Governor General, North East Frontier and Special Civil Commissioner of North East Rangpur. Later, he was elevated to the rank of Commissioner of Northeastern region. Before joining the civil service of the government, David Scott studied at Fort William College, Kolkatta. There he came under the influence of William Carey especially in the evangelical faith and missionary work. Like Garrett and Smith, David Scott's interest in evangelization was more personal and in no way did it reflect the official position of the government. The British government had made its policy of religious neutrality clear right from the beginning so that its rule in the country would remain without unrest, resistance or any political agitation. But David Scott who did not see primal religions of the hill people as no religion at all, i. e., in comparison to established religions like Hinduism or Islam in the plains, did not see any political threat from involvement in religious affairs rather saw Christian mission as an effective agency for pacifying the warlike hill people and for humanizing.

Again, as already mentioned above, Frances Jenkins too was an officer of the same level as David Scott. He too was a Protestant Christian of deep spiritual devotion and admired William Carey's missionary spirit. His service in the region

[25] *Ibid.*, p. 93.

[26] *Ibid.*, pp. 93f.

was mainly concentrated in Upper Assam and associated mostly with the American Baptist Mission in area of providing education to the plain people of Assam.

2). Serampore Mission Activities in the Region:[27] The main activities of the mission in Northeast India were evident in at least two areas, viz., Bible translation and education.

True to the basic and primary objective of the founders of the Serampore Mission, the Serampore missionaries in Northeast India committed themselves to the task of translating the Bible. It was reported that the first effort in translating the Bible was done in respect of the Assamese language. The work was started off since the year 1811, i. e., before the deputation of Rev. K. C. Pal and could have taken place at Serampore itself. Shri Atmaram Sarma from Kaliabor, Nagoan, Assam was appointed to carry out the translation work. The New Testament in Assamese was brought out in 1819. The whole translated Bible in Assamese was completed by 1833. Though this translation was a great achievement but a poor translation did not make it effective. However, the Serampore Mission deserved appreciation for it being the first to have begun the work.

The translation of the Bible into Khasi was another achievement. It was Rev. K. C. Pal who took up this initiative at Pandua in 1813 itself. Under his supervision, the translation of the New Testament was published in 1831. The mission adopted the Shella dialect in the translation and used the Bangla alphabet. Like the Assamese translated Bible, the Khasee New Testament was not useful to the community. Its imperfect translation made even those who speak the Shella dialect unable to make sense. Rendering of Bangla alphabet in the translation was also incompatible with Shella phonetic system of spelling and pronunciation.

Another translation was made into Manipuri language. Though the Serampore Mission did not send any missionary to work in Manipur but the records indicated that the translation of the New Testament into Manipuri language was completed by 1827. This translation too was so poor that required an entirely new translation.

In spite of these imperfections, the Serampore Mission had done its part to venture and invested into this unexplored daunting task. It got the credit of being the pioneer in doing the job. It was through these attempts that Khasi language was included in the list of major Indian languages. Besides that, the translation was an indication of the promotion of indigenous languages and literatures. These attempts carried far national integrative interests.

3). Starting of Educational Schools:[28] Rev. Pal's missionary work at Pandua was successful and productive. Those who were baptized at Pandua formed the first

[27] Read Ngapkynta, Hamlet Bareh **William Carey in a New Perspective** (2004) – a book written from a Northeast India angle. Also Cf. Drewery, Mary **William Carey: Shoemaker & Missionary** (1978) – a view from a woman's eyes.

[28] For a detail story of Lish's activities, see Lish, A. B. "A Brief Account of the Khasees" **The Calcutta Christian Observer** (January to December 1838), pp. 129-143. Also Cf. Snaitang, O. L., *op. cit.*, pp. 90-92.

nucleus of a Christian community. However, as Rev. Pal went back to Serampore and concentrated at the supervision of the publication of the Khasi New Testament, the sprouting Pandua Christian community just disappeared in the absence of pastoral care and leadership. It was difficult to trace why Rev. Pal left Pandua in haste. One of the reasons could have been because he was not happy with excessive interference from the British officials in Church's activities. Ecclesiastical affairs that should have been dedicated in devotion and sacramental attention have by contrast been made part of the government's extended department. The Pandua church had just a historic beginning but did not leave any trace of continuity.

The work was started again under the supervision of Rev. Alexander B. Lish.[29] Unlike Rev. Pal who worked in the plain area, Rev. Lish chose Sohra, the hill proper, to carry out his evangelistic mission and this took place almost two decades after Pal's departure. Sohra was then a British station for Khasi-Jaintia hills. Landed at Sohra in 1832, Rev. Lish devoted to his educational mission. Rev. Pal's objective was to translate the Bible into Khasi, distributed it to the people, allowed them to read it and to make decision themselves. He did not bother whether the people could read or write. He took it for granted that they could read. At the same time, he tried not just to follow the Serampore trio's mission agenda in letter and spirit but to please them.

Rev. Lish's missionary vision was somewhat different. His missiological perception was that education should go to the indigenous people first so that they could read the Bible and other writings when placed before them. It is useless to give the translated Bible to the illiterate people but it becomes useful only once people have become literate. His missionary vision was for starting school education first. Hence, Rev. Lish was able to start elementary schools at Mawsmai, Mawmluh and Sohra. These missionary ventures were indications of Rev. Lish's dynamic vision.

Following Rev. Pal's initiative, Rev. Lish too taught the Bangla alphabet to the Khasi pupils. While Pal knew the Bangla language and alphabet and could work well with them, Lish had to struggle himself. That was the reason why before closing down the mission enterprise in Sohra he had contemplated of switching over to the Roman or Latin script. He found that the Khasi linguistic system could go out well with the Roman alphabet rather than with the sophisticated Bangla symbolic letters. At the same time, one should not forget that British officers were in favour of introducing Bangla letter and language for the Khasis so that they could administer well through their Bengali assistants and the Khasis too could successfully benefit in their business, trades and economic transactions in border markets.

The Chief of Sohra Syiemship and his durbar were receptive to the British government. They had given a portion of land at Saitsohpen area to the British for establishment of office buildings, quarters and health resorts. Rev. Lish selected

[29] *Ibid.*, p. 91.

Sohra because of the presence of the government who could assure him and his missionary operation some protection and help. Though the Sohra Chief and his council of ministers received the new colonial power with open hands, their actions did not mean positive acceptance of Christian missionaries. Realizing such danger, Rev. Lish stationed close to the ruling masters' office and residence.

Christian service in Sohra went out in good progress with positive response from most of the local people. However, in spite of their phenomenal development, Rev. Lish had to leave the region and liquidated the already established schools in 1838 because the Serampore Mission could no longer look after the long distant Khasi hills mission field. Another reason was that after the last Serampore trio, Joshua Marshmaun, who died in 1837, the Mission headquarter in Serampore could no longer get successors to the trio's calibre. The Baptist Missionary Society that took over the Serampore Mission preferred the policy of limiting missionary operation and staved off extra missionary burdens like the one in Khasi Hills.

Another area that the Serampore Mission had started educational mission was Guwahati.[30] This activity was carried out at the initiative of David Scott. Starting in 1829, the Mission sent Rev. James Rae and Ram Chandra Nath to work in Guwahati. David Scott worked hard to send 12 (twelve) students, 9 Garos and 3 Khasis to the Guwahati school. The objective of giving training of these hill students in Guwahati was that after completing the course, they could go back to their respective places and carry out mission service themselves. In other words, raising of native leadership would enable the students to start their mission work by standing on their own. Rev. James Rae was also active in mission and evangelism. He was able to build a church in Guwahati in 1837. The sending of William Robinson later had strengthened the Guwahati mission but the sudden change in Serampore Mission leadership, the Guwahati mission like that of Sohra mission came to an abrupt ending in 1838.

Besides the establishment of educational primary schools at Cherrapunji area and Guwahati through the Serampore Mission, David Scott whose main interest was for the advancement of the Garos and also of the Khasis, started a school at Singimari in Garo hills proper in 1827. Although Bishop Heber of Calcutta appeared to have proposed a strong recommendation for the school, the Singimari school was initially a school without any connection with Christian mission.[31] However, Scott's primary intention was to evangelize the illiterate Garo people. The school served as a model because of its comprehensive nature. It adopted not only teaching text books in school's curriculum but included in the educational study practical programmes of animal husbandry, farming and agriculture. This school could not survive because of Anglo Khasi War.

---

[30] Downs, F. S. **Christianity in North East India: Historical Perspectives** (1983), pp. 24f.

[31] *Ibid.*, p. 58f.

Chapter 5

Survey of Stable Christian Missions in the Region

I. The American Baptist Mission

1. Brief Introduction: The American Baptist Mission started its missionary work in Northeast India in 1836. Its work in Upper Assam and Nagaland are well described and narrated in most recent publications.[1] It is always stated that though the first objective of the Mission was to reach the Shan people in Myanmar it however landed in doing extending but serious evangelistic work among the unreached tribe among the Garos in Meghalaya. It was they who provided stable and well coordinated work among the Garos in Garo hill areas. Though a description of its missionary labours in different parts of the region is important but for the present study the concentration will be its work among the Garo people in Meghalaya – a study that has so far not given sufficient attention. At the same time, given the rise of conflicting arguments from indigenous writers like N. Toshi Ao, **Mission to the Nagas: A Tryst with the Aos** (1995) and the response from the Molungyimsen Baptist Church under the title **The Book Mission to the Nagas: Clarified** (1997) concerning the origin of Christianity in Ao area and my inability to check and verify the facts, I have chosen to devote only to the development in Garo hills at least for the present volume and its development in Nagaland, Assam and other areas in the region will be published in another related volume.

2. Mission in Garo Hills: Before the arrival of the American Baptist Mission, David Scott of the British government had already initiated missionary operation among the Garos of Singimari way back in 1827. The Singimari mission centre was significant because of its holistic approach. Though its aim was to bring about spiritual transformation among the enslaved religious Garos

[1] For detail information about the American Baptist Mission works in Northeast India, see Downs, F. S. **The Mighty Works of God** (1971); Puthepurakal, J. **Baptist Mission in Nagaland** (1984); Philip, P. T. **The Growth of Baptist Churches in Nagaland** (1976/1983).

its involvement however targeted the objective of liberating the people from their backwardness, poverty and illiteracy through education, agriculture and animal husbandry. Besides David Scott, it was Frances Jenkins, a Commissioner and Agent to the Governor General of Bengal in Assam who showed intense interest in missionary work among the Garos. His vision was to offer training to Garo boys in such a way that after getting education they would go back to Garo hills and help civilizing them. So, he started a school at Goalpara in 1847. Omed Momin and Ramke Momin who were reputed as the apostles of the Garos, were among the first batch of the students in Jenkins' school.

Even when the Serampore Mission abandoned its missionary work in the region in 1838, the fruits that it had reaped in the persons of Omed and Ramke Momin had not gone out of mind. It was the American Baptist Mission that took over the abandoned field among the Garos.[2] Pastor Kandura of the Guwahati Baptist Church was instrumental for ushering the connection with the American mission. Under his initiative and direction, Rev. Miles Bronson of the Baptist Mission in Nowgong traveled to Guwahati and baptized Omed and Ramke in the river bank of Brahmaputra on 8th January, 1863.

Now that the native converts had accepted the new faith, the interest in Christianization the Garos had come from the indigenous people themselves. In response to the Garos' written request – a Macedonian call, Rev. Bronson set out his journey from Nowgong to Garo hills – a distance of more than 200 miles, and reached Rajasimla on 13th April, 1867.[3] He and Omed baptized a total of 37 adult men and women. The incident resulted in the starting of the Baptist church at Rajasimla, the first in the entire Garo hills. Five months later, Dr. and Mrs. Stoddard of the American Baptist Mission who were given specific assignment among the Garo tribes, came to the region and landed at Goalpara on 3rd October, 1867. Their presence added strength to the newly started indigenous missionary venture.

The church began to gain significant presence among the people in the hills proper. Most Garos responded positively to the new faith. Their confidence in the Christian church was strengthened by the presence and role of Rev. Omed Momin and Rev. Ramke Momin. While the missionaries provided the needed guidance, administration and financial support, those who did the practical work of evangelization were native converts and evangelists. The success story of the Baptist church in Garo hills rested with these indigenous church workers. It was such development that made the people to have an understanding of Christianity not as a foreign religion but as a response to people's inner voice and a collective participation in the life of the community.

---

[2] Aier, K. I. **The Growth of Baptist Churches in Meghalaya** (1978).

[3] *Ibid.*, pp. 31ff.

Like the Khasis, the Garos too possessed numerous unintelligible dialects. It was the American missionaries who adopted the A'we dialect as a standard language for the entire tribe. Once it was introduced, they put it in use as a lingua franca or a universal linked language in education, literature, church service and public meetings. They also introduced Latin alphabet. The alphabet was a gift to the Garos in a way that it enabled them to function effectively in a modern situation, liberated them from the bondage of illiteracy and protected the community from outside literary oppressive forces.

The other area of the Church's contribution was in the introduction of educational schools and colleges. Although the main objective of the educational mission was for evangelization, the contribution that it had was on shaping the destiny of the community as a whole. It helped in raising the standard of living and thinking as well.

The Church takes care of the physical well being of the isolated hill people. Starting of health care and services through dispensaries and hospitals has brought tremendous benefit to the people. Medical mission had also the consequence of stamping out people's fear and superstition. Missionaries paid attention to the neglected orphans, the poor and the aged. Orphanages and other humanitarian services showed people the way to a new life of hope and service.

As of now majority of the Garo people have become Christians. Membership is evenly distributed in the entire Garo region except in areas with significant presence of non-tribal Muslim population. Ecclesiastical institutions provided the people meaningful occasions for fellowship, unity and solidarity. They also experience a new meaning in their life and espouse a dynamic worldview.

Baptist missionaries had prepared indigenous leadership right from the beginning of the mission operation in 1867. As a result of this preparation, many major ecclesiastical responsibilities were handed over to the Garo Christian leadership even well before India attained political independence in 1947. The post-independence scenario witnessed an indigenized Baptist church in all areas of administration, education, health services, evangelization, financing and theological academy as well.

II. An Introduction to the Welsh Presbyterian Mission History

Like the American Baptist Mission, the Welsh Presbyterian Mission is another Protestant mission that had come and worked among the Khasis and Mizos in the region in the 19th century and provided a stable and permanent ministry. This brief survey will touch upon its origin, growth and development especially its mission activities in Northeast India from 1841 till the present.

1. Beginning of the Welsh Mission and the Choice of Northeast India Field: The Presbyterian Church had its origin in the 16th century reformed tradition.[4] Huldrich Zwingli (1484-1531)[5] and John Calvin (1509-1564)[6] were pioneers of this tradition. Under their leadership, the reformed tradition came out in protest of the medieval authoritarian church, nominalism and sale of indulgences and others. Their main emphases were on God's sovereignty, importance of faith by divine grace for the attainment of salvation, the supremacy of the Word of God in matters of faith, practices and life, people's involvement in the Church through a well designed democratic structure and freedom of an individual's decision. John Knox from Wales who had studied under John Calvin in Geneva was the pioneer for spreading the Presbyterian Church in Wales.

The new faith brought about tremendous change in Welsh's social and religious life.[7] The Welsh were initially people of humble origins but were blessed with good quality coal deposits. Leading English businessmen from London and Great Britain, who had undertaken acquiring Welsh lands, had also begun digging the precious minerals and sold to factories outside Wales. The Welsh people who appeared less business minded were mostly engaged in manual labour force and daily wages. It was in the midst of these economic and physical sufferings and constraints that the role of Calvinistic Methodist Christian spirituality was so significant that they could heave a sigh of spiritual relief and solace. The new Christian theology brought the people together in praise and worship and in solidarity.

The rise of the Pietistic movement in the 17th century Germany and its subsequent influence on churches of Protestant traditions in Europe was so significant and it played a dominant role on the Welsh revival.[8] The emergence of the Puritan Movement in England in the 18th century had also added evangelical weight to the Welsh progressive Christianity. Evangelical and revival movements that resulted in the Howell Harris Revival in Wales in the 18th century infused deep Christian devotion and commitment to the Welsh people. These developments were influential factors that gave birth to the rise of missionary movements in Europe and North America. Though the Catholic Church was the pioneer in major missionary venture, it was the Moravians at least among Protestant Christianity who had initiated serious cross cultural mission and evangelism.

---

[4] Some authoritative studies in English on the 16th century reformation in Europe, read Bainton, R. H. **The Reformation of the Sixteenth Century** (1952); Elton, G. R. **Reformation Europe, 1517-1559** (1963); Grimm, H. J. **The Reformation Era, 1500-1650** (1973).

[5] For the life and works of Huldrich Zwingli, read Courvoirsier, J. **Zwingli: A Reformed Theologian** (1963).

[6] Cf. Wendel, F. **Calvin** (1963/1974). N. B. The Calvin Study Centre of Aizawl Theological College, Durtlang, Aizawl, Mizoram is the only study centre specifically on Calvin's life, works and thought, in South Asia.

[7] For further information about the Welsh history and culture, Cf. Williams, Gwyn A. **When Was Welsh?: A History of the Welsh** (1985/1991).

[8] Information about the Welsh Revival, see Orr, J. E. Evangelical Awakening in India (1970), pp. 50-59.

Pietism, evangelical and revival movements and other evangelistic groups have further bolstered Protestant missionary movement.

As a reiteration, though it was the Danish-Halle Lutheran mission that introduced Protestant Christianity in India in 1706 at Tranquebar, South India,[9] the arrival of the Baptist Missionary Society missionaries through William Carey in the late 18th century ushered a new chapter in Indian Christianity.[10] It was this Serampore Mission that sent Rev. Krishna Chandra Pal to Khasi hills in 1813. In almost the same period, churches of reformed tradition in the United Kingdom became interested in world evangelization and formed the London Missionary Society. Though the Welsh Presbyterian Church was a major partner in its formation but the non-Welsh who were predominantly English tended to have passed over the presence and contribution of Welsh Presbyterian church leaders. In most probability, the Welsh people might well be regarded as "dalits" of Great Britain.

The English leaders who hailed mostly from the Congregationalist church whose prejudicial approach and decisions in running the newly formed London Missionary Society and in selecting candidates for overseas missionary works, left a sense of Christian set back on the part of the Welsh partners. The other alternative to the Welsh was to stand on their own feet and to start a new mission society. In other words, leaders of the Welsh church who was disillusioned by the English attitude and decisions saw no other way except severing links with the London Missionary Society. This development led to the formation of the Welsh Calvinistic Methodist Foreign Missionary Society (WCMFMS) in January 1840.[11] Though the process that resulted in its formation went out with zeal, zest, understanding and determination but when the question came as where the Welsh Mission would work just hang on in conjecture. Experienced itinerant missionaries like Rev. Jacob Tomlin and Dr. Wilson appeared to have suggested unevangelized fields in places of Gujarat, Manipur and Khasi hills to the newly formed Welsh Mission. Their decision that favoured the Khasi hills was because of receiving an offer to subsidize missionaries' traveling tickets up to Kolkata and Khasi field was nearer to the ship arrival port. This incident was seen more providential than accidental.

Rev. Thomas Jones who was a chief exponent and architect of the Welsh Mission was the first missionary of the newly formed society to Khasi hills.[12] He and his wife landed at Saitsohpen, Sohra-the then British military outpost, on 22nd June, 1841. Their arrival had greatly contributed to filling up the gap left by

---

[9] Cf. Lehmann, E. A. **It Began at Tranquebar** (1956).

[10] Potts, D. E. **British Baptist Missionaries in India, 1793-1837: The History of Serampore Missions** (1967).

[11] Morris, John Hughes **The History of the Welsh Calvinistic Methodists' Foreign Mission, to the End of the Year 1904** (1919), pp. 3-5, 25ff.

[12] More about Rev. Thomas Jones' works in Khasi hills may be referred to *Ibid.*, pp. 77–90.

the Serampore Mission. The time of their arrival was quite memorable because of continuous heavy rainfall, dense cloud, a shivering flash of lightning and thundering. These natural phenomena did however not deter their missionary zeal, commitment and goal. Their sojourn at Saitsohpen was no more a home away from home but a home out of sight and mind. A little solace that they could heave was a protection from the British outpost and help from Alexander Lish's former pupils, U Jungkha and U Duwan Rai.[13] It was these experienced Khasi students who gave some orientation to Rev. Thomas Jones about the place, the local people and more importantly about the Serampore missionaries and their activities. It was most apparently at the behest of their suggestion that witnessed starting of elementary schools at the same villages that Lish had started before abandoning them in 1838. These schools were located at Mawsmai, Mawmluh and Sohra. These initial developments were so crucial and appeared to have provided a kind of continuity to the former abandoned Serampore Mission.

Given that, however, Rev. Thomas Jones set up a new literary design by adopting the Sohra dialect as a medium of instruction and communication and introducing the Roman or Latin alphabet instead of the Serampore Mission adopted Shella dialect and Bangla alphabet.[14] Given the fact that colonial powers saw economic productivity of the Khasis by learning the Bangla alphabet in addition to their administrative convenience, Rev. Thomas Jones went ahead with the introduction of the Roman alphabet. He did so not because of any antagonistic attitude to the Bangla people and their literature but because the pioneer Welsh missionaries did not know anything about the Bangla alphabet or its language. The change of the already adopted Shella language to Sohra was also circumstantial, that is the dialect spoken locally at the mission headquarter was Sohra and not Shella.

2. Growth and Development of the Church: The Welsh missionaries were serious about giving education to the Khasis and were not in a hurry in making converts. They gave elementary teaching to the natives and desired to see them learnt the simple knowledge of reading and writing in addition to a simple counting. These literary aspects were made mandatory and obligatory also to the Khasis before admitting them to the Christian church. In other words, the Welsh mission in its initial period of missionary operation raised the standard of church membership and that no native Khasis would be granted membership unless he/she had learnt the art of reading the introduced Roman alphabet and writing alike.[15] It was such concerns that made the missionaries devoted to the literary and educational mission first and looked at it with a spirit of urgency. Keeping this objective in mind, the Welsh Mission's conversion of the native went out with

---

[13] Jones, G. Angell **Ka History Jong Ka Balang, 1841-1966** (1966), p. 8.

[14] Snaitang, O. L. "U Rev. Thomas Jones I u la wan ha u bnai June 1841" in Ka **Jingshai Ka Gospel** (June 2008), pp. 22-25.

[15] Morris, John Hughes *op. cit.,* p. 91.

larger educative processes. Besides, they gave the freedom of choice or free will to the natives either to change their primal faith and join the church or not.

Keeping their standing rules of examining a person before registering into a Christian Church, the pioneer missionaries did not admit straight away four Khasi adults who approached the missionaries for the decision to change their primal faith to Christianity. Instead, they crossed examined the candidates first in which U Amor and U Rujon were qualified, admitted into the Church and baptized at Nongsawlia on Sunday 8th March 1846.[16] Judging by years of their labours, the progress of the church was rather slow but given the imposition of specified literary procedures, church's members formed a nucleus of a qualitative community. Since then, however, the church witnessed its gradual growth in membership and the Nongsawlia Church became the first organized Church in the region.

It was after more than two years later that the Church could register admission to the first native Khasi woman, Ka Nabon Sawian[17] from Mawmluh, and baptized on 16th July 1848. With an exception of confession of faith and knowledge of reading and writing, the acceptance of native converts was never determined from approval of parents, uncles or relatives. This was the case with Ka Nabon Sawian. Her joining the Church was marked with disapproval, severe protest, opposition and threat from her parents, uncles, relatives and local village. Even men who changed their faith to Jesus Christ had to pass through hardships, public ridicule and even persecution. Ka Nabon Sawian, then, braved herself for the sake of the new faith even at the cost of her personal sacrifices.

Another monumental happening was the conversion of U Borsing Syiem[18] as early as 1872. He hailed from the legitimate royal line to the Sohra ruling chief. He stood next to his uncle, the sitting Chief of Sohra Syiemship, and would have succeeded to the royal throne should his uncle abjure the throne or died. The customary law in regard to holding the prestigious Sohra royal throne was that the chief is tied down to the traditional religion in addition to the other state's requirements. In other words, a Sohra Chief must remain unconverted to another religion.

U Borsing Syiem and his family have renounced their traditional religion and became members of the Presbyterian Church. By doing so U Borsing Syiem and his family have done from the perspective of their personal convictions and decisions and there was no outside compulsion.

Therefore these incidents, the conversion of Ka Nabon Sawian and U Borsing Syiem were examples of people's search for a new spirituality and it

---

[16] *Ibid.*, p. 93.

[17] *Ibid.*, pp. 102ff.

[18] Jones, G. Angel *op. cit.*, 54-57.

was not for personal material gains.[19] Ka Nabon Sawian, being a daughter in the Khasi matrilineal family deserved custodian rights to the family's property and belongings. However she lost all her rights because of her conversion to Christianity. She also became poor and for the sake of the Church and his mission she had gone and served as a school teacher at Shella with a negligible and meagre income.

U Borsing Syiem too became a pauper and an ordinary citizen because of his acceptance of Jesus Christ. He lost not just the status of the Chief of Sohra state but also economic benefits from markets from the border areas with Bangladesh. Therefore there was no material motive in the Khasi people's conversion to the new faith, at least in the initial period.

The Nongsawlia Church gradually witnessed increase in Church membership. Regular worship services were held on Sunday. Evening services were also introduced especially on Saturday evening as a preparation for congregational preaching sources and sacrament on the Lord's Day. However since the objective of the missionaries was to educate the people, it was thought it appropriate to introduce Sunday School also and they did so way back in 1849. Though the aim of introducing Sunday School was to teach the members in the knowledge of the Bible and of Jesus Christ, but it also served as an avenue for teaching the members in the art of reading and writings. In the early years, therefore, Sunday school could well be called as institutional means for mass education. Those members, who could not get the opportunities to attend daily elementary schools, could get their chances of learning in Sunday school.

Another significant development was the introduction of the concept of responsibility in running the affairs of the church through collection of offering in Sunday's services. In this way native converts were made to become aware the need of supporting the church through the gifts and offerings to the church. Though this development was introduced in a humble and modest manner it was however crucial and decisive for subsequent indigenous responsibility and sharing in taking care of the church and its mission to the neighbouring places in the region.

It was not just the importance of raising financial resources that the missionaries had introduced but they also guided the church in the ministry of lay leaders. Again the introduction of lay membership took places in 1849 by the ordination of U Tira Sing to the position of an elder of the Nongsawlia Church.[20] He was therefore the first native elder of the Welsh Presbyterian Church in India. The ministry by the elders in the Church was an integral part of the Presbyterian principle and discipline. Though elders could not perform the sacramental duties like Baptism and the Lord's Supper, they however played an important role of

---

[19] Most early hill people converts to the new faith had passed through the test of untold opposition and ill-treatment.

[20] Jones, G. Angel *op. cit.*, p. 27.

caring and nurturing the Church through their visitation to Christian homes, especially visiting sick persons and bereaved families. They also run the daily activities of the church through the designated church committees.

The Welsh missionary took serious note of raising the standard and quality of Christian families. Members of the church were instructed that by believing in Jesus Christ and by becoming members of a Christian community, they should stop drinking traditional arracks, to discontinue practices of brewing the intoxicating drinks or involved in gambling, cheating or stealing but they should also no longer participate in traditional archery sports and religious festivals.[21] Another instruction that the missionaries gave to the members was in the area of cleanliness. Christians should maintain cleanliness not only of themselves but of their homes, compounds with proper drainage systems and also in the entire locality. It was the missionaries who taught the members how to plant flowers and trees in the compounds of their homes. More importantly, however, was the introduction of setting up Christian families through legal and ecclesiastical procedures. Members of the church should not get married improperly. This teaching was well received and accepted by native Christians. As a result, the first Christian holy matrimony between U Luh and Ka Phuh was solemnized at the Nongsawlia Church in 1850.[22]

Until 1849, the Welsh Mission concentrated their activities only in Nongsawlia-Saitsohpen, Mawsmai and Mawmluh. Running of school and church services went out regularly in these three villages. The year 1850 was significant not only for the solemnization of the first Christian Marriage but more importantly for its spread to other areas. The mission could expand its work to Shella and Sylhet in 1850. A church and a school were also established in Jowai of Jaintia Hills at the beginning of 1854.[23] Following the shifting of the District Headquarter of the British Government from Cherrapunji to Shillong in 1866, the mission too began to establish its missions at Mawkhar, Shillong in 1871 and from there the church could expand to other areas. The spread of the church was also witnessed among the Khasis who lived and settled in West Khasi Hills. Evangelization of the Ri-Bhoi area was started in 1893. Though the beginning of the mission in the area was slow but the response of the people was very positive. The mission introduced not just the Gospel of Christ for salvation but educational schools and medical services.

The spread of the church did not confine only to the Khasi-Jaintia region but also in other areas. By the middle of 1850 a school was established in Sylhet for boys of the lower caste.[24] This venture was regarded significant because of special care and attention of children who have been neglected in the society.

[21] *Ibid.*, pp. 52ff.

[22] *Ibid.*, p. 30.

[23] *Ibid.*, p. 41.

[24] Cf. **Presbyterian Church of India (PCI) Platinum Jubilee Souvenir, 1926-2001**.

From Sylhet the Welsh mission made a survey of areas in Cachar region of Assam and the exploratory survey had gone up to Manipur. Though the mission could not begin its work in Manipur, it was however able to start a school in Cachar in 1851. In spite of strong opposition to the mission work, the missionaries did not give up the work that they had begun. It was reported that four converts from Cachar were baptized in May 1852 and they became the first Christians from the Cachar plain areas. In spite of the unfavorable circumstances in the plain areas, the Welsh mission was able to open three stations in Sylhet, Silchar and Karimganj at least before the end of 1897. Later new stations were organized in Maulvi Bazaar, Sunamganj and other areas in Sylhet District. The progress of the church in the plain areas was such that it became necessitated to ordain a local plain convert. Therefore the first known local ordained pastor from the plain areas was Hem R. Sarkar from Silchar who was inducted to the priestly ministry in 1926.

From Khasi hills the Welsh Mission deputed Rev. Williams to make an exploratory survey of the distant and most inaccessible areas of Mizoram in 1891.[25] The survey was productive in that Rev. Williams requested the Welsh Mission authority to include Mizoram and Manipur in its missionary operations. The Welsh Mission Society conceded to Rev. Williams' report but disastrous natural calamities and death of missionaries had prevented the Welsh missionaries to enter into the Lushai hills immediately. In 1897 the Welsh mission took over the missionary work in Mizoram from the Arthington Aborigines Mission and began its permanent mission work among the people. The work in Mizoram though did not make much impact in the initial years but following the outbreak of a revival in 1906, people's response to the new faith was in great numbers that by the 20th century all Mizos in Mizoram have renounced their primal faith and became Christians.[26]

3. Language and Building Up of Indigenous Literatures: The Welsh missionaries were pioneers in picking up a dialect for a particular homogenous community and making it a common standard language and in promoting indigenous literature.[27] Major communities in Welsh Mission evangelized areas like Khasis, Mizos, Cachar hill tribes and others were people without written alphabet and without any single common language.

In respect of developing a standard language, the Welsh missionaries normally adopted a dialect spoken at their mission centre and converted it into a common language for a community that shared cultural similarities, like Sohra dialect for the Khasi-Jaintia people and Lushai for the Mizo people in Mizoram. There were no scientific or linguistic procedures in determining the choice. It was never judged from its being sweet sounding, the best or the purest but on

[25] For more information about the origins and activities of the Welsh Presbyterian Mission in Mizoram, read Lloyd, J. Meirion **History of the Church in Mizoram: Harvest in the Hills** (1991).

[26] *Ibid.*

[27] Bareh, H. **A Short History of Khasi Literature** (1979).

the condition that the missionaries settled, lived and set up a main office at a particular place, mixed with the neighbours in their residential premises and talked with them in their daily dealings and works.[28]

The adopted spoken language was made compulsory to be used in literature, educational institutions, church services, official meetings, Sunday schools and official application forms and sale deeds. This procedure was found it difficult and hard in its initial period but once it secured its foothold among the people who were fragmented into several unintelligible dialects, it became so significant that over a period of time had the consequence of solidifying the people to a common sense of identity, like the Khasi-Jaintia in Meghalaya and Mizo people in Mizoram.

After deciding to adopt a standard language, the next step was the introduction of the Roman or Latin alphabet. Before that, some tribal groups like the Khasis of Meghalaya had exposed to Bangla language and literature. We have seen that the missionaries of the Serampore mission had imposed Bangla alphabet. They were able to bring out a translated New Testament Bible in Khasi using the Bangla script and Shella dialect as early as 1831. Even indigenous tribal intellectuals like U Jeebon Roy had not only supported the imposition of Bangla script for the Khasis but had also started a Bangla School at Mawkhar, Shillong.[29] The British government was in favour of the Serampore mission literary policy.[30] When the Welsh missionaries changed the literary policy to the Roman or Latin alphabet, it did so not on the condition of opposing to the Bangla alphabet but on the basis of their knowing neither the Bangla language nor its script. At the same time, they found at least upon the orientation of the ex-students of the Serampore mission in Cherrapunji that learning of more than forty Bangla letters was complex and the phonetic sound did not go out well with Khasi linguistic mode of pronunciation. Therefore in order to speed up their evangelistic mission the Welsh's missionaries introduced the Roman alphabet and script.

The main area of the contribution was in the production of prose literature. The first thing that Rev. Thomas Jones did was in translating the **Lord's Prayer**. His decision to translate it first had far implication for building of a foundation of Christian homes in addition to building up a strong Biblical Christian Church. Then he translated the Gospel according to Saint Matthew, the Mother's Gift[31] and others. Other missionaries who came later contributed to translating the

[28] Snaitang, O. L. "U Rev. Thomas Jones I u la wan ha u bnai June 1841", *op. cit.*, 24.

[29] "Ki Khasi ki dei ba'n pule Bangla" **U Khasi Mynta**, 31 (Lber 1, 1899), pp. 1f.

[30] For a specific illustration, Cf. **Proceedings of the Lieutenant Governor of Bengal,** Education Department, October 1863, Pro. Nos. 17-19.

[31] The original title in Welsh was **Rhodd Mam** but rendered into Khasi as **Ka Kot Tikir**. Tikir was probably a Khasi rendering of the English catechism.

entire Bible,[32] brought out an Anglo-Khasi Dictionary, the Grammar[33] book and primers or readers[34] for use in schools.

The Welsh mission also pioneered in developing a modern poetry. A Welsh. missionary, Hugh Roberts, took the initiative to collect and edit the Khasi Hymn Book and published it in at least by 1870. It composed mainly of translated western hymns and western tunes. Though these hymns were meant for use in Christian services but the composition of either the four line or eight line stanzas by applying the modern forms of poetry with rhymes they could well be called examples of modern forms of poetry.

Khasi literature was further developed and enriched by the introduction of journals. Rev. Williams brought out the first Khasi journal entitled **U Nongkit Khubor** in 1889.[35] It became the first ever journal produced in Khasi language. Other journals like **Ka Pateng Khristan**[36] and **U Nongialam Khristan**[37] were subsequently brought out by the mission. These journals contributed not only to the development of a Khasi literature but also in creating reading awareness and literary interests among the Khasi-Jaintia people.

The other contribution to the Khasi literary mission was the establishment of a printing press in 1869. However in the absence of a printing operator, the printing press had to be disposed off to the Government in 1874.

Another contribution in the promotion of tribal language and literature was in the establishment of publishing houses and book services. These became significant missionary operations for wider distributions and circulations of books and Christian literatures among the people in the region.

4. Educational Mission: The role of the missionaries in the promotion of tribal languages and literatures was noteworthy and significant. They were means that raised the alienated tribal people to the literary level. As already indicated above, tribal languages and literatures were implemented mainly in educational institutions. As a matter of fact, educational schools were started simultaneously with the adoption of a standard language and literature. In certain areas like the Jaintia hills of Meghalaya, educational schools went first before a church that both were in the minds of the Pnar people synonymous that till the present, the church is called a school (ka skur).[38]

---

[32] See Jones, G. Angell, *op. cit.*, p.73.

[33] Cf. Roberts, H. **A Grammar of the Khasi Language** (1891/1995).

[34] While Rev. Thomas Jones brought out the First Reader, the remaining three Readers were written and produced by Rev. Dr. John Roberts.

[35] Though **U Nongkit Khubor** was the first journal in Khasi, most of its earlier issues have not been preserved properly and appeared to have gone out missing.

[36] First published in 1897 but remained defunct in 1903. It was revived again in 1937 and continues serving the Presbyterian Church and the society till date.

[37] **U Nongialam Khristan** remained in service only from 1902 to 1936.

[38] Snaitang, O. L. **Christianity and Social Change in Northeast India** (1993), p. 52.

The Welsh mission, which had revived the Serampore mission abandoned schools at Mawsmai, Mawmluh and Sohra in 1842 had been successful in producing brilliant Khasi students like U Larshai, U Nising and U Jom. They became effective native leaders and were later appointed as school teachers. In this respect, though the missionaries had come with specific religious objectives but the fact they have raised indigenous leadership should in no way be remarked as anti national. Though the missionaries were pioneers in starting missionary activities in the region but the credit of larger impact and spread of the Church to rural areas should be attributed to the role and services rendered by these indigenous native leaders.

The growth of educational institutions was evident by their spread into several rural areas. It was reported that by 1866 the number of lower primary schools had gone up to 65 with total enrolment of 2000 in all. Even the Zilla High School[39] in Shillong was amalgamated with a Mission School and placed under the supervision of the Welsh Mission before it was converted into a government school with a name Shillong Government High School. Its spread to the plain areas was also phenomenal. In at least one source of information, it was reported: "According to 1911 census, 600 Namasudra boys and 300 girls were reported in the Karimganj district under education; 20 schools were opened in Sylhet with 370 scholars; 12 schools in Cachar and 8 in Maulvi."[40] Later, educational mission was introduced in Mizoram in the late 1890s and by the latter part of the 20th century Mizoram became the leading state in literacy in Northeast India and stood second by the national literacy rating.

Another contribution in the educational field was the starting of schools for women. The Welsh missionaries have done this in Khasi hills and the support that the Khasi-Jaintia people had shown by sending their daughters to schools was encouraging. The Welsh mission educational work in the plain areas was mostly concentrated on the education of women. It provided an alternative to what the government and municipalities had opened schools only for boys. Running of girls' schools was not a problem to the missionaries but native opposition, derogatory remarks and contemptuous shouts were humiliating and discouraging. They however, did not bow down to these negative pressures. The girls' school in Silchar, which was developed into a high school level in 1913, was remarkable in two grounds. It gave education to women from all walks of life without any discrimination. Secondly, it created a special attention to giving training to Hindu widows and assisted them so that they could live a life with a sense of dignity.

The other area that the Welsh Mission had initiated was in the area of theological education. While the Welsh Mission School of theology was started in Cherrapunji in 1888, the Aizawl Theological College was organized in 1907 but had now been upgraded up to the Post Graduate level. These colleges have

[39] Started by U Jeebon Roy of the Seng Khasi.

[40] **PCI Platinum Jubilee Souvenir, 1926-2001**, p. 31.

contributed to serving the Church and society in the region. One could comment that the farsightedness of the missionaries in starting theological education could not be downgraded because it was through these institutions that had contributed to the rise of indigenous leadership[41] who took over the Welsh mission missionaries' leadership after leaving the region by the mid 20th century.

5. Medical Services among the People in the Region: The Welsh mission undertook pioneering works in healthcare and nursing. Though the missionaries believed in divine healing but that was by no means putting off their commitment to rendering modern medical care and treatment to the suffering humanity. The pioneer medical missionary, Dr. Griffiths, started the ministry with love, zest and determination. Arriving Khasi hills in early 1879, Dr. Griffiths was able to begin a dispensary at Mawphlang.[42] The outbreak of a plague in Shillong in June 1879 had claimed many precious lives. Many were affected and some have left homes for jungles. The services rendered by Dr. Griffiths and other missionaries have set an example of Christian love, care and sacrifices.

The Mawphlang dispensary was later shifted to Shillong. Following the coming of Dr. Gordon Roberts in 1920s, the mission could start a hospital at Jaiaw, Shillong in 1923. A dispensary that was started at Durtlang, Aizawl now had developed into a fully fledged hospital. Though native people did not believe in the efficacy of modern medical treatment and allopathic medicines but experiences of healing and recovery dispelled their traditional fears. In this manner, modern medical services and medicines had the effect of stamping out tribal people's superstitious beliefs. Traditionally, people had some kind of understanding that sickness was caused not by germs by some supernatural punishment. The cause of sickness was sort out through series of sacrifices and tried to identify whose natural spirit had the patient displeased. Sacrificial procedure was done first before treatment. In this respect, modern medical care and medicines could give the people with a reasonable sense of rationality.

Another impact of medical mission was in the area of taking care of the injured or wounded persons and attending on those who died unnaturally. Tribal people normally looked at such persons with some kind of religious taboo. Their fear was of *Ka Tyrut* (a goddess of unnatural happening or death), lest it might smite back on those who extended helping hands.[43] If any service is done it has to go through processes of offering sacrifices called *ka mait tyrut* (meaning cutting off or slicing the goddess of unnatural death). The new faith in Jesus Christ – the One who has overcome death, and the courageous spirit of care and help, had in the process endowed with a new worldview and a good Samaritan spirit.

Medical institutions were avenues that witnessed practical applications of Christian love and a compassionate welcoming heart. There was no discrimination

[41] Snaitang, O. L. *op. cit.*, 154f.

[42] Jones, G. Angell, *op. cit.*, pp. 58ff.

[43] See Chapter V.

in medical help. Hospitals opened their doors wide to all sorts of sick persons and took care through nursing, examining and rendering of medical treatment in a disciplined and orderly manner. These institutions too contributed to imbibing a new attitude to human beings who were in need of medical care and treatment and made the people realized how important humans were in God's sight.

Side by side with the starting of a medical mission to the suffering humankind the missionaries took special care of the orphans, rural folks and the aged. These activities added up to the holistic ministry of the church. Again, although the primary objective of these medical and humanitarian activities was evangelistic but the contribution that came about was upon the native citizens of the country irrespective of caste, class, creed or language.

6. The Presbyterian Form of Administration and People's Solidarity:[44] The Presbyterian Church believed in a democratic form of government. It maintained collective participation of the people through the local church, district, presbytery, synod and up to the highest assembly level. This administrative pattern was put into practice only after the church registered its numerical growth, increase in local churches and geographical spread. The ecclesiastical structure though aimed at maintaining discipline, orderliness, equality and fraternity but had the effect of bringing the Presbyterian communities to a sense of unity.

The local church is a basic community that takes care of people's spiritual welfare and active participation. The local church committees that included elders and elected adult communicant members run the church's affairs in a clear and transparent manner. Local churches of four or five could together be formed into a District level. The District authority maintains closer unity with the local churches. Though this level administrative pattern was introduced much later, the Welsh's mission authority had ushered a comprehensive ecclesiastical organization, the presbytery for the Presbyterian churches in Khasi-Jaintia Hills, in 1867.

The introduction of the Presbytery in the community though was meant for church's business and religious matters but given the fact that members, delegates and elders attended the meetings at Nongsawlia in 1869 as representatives from different regions in Khasi-Jaintia hills, the presbytery became the first Khasi-Jaintia solidarity movement.[45] There was no effort in the community before the formation of the Presbytery that could draw together the fragmented Khasi-Jaintia society to a unified forum for participation in the decision making committee, for staying together and for collective worship and proclamation. It also provided awareness to the indigenized church for standing on one's own feet in terms of financial support, administration and evangelization.

It was this body that laid down rules and guidelines for processing admission of converts into the church. This was seen highly significant given the objective of maintaining a high standard of church's membership. The unity of members was

[44] Snaitang, O. L. *op. cit.*, pp. 168-176.

[45] *Ibid.*, p. 171.

also made through the maintenance of an enrolment register both in the Church and Sunday Schools. It was the Presbytery that accorded final recognition and approval of chosen elders and evangelists in addition to supervising activities in the new stations and mission fields.

The growth and expansion of the church in Khasi-Jaintia went out at a fast rate that required further administrative organizations for ecclesiastical integration and consolidation. This phenomenon gave rise to the creation of five Presbyteries in 1895, namely the Cherra-Shella, Shillong-Mawlai, Mawphlang-Khatsawphra, Jaintia and the Sylhet plains.[46] This reorganization policy functioned effectively and enabled to dispense ecclesiastical duties in a more progressive and dynamic way. Members of the church, lay leaders and ordained ministers could come together with a sense of unity under each respective demarcated ecclesiastical jurisdiction.

Given the fact that the Presbyterian polity was for a well maintained unity and uniformity in addition to implementing the policy of solidifying, the action that led to the setting up of five Presbyteries appeared to have paved the way towards being autonomous and independent. However, in order to bring all these created Presbyteries together under a common roof, the missionaries introduced a comprehensive structure, an Assembly of the Presbyterian Church in the region, in 1896.[47] Though missionaries and pastors were ex-officio members of an annual Assembly meeting, others included those delegated members from Presbyteries. The first Assembly meeting was held at Shella on 15th to 17th February, 1896. The meeting demonstrated its special characters in a sense of shared responsibilities between missionaries and native Christians. That is, while a Welsh's missionary, Rev. Robert Evans served as the Assembly Moderator; its Secretary was handed over to Rev. Amirkha Chyne, a Khasi Pastor.

The development that had happened in Khasi-Jaintia hills and the plain areas had also taken place in Mizoram. With the creation of the Presbytery in Aizawl in 1910-a Presbytery for the Presbyterian churches in what is known today as Mizoram;[48] the jurisdiction of the Assembly was widened. Again, the church in Mizoram witnessed significant expansion through missionary outreach activities in Tripura and Manipur. As the church spread to other areas in the region and among numerous ethnic groups, it became necessitated for further administrative re-organization so that all created constituent units were brought together under a single structure. This vision resulted in the creation of an all inclusive supreme authority, the Synod of the Presbyterian Church in Assam in 1926. Today, its name was changed to the Assembly of the Presbyterian Church of India.

The Presbyterian form of government contributed not only to the solidification of divided sub-ethnic groups in a single homogenous community but

---

[46] Jones, G. Angell, *op. cit.*, p. 77.

[47] *Ibid.*

[48] Cf. **PCI Platinum Jubilee Souvenir, 1926-2001.**

also in bringing together ethnic communities to a common platform. Members of the Presbyterian Church in Northeast India belonged to numerous ethnic, linguistic and social groups, like the Khasis, Mizos, Bengalis, Nepalis, Assamese, Biates, Hmars, Cacharis and many others. The Presbyterian administrative organization functioned in such a way that all of them are brought together under a single family and thereby created a sense of unity even in the midst of diversity.

III. History of the Church of England or the Anglican Church, 1876[49]

The Anglican Church or the Church of England was another Western Christian agency that had come and worked in Northeast India. However, unlike the other Christian Missions, the Anglican Church came as an integral part or department of the British Government in India. Its name the 'Church of England' is implicit in the British colonial polity and rule. As an official religion of the new administration, the primary objective of the Church of England was to attend to the spiritual need of the British officials and personnel and their families.

1. British Administration and Evangelization: The British came to India and the Northeast for the purpose of ruling, trading and exploiting the resources for their benefits. In order to achieve such intended objectives, the British masters adopted a policy of non-interference in native religions. They did not want to see unrest, resistance or disturbance of any form in the course of their administration. Knowing that Christian Missions, both Catholics and Protestants, were interested in conversions of the people in India the British maintained religious neutrality. In other words, no missionary works were allowed in British administered territories.

Though this restricted policy had undergone a change by 1813, it had however not found immediate effective implementation in the country. As a reiteration, the Church of England did not engage in evangelization and church planting. Mentioned was made earlier that the British officials resident in Sylhet who were interested in Christian activities in Northeast India had extended their invitation to the Serampore Mission to take up the job of evangelization. This initiative resulted in sending the Bengali convert, Rev. Krishna Chandra Pal in 1813. David Scott and Frances Jenkins too were seriously involved in encouraging Christian activities among the people in Northeast India. However, though these officers were officers under the British Government, their evangelistic interests were not with the Church of the colonial masters, the Church of England but with the Serampore Baptist Mission and the American Baptist Mission. Even the Welsh Presbyterian Mission that accepted grant-in aid for running schools in Khasi-Jaintia hills did not belong to the Church of England. Therefore, the

[49] Information about the Anglican Church in Northeast India, read Lyngdoh, Bishop P. "The Diocese of North East India Church of North India" in **Souvenir: The Church History Association of India** (2009), 13-17. Also see Ngapkynta, H. B. **The Church of England Now The Church of North India in Bengal, Assam and Meghalaya** (2009).

Anglican Church was not a missionary religion in a strict sense of the term because of the standing policy of religious neutrality.

2. Beginnings: The last bastion for British occupation in Northeast India appeared to have been up to the plains of Bangladesh alone and never up to the hill areas or even in the plains of Assam. While their interest on annexing the plains of Assam Valley was hitherto put on hold, the unprofitable hill areas remained apparently beyond their agenda. However, unexpected changes in indigenous chiefs' policies in regard to the British power, their opposition to the continued presence and rule of the Burmese regime and the exploration to build road connection between Sylhet and the plains of Assam led to their need of passing through the hilly terrain of the Khasi-Jaintia hills region made the new colonial administration to apply the 'forward policy' and it resulted in the annexation and occupation of the Northeastern region. In the process, there witnessed the presence of British officials in Guwahati, Shillong, Aizawl, Kohima, Imphal, Tura and elsewhere. Important stations in the Brahmaputra valley like Guwahati, Dibrugargh, Tinsukia, Sibsagar, Tezpur, Jaipur, Lakhimpur, Nagoan, Goalpara and others also witnessed the presence of not only British officials but tea planters alike.

These British personnel, officials and traders have come with their families. Their settlement in these designated locations in the region became stable. Residential buildings were built, kitchen gardens grown and the British could play and spend their leisure time in other activities. In the process, families were increased through births. Grown up children too began to reach marriageable ages. While their works and upbringing passed on naturally, they were however not forgotten of their religious life. What were most needed in their Christian religiosity were the performances of baptism on infants and marriages as well. These rites were fundamental sacraments of the Church. Had not these sacraments been performed, most Christian families would carry with them a sense of incompleteness. These British Christians and families by virtue of their settlement in the region could have enjoyed their stay and movement but when it came upon their religious practices they found themselves wanting.

It was in this context that the British authority sent a notice to Major Frances Jenkins in 1839 in respect of performing the ecclesiastical duties in baptizing the unbaptized children and marriages as well. Rev. A. Garstin, the then Chaplain in Sylhet, was reported to have visited the upper Assam valley in 1841- the year of the arrival of the first Welsh missionaries in Cherrapunji, most likely for the objectives of performing the required and needed sacraments among the faithful adherents. This was the first ever visit by an Anglican priest in the region. In this connection, the British interest in ecclesiastical affairs in the Assam plains and the hills alike was for the sake of providing spiritual ministrations of baptisms and marriages to the British subjects.

1). Building of Churches: Rev. Robert Bland was the second clergy from the Church of England who had visited the Brahmaputra valley. His stay over the valley stretched out from 1844 to 1862. Like Rev. A. Garstin, Rev. Bland's visit was also in response to the government directive. By the time of his sojourn in the region, the British families in the valley had grown in certain sizable numbers following the progressive starting of tea gardens. Even in the midst of the presence of British Christians in different stations, Rev. Bland was the only clergy who looked after the ecclesiastical ministries. His role and ministry was memorable because of two things. First, he was able to pay a personal visit to strategic towns where British families were concentrated, like Guwahati, Dibrugarh, Sibsagar, Jaipur, Nagoan, Tezpur and Goalpara. This visit could have resulted in the performance of sacraments to these families. There was no evangelistic objective in these visits.

Second, another memorable incident through his sojourn in the valley as an official priest of the British administration was in the building of churches in Guwahati and Tezpur. The church building in Guwahati was completed and dedicated under a name the Christ Church on 23rd August, 1844. The next church was in Tezpur. It was named the Epiphany Church and consecrated in 1847. While Rev. Bland saw the importance of performing religious duties in homes and public places, but what was more important in his ecclesiastical vision was in building sacred sites specifically for such spiritual ministrations. His role had contributed to the stabilizing the church and Christian communities.

Guwahati was then a growing city and a place with significant concentration of British Christian families. It was also a strategic place for Christian interaction and a centre for areas like Goalpara and other areas in Kamrup district. Tezpur became significant for Christian families scattered in upper valley and the construction of the church there was to bring them to a spiritual sense of unity and worship.

2). Chaplaincy in the Region: The first known chaplaincy for the region was the Chaplaincy of Sylhet. Rev. Garstin was a chaplain of Sylhet at the time of his visit the Brahmaputra valley in 1841. Though towns and centres in the Brahmaputra valley were important in terms of the presence of British officials and families and others, the ecclesiastical attention tended to have been on Cherrapunji and Cachar besides Sylhet. These centres were closer and lay mostly within the same political boundary. Cachar appeared significant perhaps because of the presence of a sizable Catholic Christians at Bondashil and ecclesiastical manageability. Cherrapunji became a district headquarter for the Khasi-Jaintia hills district and a health resort. Given that, the Sylhet Chaplaincy was made inclusive of Cachar and Cherrapunji. Rev. F. Hinde was apparently the first chaplain for Sylhet, Cachar and Cherrapunji as early as 1862. Following the shifting of the district headquarter from Cherrapunji to Shillong in 1866, there witnessed the growing importance of Shillong in terms of administration, physical salubriousness and ecclesiastical spirituality. As a result of this change, it appeared that Shillong was made the centre for the said chaplaincy. It was reported that in 1870 Bishop Cotton sent direction to Rev. Hinde, the Chaplain, to visit Sylhet from Shillong at least not less than six times in each calendar year. The order was made in such a way that the Shillong chaplaincy should continue without interruption or vacancy.

The importance of ecclesiastical ministrations among the Christians in the region was well recognized and that it necessitated appointment of another responsible clergy. Rev. A. Ayerst was appointed chaplain in-charge the tea gardens in 1863 in addition to Rev. Hinde. Rev. Ayerst who should have been an asset in serving the needed Christian families in such scattered locations in Northeast, was unfortunately knocked down by a sudden deficient in health that left of no use in the service. Again, Rev. Hinde was left alone to look after the ministry in the capacity as Chaplain for this long stretch of geographical area and among the scattered Christian families and individuals.

The increasing pastoral ministry among the British families in the tea gardens had drawn more attention because of the presence of numerous Christians in railway services, civil offices, coal mines, army and other institutions. Some native people like the Kacharis and tea garden labourers have become Christian and joined the Anglican Church. The United Society for the Propagation of the Gospel (USPG) that had understood the spiritual need of these Christians in the valley and the burden that Rev. Hinde had to shoulder alone, especially after Rev. Ayerst became invalid, took the initiative in looking into this need. They sent Rev. C. Hesselmayer to tend to the spiritual aspects of the British Christians and more importantly among the tea garden labourers and Kacharis.

The tea garden chaplaincy though appeared insignificant in the beginning because of the concentration among the British personnel and families, turned out to be at the forefront because of the rise of the indigenous Christian population. Besides Rev. Hesselmayer, the USPG commissioned another chaplain, Rev. Sydney Endle. He reached Tezpur in 1864 and found solace and strength at the warm welcome he received from his predecessor, Rev. Hesselmayer. Though Rev. Endle was just 23 years of age by the time he took over the ecclesiastical duty, he however joined the work with great spiritual maturity. He concentrated his missionary works mostly among the Kacharis and the Bodos. His ministry did not remain confining only to the word and sacraments but touched upon the culture of the native communities especially in the development of their languages and literatures. These tea garden labourers, the Kacharis and the Bodos found in him not just a faithful chaplain but a helping brother in the most needed times. He was no longer a visitor but a spiritual leader in residence. His uninterrupted ministry among the people was right from the time of his arrival in 1864 and continued till his death in Lakhimpur in 1907, that is, a labour for a period of 43 years.

Many churches have been built among the tea gardens, the Kacharis and the Bodos. More importantly were the St. Paul's Church, Bengbari in 1865, St. Patrick's Church at Athabari in 1890 and the Church of Resurrection at Digholia and several among the Bodo Christian community. These activities were testimonies of his ministry not just as the British official chaplain but a missionary. He and his wife were instruments in shaping the destiny of these indigenous Christians in the Brahmaputra valley and under what was known as the Tea Garden Chaplaincy.

3. Laying on the Foundation Stone and Inauguration: 1). Laying on the Foundation Stone in 1874: Though British and native Christians appeared to have grown so significantly in the Brahmaputra valley, the emergence of Shillong as the administrative importance for the entire region was in the eyes of the colonial masters, unstoppable. Side by side with the administrative vision and preparation, the Church of England had felt it greatly that Shillong chaplaincy should never be allowed to remain without a chaplain since 1870. The shifting of the centre of chaplaincy from Sylhet to Shillong was also conspicuous in this preparation.

The British authority laid the foundation stone of the Church of England in 1874. That was the year in which the office of the Chief Commissioner of the erstwhile composite Assam was shifted from Guwahati to Shillong. The ecclesiastical importance of Shillong did not depend on numbers but in terms of the presence of civil administration, the military cantonment, the Gurkha Training Centre, the Assam Rifles, military hospital and a vast network of communication.

2). Inauguration: This development was by no means ignoring the growing churches in the plains of Sylhet or Assam. It was just an effort to run a pace with the establishment of an administrative centre in Shillong. When Assam was elevated to the level of a province, which means with the setting up of a permanent residence and office of a Governor, Shillong became its capital. Gradually, the church in Shillong began to witness the growing Anglican communicants. Two years after the laying on of the foundation stone, the church was inaugurated. In the words of Bishop P. Lyngdoh, "...the Divine Service was held on Trinity Sunday, 11th June, 1876, which was also attended by a few Khasis who were originally from the Presbyterian stream but had joined the Anglican community through circuitous routes and some through marital relationships with Anglicans."[50]

4. Spread of the Church: Although the Anglican Church did not directly involve in evangelization because of the standing official religious policy of neutrality, its spread in the region was inevitable. First, the growing Anglican population was through the British personnel in the capacity as official or tea planters in the prospective gardens of the plains and hills in Assam. Their occupation and settlement in the region saw their growth through births and reinforcements. In other words, it was biological and increase in employment

[50] Cf. Lyngdoh, Bishop P. *op. cit.*, 14.

that led to the Church's growth in the plain areas. Anglican communities became concentrated in Sylhet, Guwahati, Dibrugargh, Tezpur, Jaipur, Tinsukia, Sibsagar, Laakhimpur, Goalpara and Nagoan. It has been noted that churches have been erected at Bengbari, Athabari and Digholia in addition to some places among the Bodos.

Second, the growth was also attributed to conversion of certain tea labourers, the Kacharis and the Bodos and some Assamese. The other factor that had contributed to this growth was the joining of fellow Christians through the 'circuitous routes.'

Meanwhile, some places have over a period of time begun to grow into important commercial towns both in the plains and hill areas. Its spread to lower Assam like Dhubri and Goalpara was also well noted. The Anglican Church in these plain towns received sacramental ministrations from the chaplains in Shillong and Guwahati. While these chaplains were responsible for the overall administration of these churches in Dhubri and Goalpara, the running of the life of the church in these areas was mainly in the hands of dedicated and recognized lay leaders. One might say that these churches were churches of lay people.

The spread of the Church in the hill areas was mainly in Tura, Garo hills, Halflong in North Cachar hills and Jowai in Jaintia hills. The building of the church in Jowai was completed in 1913. Bishop Lefroy of the Calcutta Diocese dedicated it to St. Michael and All Angels on 29th September, 1913. Though the Church secured its presence in most places through the presence of Anglican members but in Jowai its prominent presence was mostly through the role and work of a local convert Revd. Lowell Gatphoh. He was dedicated to the level of the Archdeacon of the Church of England in Jaintia hills.

5. Creation of the Diocese of Assam, 1915 and Its Subsequent Development: On the basis of the gradual growth of members in the Church in the region and the geographical spread in both plains and hill areas, it was seen a necessity to raise the level of Chaplaincy in the region to that of a fully fledged Bishopric see. Following years of evaluation, consideration and scrutiny, the authority created the Diocese of Assam with its headquarter in Dibrugargh in 1915. Long before this date, the Anglican Church or the Church of England in Northeast India was under the control and supervision of the Calcutta diocese. Elevation of the ecclesiastical jurisdiction to the level of a diocese served as a precursor to the raising of Assam's political status of a Chief Commissioner's level to the level of a Governor's Province in 1921. The decision that led to the creation of a separate diocese was a farsighted and a well thought out decision for greater elements of independence, maturity, autonomy and 'come of age' for the Church, native Christians and political identity in Northeast India.

Indigenous Anglicans and churches in the plains and hill areas of the region were jubilant because with the granting of a separate diocese, there developed a sense of belonging, a responsibility and authority. Upon the inauguration of the

Diocese of Assam on 10th January, 1915 the Church's authority assigned the first higher ecclesiastical position to Bishop Herbert Pakenhem Walsh and provided satisfactorily service to the Church, the government and the people till 1923. His residence was at St. Paul's Church in Dibrugargh. Again, the decision to have the bishopric headquarter at Dibrugargh was based most apparently from the perspective of the large concentration of the British personnel, tea owners and planters not just in Dibrugargh region but in its surrounding towns like Tinsukia, Jaipur, Sibsagar and other areas. The jurisdiction of the Diocese covered areas under East Bengal as well and included mission activities carried out by missionaries of the Oxford Mission.

Besides the ecclesiastical reorganization in the region, another development in the region was the arrival of the next USPG missionary, Revd. St. Quinn Wyld in 1920. His first assignment was the taking over of the Chaplaincy of Lakhimpur. While this place was regarded as the centre for the tea garden areas in upper Brahmaputra valley, it was however thought otherwise in the thinking and vision of the new incumbent, Rev. St. Wyld. He got it relocated at Tezpur in what it was a middle Assam valley. The shifting had however not affected the smooth running of the Church and its expansion. He rendered a successful service for a long period of 54 (fifty four) years until his death in 1974.

George Clay Hubback of the Oxford Mission succeeded Bishop H. P. Walsh in 1924. Unlike his predecessor, Bishop Hubback could serve substantively among the people not just in terms of more than two decades but in terms of establishing institutions. His vision was not in just maintaining the bishopric continuity but in imparting sound and solid teaching in the doctrine and ministry of the Anglican Communion. The Annual Clergy Meet that he started was introduced with the objective of giving training to the priests, deacons, catechists and Bible men and women. Along with that he undertook refreshers courses so that the distinctive theological identity and discipline are maintained in standing order. It was he who was responsible for the starting of a renowned St. Luke's Hospital at Chabua in 1930. Another achievement during his ministry was the completion of the building of hostels for boys and girls in Dibrugargh. This was a need long felt by the people as their concern was for the educational pursuits of their children in schools in a city like Dibrugargh. Bishop Hubback who was so concerned for the Church's ministry in the tea gardens, was responsible for getting sponsorship from the India Tea Association, Calcutta for the appointment of 6 (six) chaplains from 1926. The supporting force began to dwindle from 1950s until it was completely terminated in 1965. His successful service to the Church in the region came to an abrupt ending following his transfer and promoted to the post of a Metropolitan in 1945.

Bishop Nirod Kumar Biswas of Bengal joined the office of a Bishop of the Diocese of Assam in 1945 following Bishop Hubback. His interest was mainly in providing pastoral ministry to the Church and its people. His ministerial services tended to have confined to the sacramental duties and preaching. His love and passion in singing drew the attention of the public and in the process most members of the church thought it right to call him the "flute of Jesus." Though the institutional means that his predecessor had established had moved on with support and supervision from the leading members of the Church, Bishop Biswas appeared to have played a low profile in them. That was apparently the reason why his mission did not pass through rough periods of difficulty. He died in 1948.

The enthronement of Bishop Joseph Amritanand in 1949 opened a new chapter in the history of the Church of England in Northeast India. His service continued till he was transferred in 1962. Changes that have taken place during his period were so remarkable that one could not pass over. First, his job was to follow the policy of the British Government in transferring its capital from Guwahati to Shillong and that he initiated for the shifting of the Bishop's residence from Dibrugargh to Shillong in 1949. The decision was determined from the general British administrative policy and hardly did it have connection with the nature of its adherents. The Bishop's office remained in Dibrugargh and it was looked after by the Chaplain of Lakhimpur. A year after the relocation of the Bishop's residence, a disaster of unimaginable magnitude happened in Dibrugargh following the devastating great tremor that hit the Dibrugargh region in 1950. Rt. Revd. P. Lyngdoh reported, "As a result of the great earthquake of 15th August, 1950, the Brahmaputra changed its course in 1954 and swallowed the St. Paul's Church, the Bishop's bungalow, Office, Hostels, the entire 5 acre property located beside the river. This led to the permanent shift of Bishop's establishment from Dibrugargh to Shillong."[51] Though the great Brahmaputra river had swallowed up the church and its designated locations including the hard earned investments, by the fury of a natural disaster, it had however not able to swallow up the living members of the Church. The body of Christ is alive and continues to witness to the world the mighty works of God.

Secondly, Bishop Amritanand was instrumental for endowing an indigenous mission of self-supporting in financial matters. This was a ripe and encouraging idea and it had created a strong awareness among the members of the Church of being self-reliant and independent. Last but not the least, he was so concerned about the future ministry of the Church especially after India's Independence. In order to achieve his vision for the development of indigenous leadership, Bishop Amritanand took the initiative in calling young people to come forward for enrolling as candidates for theological training and education and that to join the ordained ministry of the Church in the region.

The challenges faced by the succeeding Bishop Eric Samuel Nasir (1963-1968) were so enormous that he himself and the Diocesan office were kept active and busy. It was during his tenure that witnessed large scale immigration of Garo refugees from the then East Pakistan (today Bangladesh) to Garo hills. Many of

---

[51] *Ibid.*, p. 16.

these Garo immigrants were already members of the Church of England. Their arrival and settlement in West Garo hills made the Bishop and the office engaged in the ministry of rehabilitating, caring and tending. It was reported, "Tura, once again, assumed great importance and considerable Diocese energy was shifted to this area."[52]

The Church also witnessed the building of a Chapel at the newly constructed Cantonment at Narangi. This new Cantonment is located close to Guwahati city. Though it was Lieut. Col. Dawson who initiated the construction of the new church building, it was however Bishop Nasir who dedicated and christened it as the Ebenezer Chapel on the 21st of April, 1968.

The appointment of Bishop Ariel Victor Jonathan as a successor to Bishop Nasir in 1968 was rather short because before his service could enter upon the period of stability, he was transferred in 1970. The year was also memorable in the history of the Anglican Church in North India including the Northeast, because of the inauguration of the Church of North India-a Church in which the Church of England was a major partner.

6. Ecumenical Involvement of the Anglican Church: Long before the formation of the Church of North India in 1970, the Anglican Church in South India had joined solidly in the formation of the Church of South India in 1947. This ecumenical incident was unique in a sense that it was made compatible the union of both episcopal and non-episcopal communions. The formation of the Church of North India was almost on the same pattern.

Meanwhile, the much anticipated creation of the Church of North East India by the union of the Presbyterian Church, Baptist Churches and other constituent affiliated churches of the North East India Christian Council (NEICC) just proceeded on the regular annual concilliar fellowshipping. While the Church of England thought it right not to miss the golden ecumenical opportunity with the larger North Indian counterpart and given the conservative and individualistic Christian mentality of major protestant traditions whose indecision and slow process in the hierarchical democratic committees and made the Church moved on a snail pace, leaders of the Anglican Church in the region anticipated not to undergo an ordeal of losing the opportunities, then associated with the Church of North India movement without a second thought. Then at the time of the inauguration of the Church of North India in Nagpur on 29th November, 1970, the Diocese of Assam was already its integral constituent unit.

History is proof that the Church of England in India was well ecumenical. Their ecumenical spirit remained explicit in their openness, commitment to 'unite in order to unite' and cooperation. In order that the ecumenical process in the country should stand translatable, the Anglican Church leaders placed the Church in the process of being adjustable, compatible and workable. They did so with the full backing of the Church. Before that, the building of the Ebenezer

52 *Ibid.*, p. 16.

Chapel at Narangi, Assam in 1968 was meant not for use by the members of the Anglican Church alone but by Christians of all denominational persuasions. It was an ecumenical place of worship.

By joining the Church of North India, the Anglican Church joined hands with the Presbyterians of the United Church of Northern India, the Baptists of the Council of the Baptist Church in Northern India, the Methodists of the Methodist Church of both British and Australian Conferences in India, the Brethren of the Church of the Brethren in India and the Disciples of Christ.

The Church plays an important part in the National Council of Churches of India and other ecumenical bodies in the country. Its commitment to the ecumenical Church and institutions has enabled their full participation at the World Council of Churches, Christian Conference of Asia, the Anglican Church in the United Kingdom and others. It could address public issues and national problems as a collective and united body of Christ. There was tremendous integrative national dimension in it.

7. Anglican Developmental Activities in the Region: Following its integration with the Church of North India, the Diocese of Assam became a constituent see of the united church. Bishops who have served the region since 1970 included the Rt. Revd. D. D. Pradhan (1970-1986); Rt. Revd. E. W. Talibuddin (1986- 1996) and Rt. Revd. Purely Lyngdoh (1996 till date). The role and contribution of Bishop Lyngdoh was so significant that the Church of North India Synod voted him for the most prestigious post as its Moderator. While this chair has raised the status of the Diocese of Assam to a well recognizable level, his very presence was an honour to the Khasi-Jaintia community. In order to make the Church in the region runs at par with the changes in political administration, the CNI Synod in its meeting in 1995 approved the change of name from the Diocese of Assam to the Diocese of North East India.

The activities of the Church among the people in the region could well be seen in medical mission, establishment of boarding homes, educational activity, identification with the rural congregations and encouragement of indigenous local leadership.

1). Promotion of Medical Services: Despite the fact that its presence here was to meet the spiritual needs of the British personnel and other members of the Anglican Communion, the Anglican Church gave sufficient attention to the medical requirement of the people in the region. The first effort in medical service was traced to the arrival of Miss Helen Slawson in Chabua in 1923. Her coming was made possible by the USPG. Miss Slawson was a trained Community Health Worker. Another worker who had joined this community health programme was an Indian by the name Francis Tirki. Their main job was by touring rural areas and gave instruction in home nursing first aid. They also conducted training for selected rural folks in midwifery.

Following this modest and humble attempt, Bishop Hubback apprised of the need of starting a medical mission in upper Assam valley. The USPG attended to the Bishop's requests and sent Dr. Wenefrede Thompsom. His coming resulted in the starting of the St. Luke's Hospital at Chabua in 1930. As the medical ministry was on, another strengthening effort was made during the tenure of Rt. Revd. D. D. Pradhan in the 1970s. Following receiving financial assistance from the KNH, Germany the plan to start a hospital in Tinsukia was implemented in right earnest. The 150 bedded Tinsukia hospital dedicated to St. Luke was inaugurated in 1979. The establishment of this hospital went out side by side with the revitalizing the Chabua St. Luke's Hospital.

The St. Luke's Hospital in Tinsukia witnessed the running of a school of nursing. This was regarded important and a necessity in the midst of the growing fully fledged Hospitals in the area. Besides that, the Church gave tremendous importance to the promotion of community health centre. Its commitment to social health care and service led to the construction of the Community and Health Centre in Guwahati. It was commissioned on 23rd April, 1995 under the name of the first Bishop in the region, Rt. Revd. Herbert Perkenhem Walsh.

2). Establishment of Boarding Homes: Though the Church had not engaged in any full scale educational mission, it had nevertheless involved in building hostels for boys and girls separately in Dibrugargh as early as 1936. Similar hostels were also constructed in Tinsukia and Jowai in Jaintia hills. These boarding homes facilities received improvement, renovation and broadening following support from the KNH, Germany. Through this support, the Church was able to carry out development in the infrastructure. It had enabled to increase the in-take of children. Further, the Church could hold training of hostel personnel as well.

Though these hostels aimed primarily at accommodating boys and girls from the Anglican Church but they also extended open hands to school going children from all walks of life. In the information provided by Rt. Revd. Lyngdoh, it said "Through these Hostels, a great number of men and women have come out who hold responsible positions in the Government, the Society, as well as leaders in the Church."[53]

3). Educational Activity: It has been mentioned elsewhere that Protestant and Catholic Missions in the region have invested so much in running schools and colleges. These educational activities did not confine to the urban centres but also deeply into the interior among the rural people. The Anglican Church though had given substantive investment in building hostels and in providing the needed facilities for the benefits of the children their investment in educational field is rather concentrated on a small scale. Significant schools were set up in Jowai, Shillong and elsewhere. These were co-educational schools.

---

[53] Cf. *Ibid.*, p. 17.

Given the presence of numerous first class educational schools in Shillong at least that belong to the Presbyterian Church, the Catholic or other Christian traditions one could no longer say otherwise because their contribution was mainly in the upliftment of several tribal communities. However, there was a community of Punjab origin right at the middle of the city. It was the British who were responsible for bringing this serving community mainly in the cleaning of filths and dirt in homes, compounds, drains and public roads. While this community could not be integrated in the larger local community, they were alienated in most spheres. While other Christian Missions have stood aloof from helping this servicing community, it was the Anglican Church that had started a school specifically for children from this community. That is the glorious service that deserved appreciation.

4). Identification with the Rural Congregations: Most of the Anglican priests and workers gave adequate care and attention to the churches in rural areas. We have seen that Miss Slawson and Bro. F. Tirki served the Church by devoted their time and ministry among the people in villages. Most of these rural folks were uneducated and isolated. The fact that they have chosen to identify and participate in the rural life was a memorable work.

Some Bishops too who have witnessed the growing rise of Anglican local churches and members in several towns and villages have embarked on constant tours and visits to almost each and every local congregation. It was such humble ministries that had endowed the local Anglican communities with greater sense of spiritual trust and confidence.

The Anglican Church has been well established in the region. It covers most of the states in Northeast India. Though the previous leadership had concentrated in the development of the Church at the ministerial level and initiated works for social upliftment, its vision under the present leadership is to make the Church getting involved in the overall holistic mission that touched upon different aspects of the people like social, economic, ecological, political and ethical spheres.

IV. An Historical Overview of the Catholic Mission

1. Beginnings of Catholic Missions: Though Catholic missionaries had made sporadic visit to Northeast India well in the 17th and 18th centuries but their permanent missionary operation in the region began in 1890 only.[54] It was German Salvatorians who started the work but before they began to secure stable foothold among the people, there was a sudden setback because of the internment of the missionaries following the outbreak of the First World War. As a result of this incident, the work in Meghalaya was placed under the supervision of the

[54] More stories about the Catholic Church in the region, read Becker, C. **History of the Catholic Missions in Northeast India** (1980); **Early History of the Catholic Missions in Northeast India** (1989); Karotemprel, S. ed., **The Catholic Church in Northeast India, 1890-1990** (1993).

Jesuits in Kolkata. Their preoccupation with ministries in Bengal had made them difficult to provide satisfactorily service in Meghalaya. However, judging by the numerical growth in Catholic membership during the period of internment, the work under the Jesuits was far from being static.[55]

The arrival of the Salesian missionaries in 1922 was a boon to the continuity of the Catholic presence in the region.[56] It provided not just the continuity but the stable and permanent operation. The Salesians of Don Bosco committed themselves towards the overall welfare and well being of the people.[57] They sought ways and means for their liberation and contributed much to a self-reliant life. Raising the level of life of the Khasi-Jaintia and Garo people, especially the youth was a mission priority of the Salesians.

2. Comprehensive Missionary Works: The role of the Catholic Church in education was remarkable. Unlike the Welsh missionaries in Khasi – Jaintia hills who concentrated on providing a wide network of elementary schools in different villages, the ministry of the Catholic missionaries was rather more dynamic. While introducing an extensive network of elementary schools in several places in Meghalaya, the Catholic missionaries devoted to providing higher education even up to the college level. They did this because of their missiological vision and at the same time to meet the pressing need of the people. Most of their higher educational institutions are located in Shillong, Tura, Jowai, Cherrapunji, Nongstoin, Mairang and elsewhere. Among the prominent colleges in the region included the St. Anthony's College, St. Edmund's College, St. Mary's College and many others. While these institutions admitted students from different backgrounds, they also appointed qualified non-Catholic teachers and administrative staff alike.

The contribution of the Don Bosco Technical School in the state was tremendous as it enabled the unemployed young people to start their business in various capacities without depending on government jobs. The school is also providing facility in the training on various trades. It includes training in motoring, tailoring, electrical, printing, book binding, electronic, furniture and shoe making. More importantly was their commitment in giving preference to students of poor and rural backgrounds.

The Catholic missionaries took special attention to providing education to women. The St. Mary's, Loreto, St. Margaret's, Auxillium, Holy Child and many others are among the educational institutions of high standing for the training of

---

[55] Downs, F. S. **Christianity in North East India**, p. 131.

[56] For more report, see Maliekal, G. **History of the Catholic Church among the Khasis** (2005).

[57] Further information in respect of its spread in other states in the region; see relevant articles in Karotemprel, S. ed., **The Catholic Church in Northeast India, 1890-1990** (1993). Also cf. Lotsuro, Dr. Angeline **The Nagas: A Missionary Challenge** (2000), Jeyaseelan, L. **Impact of the Missionary Movement in Manipur** (1996), pp. 100ff.

women right from the nursery class and up to the level of college education. Many women irrespective of their ethnic, religious or denominational persuasions have benefited from these institutions.

The role of theological education in giving training to the candidates for priesthood and the laity was also significant. The church runs such theological institutions, like Sacred Heart Theological College, Oriens Theological Seminary, St. Paul's Minor Seminary and other institutions right in the midst of the state and among the indigenous people. People from other states have also availed themselves of the facilities that are available in Meghalaya. The Church could set up also libraries of international standard. As of now, the Sacred Heart Theological College Library serves as a research centre in humanities, cultures and Christian theologies. Its archival documentation section gets the distinction of preserving ancient materials and rare manuscripts for the region. The establishment of a museum right within the campus of the College bolstered the theological vision of the Church. It is a gift to the nation.

Boarding homes too played another contributing role to the people. In order to help students from distant places to pursue studies in Shillong, Tura, Jowai and other places in the state, the church established hostel facilities for boys and girls separately. Through these boarding opportunities, young students from different communities could stay and study together and in the process learn to espouse vision of common interest. The unique feature of these hostels was that they entertain students not just of the Catholic community but those from various walks of life.

The other related vibrant area of the Church's ministry was in the introduction of extensive services of medical mission. The Nazareth Hospital in Shillong stands out as tower of hope to the people. It tries to provide the best medical facilities in order to meet the needed healing touch to the low income group. Health centers, clinics and dispensaries in different areas have catered to the need of the rural citizens. Orphans and the aged have also become priority frontiers for missionary work. The Church has established humanitarian institutions in order to take care of such victims in the society.

Identification with the rural folk was yet another significant venture of the ministry of the Church. It seriously takes care of their spiritual well being and establishes worshipping centers in most villages in the state. As most of the people in rural areas are farmers, the Church made concerted efforts in helping the need of the farming sections of the community. The rural resource centre that was established in Ri Bhoi district was in part an attempt to help the people mostly in agricultural sector in addition to farming and handicrafts.

The investment in academic research and publication provides avenues for the benefit of the academic communities in the region besides educational schools and colleges. Through the Don Bosco publication, Vendrame Institute and Daughters of St. Paul, the Church actively engages in the publication of textbooks for schools and colleges, religious treatises for theological seminarians and catechists and scholarly books for research scholars.

V. Origin and Growth of the Baptist Missionary Society, 1894[58]

It was the Baptist Missionary Society that worked in southern Mizoram that had contributed to the growth of the Baptist Church of Mizoram. Though a Welsh Presbyterian Missionary, Rev. Williams Williams, resident at Shella, Khasi hills was the first Christian priest to have set foot in Mizoram in 1891, the real work began with the former missionaries of the Arthington Aborigines Mission, Rev. F. W. Savidge and Rev. J. H. Lorrain. Both of them were not originally from the Baptist Church but joined it by baptism and service.

1. A Foundation was Laid Upon (1894-1898): Savidge and Lorrain came to Mizoram for missionary service under the Arthington Aborigines Mission and landed in Aizawl, Mizoram on 11th January, 1894. For unknown reasons, Robert Arthington recalled the missionaries and dismissed their services in 1898. Their missionary activities were never in vain because what they have initiated, have become specific and strong foundations for the solidification of the Mizo society. The first thing that the missionaries did was to learn the local language spoken by the people at the centre of their work. Their Church missiological vision and commitment made them gifted linguists. They could master the Duhlian dialect, i.e. the Mizo language.

After mastering the language, the missionaries decided to make it a national language or a standard common language for the whole Mizo tribe. Then they introduced the Latin alphabet. Like the missionaries in Nagaland and Khasi hills, Savidge and Lorrain introduced the European alphabet not for destroying native literary culture but for strengthening. They too did not know neither the languages nor the alphabets of the the neighbouring literate societies like the Bengalis, Assamese, Manipuri or Burmese. At the same time, they found that the Latin alphabet and pronunciation were fitting with the Mizo phonetic sound and making writing easily readable.

The next step, that is after successfully set up a primer of Mizo alphabet in both big and small letters, the missionaries translated into the people's Duhlian language the Gospels according to Luke, John and the Book of Acts. It was not neither by accidence nor by providence that led to their decision of translating these three books. They could have done so by their knowledge of the Bible and also of the Mizo people in addition to an application of missiological sound reasoning. The Gospel of Luke is a Gospel to the Gentiles that gives hope to the

[58] Significant information about the Baptist Church in Mizoram is available from Hminga, C. L. **The Life and Witness of the Churches in Mizoram** (1987); **Compendium: The Baptist Church of Mizoram, 1903-2003** (2003); Vanlalchhuanawma, **Christianity and Subaltern Culture: Revival Movement as a Cultural Response to Westernisation in Mizoram** (2007), pp. 120-123.

poor, the neglected, the marginalized and assures the new salvation to the tax collector like Zacchaeus and the repented criminal. The Book of Acts too, written by Luke, gives importance to the outpouring of the Holy Spirit and the experience was such that people from different unintelligible linguistic backgrounds could understand the spoken language without interpreters. The accounts recorded in it were about missionary tours, evangelization and planting of churches among the Gentiles. John's Gospel is a Gospel written in the context of Greek philosophy and underscores its universal nature.

All these three translated books were at least non – Jewish, inclusive, universal and missionary minded. They are books for others. It was a well thought out plan in their translations. They become the first indigenous books and set a firm foundation for the Mizo language and literature.

After publishing the translated books, the missionaries had also prepared a Lushai Grammar and an Anglo-Lushai Dictionary. These books were also brought out. They were contributing factors for the development of a modern Mizo literature.

However, despite the progress of the Arthington Aborigines Mission in Mizoram, Robert Arthington closed it down by terminating Lorrain and Savidge from services. Their termination had however not put off their missionary interests and works in unreached areas. Following that they went and worked among the Abors in Arunachal Pradesh. There too they could learn the language and produced a Grammar.

2. Securing Its Foothold: Though the Baptist Missionary Society work through the Arthington Aborigines Mission was put under suspended animation following Robert Arthington's withdrawal of the missionaries but their return to Mizoram at the request of the Baptist Missionary Society (BMS) in 1903 and the official counting of their services in 1894 placed the BMS work in Mizoram on stability and permanence. Mizo alphabet, universalization of Duhlian language, translations and publication of a Lushai Grammar and Dictionary were living testimonies of the work that started in 1894. There was no reason to question its historical importance except that their early missionary outreach was carried out in the northern region but not in south Mizoram.

The second missionary works of the duo was no longer located in Aizawl as it was by then taken over by the Welsh Presbyterian Mission but in the southern part at Serkawn, Lunglei. The selection of this southern location for the BMS Centre resulted in some mutual understanding that the Welsh Presbyterian Mission takes care of the north and the BMS of the south. As long as these two mission bodies functioned as evangelistic movements, the proposed concept of understanding functioned successfully but tended to ignore once the "evangelistic movements" became institutionalized followed by achieving the higher levels in education, communication, dispersal and migration as well to do Christians.

3. Spread of the Church: The Mizos were Gospel receptive people. In the year of their arrival at Serkawn, Lunglei in 1903, the missionaries' labours had been productive leading to the establishment of the first Baptist Church at Serkawn. From there its spread was to most areas in the sourthern region. Apart from help from local Mizo converts, the whole missionary responsibilities rested with the duo. The pioneers devoted to their evangelization through regular church services. Their priority was to build a solid gathering community of believers for corporate worship. Its collective nature was such that people from all groups – adults, youths, men, women and children, could come and participate in worship. The community service in the Church was from its inception participatory, inclusive and progressive and played a far life building measures. It contributed to a sense of unity.

Though Mrs. Savidge, who had accompanied her husband had contributed much to the education of women but the women's missionary force was further bolstered by the arrival of the second group of the BMS missionaries, viz., Ms. D. E. Dicks and Miss E. M. Chapman, in 1919. Their committed areas of service were in education and medical works. Their coming became a symbol of women's courage, ability and social dynamism in the midst of a low esteemed woman in Mizo culture. Whereas the local people and the church would welcome the second batch women missionaries but a male dominated Mizo society did not see much benefit for their women. They negatively foresaw that once native girls became educated they would no longer continue in their traditional domestic service, became lazy and would only involve in writing love letters. Though such attitude towards women was prejudicial but that was a kind of thinking in the ancient past. The lady missionaries had come to a society that did not give importance to women. Hardly however, had Mizo men shown an antagonistic spirit to the women missionaries. It was such attitude that did not hinder both the ongoing mission and evangelism and native people's response to the new faith.

It was groups of women missionaries that provided the needed missiological support to the BMS Ministry in south Mizoram. The third batch of missionaries that had gone to Lunglei in 1922 included only women. They were Ms. E. M. Oliver and Ms. M. Clark. Their main works were like the former lady missionaries, in medical and education. In other words, right from the beginning, the BMS work in Mizoram gained significant strength and stability through educational and medical services. But for the role and tenacious spirit of the committed lady missionaries, a male dominated BMS missionary operation in southern Mizoram would not have tremendous impact at a faster rate.

After that, several batches of BMS missionaries including men and women have come and laboured in south Mizoram. Their works were in educational affairs, health services, Sunday school, administration, spreading the faith, planting and organizing local churches, ordained ministry, Bible School and training of native leaders. By the time that the last missionaries left south Mizoram for good in

1970, the Baptist Church had already secured strong foothold among most of the people that it had ministered.

4. Different Activities of the Society: The activities of the BMS in Mizoram could well be explained as follows:-

1). Introduction of a Standard Language and Promotion of Mizo Literature: Language is an important cultural component of a human community. It serves as a means of unifying people and of making people have a sense of identity. Its importance is deeply felt in a society that is rife with numerous dialects. The pioneer missionaries' first job was a decision to adopt a dialect as a standard language for the whole tribe in Mizoram. Their final decision on choosing the Duhlian spoken dialect was not based on the its superior nature, sweet or the best but on the condition that it was a common spoken communication among the local people around the mission station. The presence of a common language also enabled the missionaries to communicate the Gospel to the entire Mizo people. Though the missionaries who took up such decision did it intentionally for the objective of evangelization the people, its subsequent impact was on the whole society.

The universalization of the Duhlian dialect went out simultaneously in the introduction of Latin alphabet. There was no colonial motive in its introduction. As already mentioned elsewhere, the BMS missionaries knew the Latin alphabet very well and so it was easy for them to function faster on the Latin written script. They also realized that the unsophisticated Mizo language could effectively be reduced to that phonetic sound and pronunciation of the Latin letters. Once the design of the table of Mizo alphabet was fixed, Lorrain and Savidge began their translation of the Gospel according to Luke and John and the Book of Acts. Along with the translation of Biblical books, the pioneers were also able to bring out the Lushai Grammar and a Dictionary. Many publications, both theological and social, were written by the missionaries and published in the larger interests of the Church and the Mizo society. It is no denying the fact that the missionaries were the builders of modern Mizo language and literature.

The publication of the translated books had the effect of building a foundation of Mizo prose literature. For the first time Mizo people could read descriptive essay type of stories. These helped envisioned the people and created a sense of reasoning, understanding and believing as well. It was a prose literature that shaped native people's literary minds. Closely related to this development was the production of the Lushai hymn book as early as 1908. Mizos were singing people and the publication of the hymn book had fulfilled the long felt need of the indigenous Christian community. It had contributed to the fullness of Christian worship in Mizoram. Again, although there was precisely an evangelistic objective in its publication but insofar as the hymns were composed under the conventional poetic style, rhythm and metrical structure they represented some kind of examples of modern Mizo poetry.

Besides that, Mizo literature was further widened by the bringing out of dramas, fictions and more importantly by the introduction of various educational books on various subjects. Mizo language and literature would not have become fully complete without the establishment of typing and printing technical means. Mizoram received the first Printing Press in 1938 and it was named "The South Lushai Church Press."

The missionaries made the Duhlian language compulsory in Church services, Sunday Schools, Church's assemblies and recording of official minutes and correspondences. The Bible and Hymn books were also used in churches and for personal devotions. They also made compulsory learning of the alphabet and other published books in schools. In this manner, the imposition of a single language and literature in the community got deeply rooted among the people and resulted in solidifying the Mizos.

2). Educational Activities: Lorrain was a linguist and devoted his evangelistic work in translation and producing literature. Savidge was a professional teacher and his main ministry was in starting schools in south Mizoram. His wife too was a trained school teacher and had taught at the Scottish Church Mission Girls School, Kolkata before coming to Mizoram. These missionaries, however, put up their efforts together in school education. Primary schools were started at the mission station right from the beginning. Though the primary objective of elementary schools was to enable members of a Christian community to read the Bible and sing hymns but their influence was on the society at large.

Education was an important channel in evangelization and the missionaries have taken it as a missiological priority. Their commitment to mission and evangelism had however not made their educational schools confined to studying Biblical literature and Christian teachings but in studying of other social science subjects like history and geography and also a study of elementary arithmetic. Therefore, most Christian schools in the region witnessed significant combination of Christian learning and modern elementary science. For most part of their initial service in south Mizoram, the missionaries were concerned about setting up a wide network of lower primary schools in several areas. Native Christians who have passed out their primary level of education were appointed teachers in different schools in villages. The missionaries were also pioneers in higher education. High Schools were set up though not on an extensive scale because of financial implication and scarcity of qualified personnel.

One notable contribution of the BMS educational mission was in its serious investment on education of women. Mrs. Savidge was a pioneer in this connection. The lady missionaries were also able to initiate Girls Auxiliary in 1932 at Lunglei and a Girls Middle English School in a village near Pawih in 1938. This part of the ministry was implemented at a time where a male dominated Mizo society did not have much concern about women who tended to look at them as functional being rather than personal. Lady missionaries though faced unsupportive spirit from traditional conservative sections in the society yet remained tenacious and carried out the work with love and determination.

Before Mr. Carter started a Teacher Training School in 1931, training of Primary School Teachers was initiated in Boys and Girls School at Serkawn. Many local Christian converts who have passed their elementary education enrolled in the training school for further study and learning and after completing the training programme became school masters in rural areas. There was a clear perception from the beginning that teachers of mission primary school were serving not a secular job but a dedicated ministry. Teachers were also evangelists. Education was therefore, acknowledged as an effective means for spreading the faith, evangelization and Church planting and an integral part of the mission of the Church.

Given the rise of many children who have completed their primary level of education, there was a need to have a higher level of school education in the region. As a result of this educational vision, Rev. R. F. Tucker and Rev. H. W. Carter started a High School at Lunglei in 1948. Rev. Tucker, who was an expert in teaching and administration, took over the leadership as its first headmaster and Rev. Carter served as a science master. The school became another torchbearer for the people and shaped the destiny of young people in an isolated Mizo southern society.

In almost sixty years of its committed service in education, the missionaries suffered much in running and maintaining the educational mission in a far flung hilly terrain of south Mizoram. Their serious commitment and generous investment became evident in not confining to the primary level of education but in proceeding to the higher standard of education. They have also given serious attention to providing separate education for Mizo girls. In 1963, the Baptist Mission could venture into the starting of a College. This was another breakthrough in southern Mizo history and its introduction was a boon to the whole Mizo people.

3). Mission and Health Services: The BMS missionaries were spiritual people who brought the good news of God's salvation in Jesus Christ. Their teaching on the Almighty God who could perform miracles, signs and wonders was so firm and they did not accept to compromise on that principle. While they believed in divine healing, they also saw the need of helping the sick and physically suffering people through allopathic medicines, nursing and medical care. The pioneer missionaries started their medical service side by side with the starting of a church and education. Staff nurses who have come to provide the needed support and help to the medical mission were O. E. Dicks (1919), E. M. Oliver (1922), I. M. Good (1928) and others.

Medical services too did not remain static at a clinical level but it was well upgraded to a level of a hospital. A small out-patient hospital was started at Serkawn in 1939. Dr. C. C. Chesterman, a BMS Medical officer in London, who visited Lunglei in that year, inaugurated this little hospital. Though the starting of this mini hospital sent joyous jubilation to the Church and the people but the non-availability of a resident qualified medical doctor put the much elated institution to almost a standstill. However, before all hopes for its active functioning began to dash, there came Dr. & Mrs. Stockley in 1957 who supervised and ran the hospital. Their coming was important because while Dr. Stockley was a medical practitioner; his wife was a trained staff nurse. Both came with rich experiences from the medical mission field in China.

4). Sunday School and Theological Education: Christian missionary works did not mean preaching alone and Church planting. The BMS missionaries though have given importance to proclamation and planting of community of believers, they have set up their missionary service on well coordinated, institutional and systematic procedures for an all round development and growth of an individual person and the community alike. While the missionaries have set up educational and medical institutions for their comprehensive ministries among the people from all walks of life, they have also taken special attention on spiritual life building measures. Such works became evident in the starting of Sunday School and theological institution.

Miss Chapman earned the name as the mother of the Sunday School movement in southern Mizoram. It was under her initiative that the Sunday School department under a well graded structure was instituted in the Church in 1935. That was the time when the Baptist Church in Mizoram had shown phenomenal signs of growth both in numbers and geographical spread to rural areas. Local churches and congregations have been organized in different places. Though the ordained ministry looked after the word and sacraments and was confirmed to the ordained ministers, care and supervision of local churches have been placed under evangelists and lay people. The missionaries who saw people's positive turn out to the Church and the increase in Church's attendance were able to produce the Bible and Lushai Hymn book.

Mizos were gifted singing people. Singing of western translated hymns and indigenously composed ones did not require training sessions. Once the songs were sung in the Church, the people could easily catch them instantly and could sing themselves later. The glory of Mizo songs depended on their group and congregational singing. There is harmony and strength in their collective rendition. While the missionaries could not see any need of special help in singing western hymns in Church services through the published Lushai Hymn Book, they however, could see the urgent need of teaching the members on the Bible and its teachings. The Sunday School was introduced to cater to the knowledge of the converts in regard to the contents of the Bible, the Church's theological emphases and practices. This department became a powerful teaching force in Churches and continues to serve so till date. Well prepared Sunday School lessons were printed and used in local Churches.

Starting of a theological training school in 1946, under the name Jubilee Bible School was done in response to the pressing need of qualified ordained ministers and evangelists. There was neither competition nor invitation in its inauguration. Rev. R. F. Tucker was its founder principal. Two Mizo Pastors were supporting teachers of the Bible School from the beginning itself. Though the school had a humble and modest beginning it was nevertheless a fountain for the production of dedicated and committed Pastors of the Church. Many lay leaders who have studied in the school and completed have become effective and well informed Church workers in their respective areas. Given its primary objective of edifying the Church and evangelization, the Church changed its name to Missionary Training Institute in 1991. In other words, the Church wanted to concentrate on is ministerial and missionary working aspects and left the academic dimensions to Colleges outside its purview. Most candidates for theological training were deputed to Serampore and elsewhere, i.e., Colleges affiliated to the Senate of Serampore College. It was only until 2000 that the authority of the Church began to realize the academic aspects of a Bible School and so upgraded it to a full fledged theological college and christened it the Academy of Integrated Christian Studies. Its location was relocated to Aizawl in the northern part of Mizoram.

5). Encouragement and Promotion of Native Leadership: The BMS missionaries who have laboured in Mizoram in person and the BMS office in London though have spent their time and resources have nonetheless never thought of residing in Mizoram permanently. They did not think to hold on to leadership, rule and control of the Mizo mission field for good. Their perception of the future mission of the Church was that the indigenous leaders and Churches should take over the entire responsibilities in running the affairs of the whole Church in Mizoram, supporting the needed financial resources and ownership.

The BMS missionaries were not selfish. They gave training to local leaders, both men and women in secular and theological education. Most of those who have shouldered major responsibilities during the transitional period in the 1970s were products of the BMS missionaries' tutelage.

This was an implementation of a farsighted vision. In due course, the Church did not belong to the missionaries but to the native members who have imbibed a deep sense of belonging. The Church though had its origin in western form but as it had become fully incarnated in the life and thought of the indigenous converts, it is no longer foreign but a vital and integral part of Mizo culture.

6). Reaching the Unreached Frontiers: Mizo Christians were given a sense of love, belonging and responsibility right at their initial period itself. The first converts who after given preliminary instruction in the faith and religious practices were sent to reach out people in neighbouring villages. This they did with success. Through the work of these native evangelists and lay voluntary workers, almost all Mizos had changed their faith to Christianity in less than fifty years. The love of Christ had constrained them in the faith and work for others' salvation. The community that once practiced head hunting, had by changing over to the new faith became searchers for the salvation of human persons. Most of those who did the practical work of evangelizing were lay members including men, women, students and young people.

The work of evangelization had already gone out in full swing well before the Church's authority began to take it up officially. It was reported that these volunteers have undertaken missionary outreach to Myanmar and Bangladesh in foreign lands and neighbouring states of Tripura, Manipur and in North Cachar hills in Assam. These works were productive and numerous churches have grown in the above areas. These pioneers did not leave the local churches to stand on their own but continued to provide leadership, supervision and care.

In due course, the Church took cross cultural mission seriously and started the work among the Chakmas and Brus in 1939. Later, the evangelizing work was extended to non-Mizos who have come and settled in Mizoram.

The next step of the Church's mission was to move out of Mizoram and to start missionary work among different groups of people. The formation of the Zoram Baptist Mission in 1966 had further strengthened the Church's cross cultural mission objective. Their works then got started among the different groups of people in Assam, Tripura, Madhya Pradesh, Maharashtra, Arunachal Pradesh and West Bengal. The Zoram Baptist Mission is also doing extensive missionary services outside India in Thailand, China, Nepal, Bangladesh and Bhutan.

Chapter 6

Emergence of Northeast Indian Indigenous Christianity[1]

We have seen the origin, growth and development of Christianity in Northeast India through the American Baptist Mission, the Welsh Presbyterian tradition, the Anglican communion, the Catholic Mission and the British Baptist Mission. These different Western Missions have secured significant foothold in Nagaland, Meghalaya, Mizoram, Manipur and in North Cachar hills of Assam.

Most hill people in the region have responded positively to the new faith. The new religion that was planted among the people soon became indigenized in terms of people's participation in collective worship, decision making, self – support, indigenous leadership, pastoral care and ministry and in reaching out to the outside world.

As soon as Christianity got deeply rooted in the cultural roots of the people, it began to become truly indigenous. Native converts who were no longer satisfied with the Western form and style moved out of these Western established Churches and started their own Christian movements some of such have taken place in Meghalaya, Mizoram, Manipur and Nagaland.

I. Indigenous Christian Movement in Mizoram:[2] Christianity is a productive religion among the Mizos and other people's groups in Mizoram. Their response to the faith was so progressive and dramatic that by 1947 almost all of them have changed their traditional religion to Christianity. Christian Missions that have entered upon Mizoram included mainly the Welsh Presbytarian Mission in the north and the British Baptist Mission in the south. Other Western Missions that have come and worked in the State are the Catholic Church, the Seventh Day Adventist, the Salvation Army and several groups of Pentecostal persuasion.

---

[1] Read relevant articles in a book edited by Snaitang, O. L. and titled **Churches of Indigenous Origins in Northeast India** (2000).

[2] See Dokhuma, James **Zoram Kohhran Tualto Chanchinte** (1975). Raldawna, **Isua Krista Kohhran To Bull** (c.1993).

As soon as the new faith got into the life of the people, the Mizos tended to express it in line with their cultural reality. We will now make a survey of selected indigenous groups in the state.

Tlira Pawl is the first indigenous Christian group in Mizoram. Khawliantlira, a former member of the Baptist Church from Champhai in the south was its founder member. He was born in 1876 at the time when Christian missionaries have not entered Mizoram. He was a member of Lai Pawi ethnic group and belonged to the Airawn family clan. Khawliantlira was in most probability one of the early converts to the Baptist Church. At the time when the church had just entered into a stable period of existence, Khawliantlira moved out of the established church and started his own independent Christian church, the Tlira Pawl at Champhai in 1951.

Though this new indigenous Christian group shared much in common with the Baptist Church in respect of the faith in the trinity, the Bible, the redemptive work of Jesus Christ, ordinances and Sunday worship service, it is nevertheless a separate movement that gave importance to local or native leadership, freedom of spiritual expression and self-support. The kind of Christian faith that it insisted became move evident in congregational fellowship, praying, singing and mutual co-operation. The focus on spiritual fellowship was no doubt very important in a solidified ethnic tribal community but its vision that did not encourage social and humanitarian service appeared to have insignificant appeal or impact on the society. Therefore, though its formation at the initial period witnessed energetic enthusiasm and appreciation but because of its limited vision though how indigenous it was tended to remain static. However, the Tlira Pawl is representative of some kind of an indigenous expression of Christianity in Mizo society.

While the Tlira Pawl was still at its formative stage and operated in the south there emerged another movement under the name Zakaia Pawl at Aiduzawl in the north in 1932. Zakaithanga (1908-69) was a pioneer and leader of Zakaia Pawl. He was first a member of the Presbyterian Church but became dissatisfied mostly with its structure and worship pattern that restricted people's free emotional expression and interpretation of certain theological issues. Before forming the Zakaia Pawl, its founder was well in touch and association with the United Pentecostal Church. As a sense of spiritual dissatisfaction continued to haunt him even after leaving the organized Presbyterian Church, Zakaithanga thought it right to start an independent Church – a Church that would be free from Western domination. The emphasis was on spirituality in respect of one's repented life, praying, singing and emotional expression.

Another lay leader of the Presbyterian Church, Mr. Khuangtuaha of Hmawngkawn started an organization named after himself Khuangtuaha Pawl in 1942. Its common name among its adherents was Lalpa Kohran Thar. He was a strict Bible based member and devoted much to the reading of the Book of Acts. The community life of the disciples that reflected in living together, sharing of resources, love and unity appeared to have gripped Khuangtuaha's life and thinking. Based on his understanding and interpretation, the leader tended to conclude that the Western type of Presbyterian Christianity introduced in Mizoram was incomplete because of the non-implementation of the apostolic common life. Though Khuangtuaha might have understood the apostolic context fairly well but any effort to bring such community's life in the context of a well organized and democratic Presbyterian set up simply remained impossible.

As his longing and desire to implement the Apostolic pattern of common life in the Church was virtually unsuccessful, he ventured to starting it himself as a separate movement. The initiative resulted in the creation of the Lalpa Kohhran Thar or the Khuangthaha Pawl. The explanation of the importance of the Apostolic community life was so strong and emphatic that those who associated with it were not satisfied in just attending church's services, listening to the preached word, singing and praying but literally moved to their leader's house for an experience of the community life in unity. Their meeting together was always marked with congregational singing, mass prayers, personal testimonies and discussing together on spiritual matters. This move paved the way for teaching on the Bible and to live a successful Christian life.

Just at the time when India got her independence from the British rule, in 1947, there came out another likely Pentecostal influenced Thiangzau Church at Sialsuk village in 1947. Because of its major stress on revival movement and expression, Thiangzau might well be called something of a revival church. These revival phenomena made members of the Church looked at Church's committees, rules and constitution as human made and so incompatible with a spiritual body. Like the Apostles who experienced the descending of the Holy Spirit on the day of the Pentecost, members of the Thiangzau Church too strongly believed in the experience of the outgrowing of the Holy Spirit in their community's life and worship

This indigenous church did not confine itself to individual and collective spiritual welfare but engaged in evangelistic public preaching and evangelization. This venture produced unexpected desiring results in the rise of local congregation at Champhai, Lamchhip, Samlukhai, Sailam, Serchhip and others.

The rise of Mizo **Israel Pawl** in 1951 though was an indication of Mizo fluid religious situation, also reflected much of their cultural dynamism. It was Saichhuma of Hlimen and Chola of Buallawn who came up with their interpretation that the Mizos had their historical origin in the Biblical creation and were one of the lost tribes of the Jews. As a matter of fact, such understanding was not there in their pre-Christian history. Hardly any traditional remembered folklore would subscribe to their Jewish ancestry or connection. Besides that, the Mizos whose physical appearance drew near to the Indo-Mongoloid stock did not have any Jewish surviving elements in their culture as most Jewish Diaspora communities in South India did. Therefore, it was precisely the influence of

Christianity through its Scriptures that led to their claim of belonging to the Israelite larger family.

Be that as it may, Mizo Israel Pawl was another development of people's expression of Christianity in their local segment in the society. The work that had led to the translation of the Bible in Mizo language and its wide circulation among the people had tremendous impact on their worldview. The new religion provided them an occasion of free expression and movement. Hence, though Christianity provided the necessary information about human origin, faith and practices but the move that subsequently led to the creation of independent groups was an indication of the full incarnation of the Gospel in their life and their indigenous response.

In almost 14 (fourteen) years after the emergence of Mizo Israel Pawl, two significant indigenous Christian groups came out independently on a recognizable scale. They are the **Zoram Maicham** and **Zathangvunga Pawl**. Started with the economic hardships and political negligence of the Mizos in the 1950s, their sufferings and struggles became more serious in 1960s. Though one should not pass over their religious dimension, these indigenous organizations came up in the midst of people's socio-political and economic crises.

Mr. Thanchhuma of Hmuntha who pioneered the Zoram Maicham in 1965 tried to demonstrate that Christian spirituality should find tangible expression in social service among the poor and needy irrespective of dialect, locality or denomination. The teaching of James appeared more appealing to the leaders of Zoram Maicham and so the main theological emphasis was on practical Christianity. While their attempt received important Biblical support and encouragement but it could have sprang up from people's cultural concept and practice of selfless service in the community, especially among the poor and the haves not.

In the same year, Zathangvunga led the **Zathangvunga Pawl** movement at Champhai in southern Mizoram. Unlike the Zoram Maicham, Zathangvunnga devoted to spiritual life and congregational meeting. They gave significant concentration to Bible study, prayer and holy life. Congregational services in the Church were regarded as a necessity and compulsory and so members took such seriously. There was however no compulsion in it except reasonable appeal and invitation. In the midst of numerous Christian influences, Zathangvunga Pawl carried with it far charismatic, Pentecostal and revival elements.

Christianity that was well conceived in the 19th century gave explosive birth to several instituted indigenous groups some of which I have briefly described above. Another volatile and vibrant movement that emerged in the later half of the 20th century Mizoram was the **Isua Krista Kohhran** in 1971.[3] It is an indigenous movement that attracted not just people's attention but affiliation

[3] Cf. Raldawna, **Isua Krista Kohhran To Bull** (c.1993).

alike. It grew up in the midst of numerous influences like the revival movement, political isolation, economic fall out and traditional religious replacement.

The formation of this indigenous church had its origin in some religious visions of Mr. Patlaia and Rev. Kawlthawma. Mr. Patlaia saw a vision on 14th January, 1934 – a vision that called him to lead a group of the faithful or the saved ones. Though there could have been some elements of truth in his spiritual experience, he however did not have the courage to go ahead. It was only until his friend Rev. Kawlthawma had similar vision experience on 22nd September, 1949 that both thought it desirable to form a separate church group. Although there was seriousness in their visions but given the presence of active and lively Christian Churches, they were nonetheless not prepared to move out of the church and to start a new one. It was not until after more than two decades of reflection and preparation that they formed it on 6th January, 1971. The decision that led to forming an independent Christian movement was more a cultural indigenous expression of Christianity rather than a nature of the new religion.

Isua Krista Kohhran is a movement that laid stress on the guidance of the Holy Spirit, charismatic expression of the faith and Biblical. It upholds the supremacy of the Bible and follows similar structural patterns of the established Churches in the state. The church maintains the same adopted common language and conducts similar services on Sundays and week days also. Its functioning however witnesses integration of elements found in the mainline churches, revivalism and Pentecostalism. It gives priority to involvement and participation in worship and running its daily activities.

The church came out with high theological emphasis on a person's repentance, faith and a new life. Christianity is a body of believers whose lives have been transformed. This new Christian group was initially trying to set an example of active Christian life, holiness, care and Mission. Its members came mostly from other Christian churches, who have done so on their own understanding and willingness. There has never been any case of unfair means involved in the process.

Isua Krista Kohhran is also a caring community. Pastors take serious of members' spiritual and moral life. In its initial years, lay members of the church too realized these dimensions and worked out responsibly for a distinctive indigenous Christian community and identity. Ministerial importance was also given to regular visitation to the members' homes and Bible studies in respective assigned places.

Another significant area of its service is in missionary outreach and evangelism. It carried out its missionary work both at home and outside. While much successes are still awaiting yet the way that the church has stepped in mission and evangelization is indicative of its seriousness on the Biblical principle and commitment to the Great Commission mandate.

II. Indigenous Christian Development in Manipur: Similar to the development in Mizoram, Christianity in Manipur witnessed the rise of different indigenous Christian movements. The distinction of the development in Manipur was that most Christian groups tended to get organized on ethnic identities and emerged only after India's independence. Some prominent indigenous groups that have come up in the state included the Simte Christian Association (1951), the United Pentecostal Church (1953); Jou Christian Association (1970) and the Christian Revival of Manipur (1975).[4]

The name **Simte Christian Association** suggests certain particular ethnic line of identity. It was formed at Mongawn in 1951 but its nomenclature was later changed to the New Testament Baptist Churches Association. Given the universality of the Gospel, the Simte leaders thought it appropriate to hide and remove the ethnic name. This church caters to the spiritual need of the people and provides the needed pastoral care and supervision. Its emphasis is on the Biblical principle in the person of Jesus Christ, the son of God. Although there was significant ethnic awareness at least in its initial period, the leaders could not compromise in respect of the uniqueness of the Gospel, its inclusiveness and mission.

The church underscored the universality of the Christian church. Though there is human satisfaction in confining the Christian Gospel to a single homogenous group but that was not in the vision and work of the triune God. Both the Gospel and the kingdom of God are for all manner of people without discrimination. The rise of the New Testament Baptist Churches Association, therefore, unveiled significant combination of the Biblical foundation and people's cultural setting. While the distinctive identity of people's basic community is maintained, there is tremendous openness, sharing, co-operation and solidarity in the New Testament group.

The new church does not pass over the Biblical mandate on mission. Its message normally centres on salvation through the redemption of Jesus Christ. The focus on personal experience of God's saving grace remains implicit in its Gospel message. Congregational services witnessed free expression, collective singing and prayers. Mission and evangelism that resulted in planting of local congregations and churches had produced successful results. Its spread in the neighboring villages is an indication of people's attraction to the new church.

In less than two years of the emergence of the New Testament Baptist Churches Association, another church that took the name the **United Pentecostal Church** was well introduced in the state through Mr. Sangkhum who unveiled it at Ranakot on the 14th of February, 1953. It was a rural based church and devoted to working among people in surrounding villages. It was also a lay movement in the area.

---

[4] For further stories on the indigenous movements in Manipur, read Jeyaseelan, L. *op.cit.*, pp. 106-121.

In the context of the presence of well structured, organized and democratic Western churches, Mr. Sangkhum who was looking for free spiritual worship and exercises found tangible meaning in a Pentecostal Church .

Though the United Pentecostal Church is so far an outside but national church with some international connection, its starting in the context of a rural Ranakot context got the distinction of being a symbol of local and native expression. Some people responded to this new movement because of its compatibility with tribal free life and movement.

Mr. Sangkhum's leadership though had humble beginning but made significant achievement for his ability to initiate the movement. Rev. Lerthangsung who took over the leadership carried on the Pentecostal faith but in a more dynamic way. His first main job was in shifting the office of the United Pentecostal Church from Ranakot to Salem Veng in Churachandpur. This took place in 1957. With this relocation the rural based movement began to have a rather sophisticated experience town and modern touch. There could have been some Biblical support to transferring the Church's headquarter from a village to a town or a city like St Paul, St Peter and others appeared to have done so in their missionary works but in the context of people's rural based, the relocation was rather unfortunate.

The church encourages members to active participation in worship services. Rules and regulations though how important they are in administration but in areas of spiritual ministry and congregational praises and worship they are at best on the fringe of the church. It is the outpouring of the Holy Spirit that matters and people's baptisms in the spirit that found concrete expression in speaking in tongues, slain in the spirit, singing, mass praying, dancing and other forms of physical movement and expression.

The **Jou Christian Association**, formed in 1954, was another form of Christian group that came up along ethnic line of association. It was an integral part of North East India General Mission (NEIGM).Their problem was most apparently not with the existing established churches and their teachings but with their non-theological distinctive social identity. Their objective became clear in the publication of the Jou Christian Hymn Book in just two years of its formation. There was unanimity in this venture. This development had the effect of strengthening their community and attracting those who have not associated.

However, while the social question unites the Jou Christian community, the theological factor divides. Members of the community had mixed attitude and understanding of the Bible. Those whose theological perception followed the Baptistic or Presbyterian creed accepted the Protestant Old and New Testament only as the holy word of God. There were however others who did not regard the Bible complete without the Apocrypha. These two contending parties who were not willing to come to terms on the production of the Scripture with the Catholic accepted - Apocrypha chose to be apart. The other group that made an exit went ahead with the formation of the **Zomi Christian Church**. Again, this development is a testimony that the Christian Gospel has been fully incarnated in the cultural ethics of hill people's societies.

The Zomi Christian Church struggled hard to set up a well organized structure from its inception itself. There was a proper coordination of administration right from the local level to the highest assembly or general deciding body. Decision on all crucial matters was done collectively through the designated appointing authority.

Leaders of this newly formed church took up question of mission and evangelism seriously from the beginning itself. Their focus on a Biblical and evangelical faith made them active in evangelization and church planting. Therefore, open air meetings, evangelistic outreach and personal evangelism were most common in their missionary ventures. While their main concern was with people of their own group, they also extended open invitations to others and willingly prepared to provide ministerial care and supervisions.

The other areas of their Christian services have been in social development and humanitarian ministries. Following the footsteps of the established churches, the Zomi church engaged in starting an extensive network of school education in areas that they have local congregations. Besides that, the church had even ventured in providing medical services to all manner of people in respective areas.

Another native Christian development was the rise of **Independent Church of Manipur**. Pastor Neichao was the pioneer of this church who got it organized at Hill Town, Lamka in 1970. Later, the name was changed to the Revival Church of God. The formation of this church was partly in response to some kind of nominal Christian life and fixed liturgical procedure. Its major emphasis was on a changed life of repentance and experience of God's outpouring power in the Spirit. Most significant Pentecostal elements appeared to have filtered into the church and its practices. Its call was for a full Gospel that found expression in the baptism of the Holy Spirit and a new life.

Most members from the Vaiphei, Kuki (Thadou) and Gangte communities associated with this Revival Church of God. Though these members maintain their ethnic difference; they however shared much of their spiritual commonality. People experienced a new meaning of religious life through the priority of free style of worship in congregational gatherings. The church adopted the democratic Presbyterian system of administration and always insisted on punctuality, transparency and equality.

Prayer is the backbone of the Church's life and works. While each place is a place of prayer but for the sake of people collectively in their respective villages or hamlets, the church gave clear instruction that there should be a prayer centre in a designated location so that villagers could dedicate in prayers before going out of the village or coming in. People should put up a blessing stone (malsawn suang), a standing flag with a red crossed sign to be followed with appropriate and relevant word from the Bible. Such village prayer shrine is open to all people irrespective of their denominational backgrounds.

In almost a similar line of aspiration, Rev. Seikholet started another independent charismatic church, the **Christian Revival Church** at Chienkonpang or K. Phaicham, Lamka in 1975. It was however formed to gather together members of Thadou Kuki family. His understanding of the indigenous Church was such that it could play a solidified role of the fragile and fluid community and to keep its separate identity. Along with that socio-ethnic vision, the new church sought spiritual renewal with deep evangelical conviction and promoted Charismatic type of worship.

III. Indigenous Nagaland Christian Revival Church:[5] Unlike the developments in Mizoram and Manipur where Christianity found itself fully expressed in different groups, in some states like Meghalaya and Mizoram, indigenous expressions have emerged well at the beginning of the 20th century. The rise of indigenous Christian movement in Nagaland was rather slow and it was only until 1962 that one saw the formation of Nagaland Christian Revival Church. My assumption for this slow phenomenon was that the American Baptist missionaries had appropriately introduced a well knit ecclesiastical structure in each homogenous Naga tribal groups but in due course grouped them together under a single comprehensive ecclesiastical body.

It was on 9th January, 1962 that the Nagaland Christian Revival Church came into existence. It came out in response or reaction to the nominal form of Christian life and the fixed structural pattern of western Christianity. Through an American revival Preacher, Mr. C. E. Hunter was most apparently the pioneer in introducing some kind of revival preaching in public evangelistic meetings in 1940's the real impact came from the role of Mr. Rikum whose revival meetings and crusades conducted at Longkum in 1952 swept the Naga Christian world. Encouraging instructions that had come officially from the supreme body, the Council of Baptist Churches of North East India that local churches within the Kohima Baptist field should hold renewal programme had further bolstered the wave of revival movement.

The revival movement came at the time when most people in Nagaland have changed their primal faith to Christianity. The change though had contributed to increasing membership quantitatively but the condition that tended to show signs of spiritual decline in the church then something new, something good and beautiful need to be introduced and that was a rival Church. This phenomenon did not appear to have happened out of imitation or as a result of outside

---

[5] Read Angami, Neihulie **A Brief Account of Nagaland Revivals and the Formation of Nagaland Christian Revival Church** (1987); Longkumer, M. Lanunuken "A Study of the Formation of the Nagaland Christian Revival Church with Special Reference to Ao Area" (Unpublished B. D. Thesis, Jorhat : ETC, 1997); Sale, K "A Critical Study on the Revival Movement in the Angami Baptist Churches" (Unpublished B. D. Thesis, Jorhat: ETC, 1982).

imposition. There was no official benefit from it. Revival movement in Nagaland was indigenous and it came out of people's search for a new meaningful and spiritual dynamism. There was also no borrowing of ideas but a commitment, an awakening and a serious investment for a true and practical Christian spirituality.

The Nagaland Christian Revival Church laid its emphasis on the guidance of the Holy Spirit. They understood that faith in Jesus Christ should bring about transformation from old sinful ways to the new way of righteousness, truth and holiness. Members should be able to live a free and liberated life that enabled a person to live a successful Christian life. The spirit of revivalism pertains not just to a new religious life but ushers renewal in worldview, moral behavior, social attitude and relationship and life style alike. The new movement intends to take a person to a higher order.

The Scriptures of both the Old and the New Testaments stand upper most in the faith and rituals of the revival church. The Bible is the Word of God and is supreme in faith, practices, life and mission. The Church accepts its infallibility, divine inspired, sanctified and anointed holy Testaments. The leaders acknowledged their emphasis on the Holy Spirit as Biblical. In the midst of non-existence of any written sources in hill tribal societies, the missionaries' efforts that led to making the Word of God available in respective native languages in Nagaland were an unexpected breakthrough. The translated Bible became a treasury of theological, historical and spiritual resources. In this way, the Bible became indigenously rooted in people themselves and is the basis of the Nagaland Christian Revival Church.

The Church provided spiritual direction in a personal experience of God's sacrificed acts. Though a church as a spiritual community is a collective group but it is one's own inner change that matters most. Christianity is a religion of hearts and souls and the revival church is set up to proclaim the truth of God in Jesus Christ in the life of an individual person. In this experienced spiritual community, a person does no longer indulge in drinking liquor, smoking, chewing areca nuts or consumption of any intoxicant drinks. He/she shuns violence, hypocrisy and does not involve in corruption or bribery. The community believes in upright living, righteousness and active life. There is no place for idleness, laziness or procrastination in it. Members espouse Biblical spirit of compassion, mercy and love and always pay serious concern for others' salvation.

The indigenous character of the church is in area of leadership. It was Naga Christians both ordained and lay people who have started the revival church. These people were Christians of good character, spiritually matured and Bible based. Their integrity was also in respect of birth, growth and livelihood. Almost all of them have lived, settled, worked and served God in Jesus Christ in Nagaland itself. They were persons who have passed through the process of repentance, confession of sins and a renewed faith. Their faith in Jesus Christ is well translated in their love for the Nagas, for Nagaland and for human beings. Their teachings and visions for producing spirit filled Christians went out side by side with their fight against corrupted life in public places, immorality, drunkenness and against social discrimination. Revival church leaders who condemned all forms of evil practices in the state have also a message of hope for forgiveness and reconciliation through repentance and restitution.

The building of the Church's life remains evident in the setting up of various institutional programmes and ministries that included the Sunday school, women department, youth fellowship, children services and theological education. Except the establishment of Bible Colleges and Institute that are located at Mokokchung and Kohima, the other programmes are introduced in most local churches. They are spiritual life building measures that enabled members have a wide range of understanding of the Bible and that they would grow in their Christian life and commitment to serve for others. These activities are also illustrations of the Church's dynamic vision and challenge not just for the present but for the future in particular.

The Nagaland Christian Revival Church takes active role in mission and evangelism outside Nagaland also. This dimension too has come from the Naga Christians themselves and not an imitation. It was also not a competitive mission but an obedience to Christ's Great Commission. The mission fields of the Church are now spread mostly to Assam, Sikkim, Arunachal Pradesh, Nepal and Myanmar.

IV. Churches of Indigenous Origins in Meghalaya: The twentieth century witnessed the growing rise of several instituted churches of indigenous origins. Some of these included the Church of God, the Church of Christ, the Church of Jesus Christ, the Christ National Church, the Church of God – Ecclesia and many others.[6] Most of these churches have come up immediately after the outbreak of the revival movement in 1905-06. Though a detailed description of each one of these churches is important but I am afraid it may go beyond the scope of this presentation. I will try to devote here in this section on the development of the Church of God and other indigenous churches in the state will be taken up in the next volume in the series.

The Church of God in Meghalaya was originally an indigenous church. It was Revs. Wolley Mohon Roy, J. J. M. Nichols – Roy, Jobin Roy Chyne and others who formed it in 1902 at Mylliem in Khasi hills. They were local native converts and have started the church with the objective to feed the needed spiritual food of the people in the state. However, after a few years of its formation, the church began to have spiritual connection with the Anderson Church of God in the United States of America.

While the pioneers of the church in Meghalaya were confined to the indigenous development, it was Rev. John A. D. Khan of the Church of God in

[6] For information in regard to the rise and growth of the indigenous churches in Meghalaya, see Snaitang, O. L. Snaitang, **Tylli La Ia Saphret Te: Ka History jong ki Balang Khristan ha Meghalaya Naduh 1813 Haduh Mynta** (2006).

Kolkata who had made intimate postal contact with the Anderson Church of God in the US that led to cooperation and integration. Following his meeting with Rev. J. J. M. Nichols-Roy in Kolkata in 1902, Rev. Khan visited the Anderson Church in the early part of 1903. His visit was significant. On his return to India, five faith missionaries of the Anderson Church came along with him and they reached Kolkata in 1904. The missionaries and Rev. Khan traveled up to Cherrapunji and Shillong. One of the missionaries, Miss. Nora Evelyn Nichols who had committed herself to work for the Lord among the people in India, did not go back to the US. The other four missionaries went back home soon after spending meaningful time here in India. Miss. Nichols stayed in Khasi hills and involved her ministry with the Church of God and among the isolated Khasi-Jaintia people. Later she married to James Joy Mohon Nichols-Roy in 1907.

The Church of God is one of the growing churches in Northeast India. From an insignificant beginning it has now spread to different villages in East Khasi, South and West Khasi, Jaintia hills and Ri Bhoi districts. It has also begun its missionary operation in Garo hills. Its head office is located at Qualapatty, Chapel Road, Shillong. Its total membership is now reaching close to 1, 50,000.

Reaching the unreached is the top most missiological priority of the church. Its spread is not only in East Meghalaya but in several districts in Assam. It has also secured some foothold in Manipur, North Bengal and Sikkim. During its centennial jubilee celebration in 2002, the church has on its record a total of 563 local churches. The church is also a part of the larger Church of God movement in India that has at least significant presence in South India and Orissa.

Like the other foreign missions in the region, the Church of God laid stress on the important role of a literature ministry. Even when its financial resources were almost negligible, the pioneers of the church ventured into the publication of its official magazine entitled **Ka Jingshai Ka Gospel** in June 1905 and it continues to serve so even to the present. Though the magazine is not the first journal in Khasi language it is however the only journal that has an uninterrupted publication until today. Other publications included teachings of the church and a hymn book.

The administrative structure of the church is democratic and functions on a three tier system, viz., the Church of God Business Association, the Pastors' Fellowship and the Ministerial Business Council. Whereas the latter is a comprehensive representative body of the entire Church in the region and regarded as the highest deciding authority, the Business Association is a committee of selected members and it looks mainly after the financial aspects and management of the property of the Church. The duties of the Pastors' Fellowship are on matters related to the spiritual affairs, like recognition of evangelists, ordination of pastors in addition to the general oversight of the ministry and sacraments.

The Church takes active part in mission and evangelism. Its mission fields are in Karbi Anglong, Kokrajhar area, Nepal, Sikkim, Arunachal Pradesh,

Manipur and districts in the Barak valley of Assam. Though its involvement in this dimension is of recent venture, it is however the first Protestant body from Khasi-Jaintia hills at least, to have embarked on a cross-cultural mission. The other activities included running of an extensive network of school education, Sunday school, working among women, youth and children, printing press and publication of books and journals and social upliftment.

The contribution of the church in the ecumenical movement is also well appreciated. Its pioneer, Rev. J. J. M. Nichols-Roy took a leading role in inter-church relation that subsequently led to the creation of the Assam Christian Council (known today as North East India Christian Council) in 1937. He was also instrumental in the process that resulted in the establishment of Union Christian College, Khwan in 1952. While the Church continues to cooperate with the Council, it also associates itself with the other ecumenical bodies, like the Bible Society of India, the Evangelical Fellowship of India and the Union Biblical Seminary, Pune. It is also a constituent unit of the Asia-Pacific Church of God Conference.

Chapter 7

Christianity, Nation Building and National Integration in Norheast India

I. Areas of Christian Contribution to Nation Building and National Integration

1. Adoption of a Local Dialect for the Community:[1] Language is always an important cultural component that binds the community together in unity. It engages in exchanging of ideas, conveys messages and brings action. It also builds the community, creates opportunities and helps bringing a sense of solidarity. The strength of any community also depends on the role of an intelligible spoken language. People's progress, dynamism and social development have connection to the activity of a proper understandable means of communication.

While the contribution of a common language to solidifying the community was such that a country could establish strong fortress, move, plan and achieve success, the absence of a single understandable communicating language in a community is disastrous and ethnically disintegrative. That was the situation in Northeast India. Languages and dialects in the region have become so productive that people could not understand each other. The only component that bound them together was geographical territory.

Linguistic problems in the region could be seen broadly at least at two levels, regional and ethnic. As already mentioned in the preceding sections, the region witnessed the presence of numerous languages and dialects. There was no common link language at the regional level. Sanskrit, a national and pan South Asian language, which should have served in unifying these innumerable linguistic multiplications, have unfortunately not found a place among the people in the distant past. Its affiliate, the Assamese language, spoken by majority of the

[1] Protestant missionaries in the region were pioneers in adopting a single dialect in areas that they were working and made it compulsory for the respective homogenous tribe. For information about the linguistic situation in Northeast India, see Bareh, H. **The Language and Literature of Meghalaya** (1977); Miri, M. ed**. Linguistic Situation in North-East India** (1982/2003).

people in the region like the Assamese, Boro and other people in the Brahmaputra valley remain unintelligible among most of the hill people. Variation in languages has strengthened only one group of people but weakened people's national unity. People identified themselves by the language they spoke.

Another linguistic problem was well evident at the ethnic level. As already mentioned and described earlier, there were several tribal groups especially in the hill areas of the region, like Khasis, Garos, Mizos, Nagas, Wanchos and others. These are tribal communities whose identities are connected with particular ethnic nomenclatures and settled in specified territorial areas. While a sense of homogeneity was deeply felt among each of these communities but almost all of them did not have a common spoken or understandable language. Dialects, most of which were unintelligible, have grown productive in each community that although they shared much in common, they could not successfully communicate with each other. The rise of these dialects bolstered ethnic division in different people's cultural segments. Each political segment maintained its strict territorial boundary and the stronger one like the Khatsawphra (today Nongkhlaw) state in Meghalaya attempted to engage in territorial expansion in the form of invading the weaker neighbouring states and ruled them. In other words, ethnic fragmented identities resulted in intra-tribal warfare and conflict. There was no political unifying power to bring these autonomous and independent states together. The disintegrative power had over a period of time become so strong and pervasive that the fabric of oneness was jeopardized and shattered into disarray.

Some tribal groups like the Khasis, Garos, Angamis, Karbis, Manipuris and others who inhabited on the border areas of Brahmaputra Valley, Barak Valley and Bangladesh could speak either Bengali or Assamese bazaar language in their business dealings. There were no proper teaching institutions of these tribal people in Bengali. They learnt by themselves. Some tribal leaders, like U Dewan Bakrai, who saw the importance of Bengali language for economic reasons had attempted to start tutorial classes for Khasi traders in the learning of Bengali popular language.[2] Though the attempt deserved appreciation but two reasons that had come by in the process, did not come out successfully. First, Khasis who were deeply involved in business did not have time to attend these Bengali tutorial classes. Their life was also a life between hard work and meagre living from hand to mouth. At the same time, their business though lucrative remained mostly confined to markets within the Khasi border area and Khasis were content with whatever little knowledge they had learnt the spoken Bengali language.

Second, some Bengalis though would like to see that the Khasis should communicate in their language, their desire was only at the level of their economic benefit. That is, if the Khasis could communicate without fluency, then their business remained limited to the border haats and would not facilitate exploring

---

[2] Kynpham Singh, "Khasi Hills and Jaintia Hills Upto 1874" in **Souvenir: Shillong Centenary, 1874-1974** (1976), p. 7.

beyond the weekly bazaars in border areas. In other words, discouragement of learning the language fluently would mean economic exploitation. The news that Ram Singh of Korkata who could speak Bengali more fluently than many uneducated Bengalis in Sylhet and could carry out business deep inside the main line of Bengal cities and towns and up to Kolkata had raised alarm on most business masters. That was the reason why learning of Bengali language had come from the Khasis not from the Bengalis themselves. Had they come forward to help, most Khasi-Jaintia people would have learnt this language.

Another indigenous effort in promoting the learning of the Bengali language was initiated by some Khasi leaders of villages around the Lba village of Shella Confederacy. They took the initiative to start a school at Lba, Shella.[3] It was subsequently upgraded to the high school level. Many prominent leaders like the (L) Rev. J. J. M. Nichols-Roy and others were students of this school. The great earthquake of 1897 had however destroyed the school and people's interest alike. Though Sanskrit was the main language so that students could read the ancient Vedic literatures, but the medium of instruction was through Shella and Bengali languages.

The arrival of Serampore Mission missionaries had bolstered promotion of Bengali language but its sudden closure in 1838 put a stop to the modest initiative. The British authority too was in favour of making the Bengali language as a common language among the tribal people specially the Khasi-Jaintia people at least.[4] In spite of its popularity among the Khasis and initiative from them, there was lukewarm support and help from the Bengalis.

In this respect, tribal people became an open field for someone to help that is within each ethnic community. They were looking for a change and in the midst of unsuccessful attempts at learning the Bengali language, came the Protestant Western missionaries like Edward Clark in Nagaland, Watkin R. Roberts of the NEIGM in Manipur, Lorrain and Savidge in Mizoram, Miles Bronson in Garo hills, Thomas Jones in Khasi-Jaintia hills and others. These missionaries were not against the Bengali language. They did not prohibit tribal people from learning it. The fact that they did not adopt it for the tribes was that it was not tribal people's mother tongue and at the same time they knew nothing about it. Though like William Carey, Joshua Marshmann, William Ward and others, they could have done so but insofar as the tribal people's languages were entirely different they had to learn the local language of the people.

The missionaries who had come for evangelization had invested themselves even at the cost of personal devotion and sacrifices. Their first job after choosing the mission field was to settle down at a well accepted convenient and designated

[3] Nichols-Roy, J. J. M. "Memorandum Supporting the Demand for Separate Hill State" (c.1955).

[4] Cf. **Proceedings of the Lieutenant Governor of Bengal, Education Department, October 1863, Pro. Nos. 17-19.**

village and built a permanent mission centre. The base was for them the most important missiological strategy and the power house for missionary broadening.

The mission centre and residence became a nucleus for missiological articulation, designing, vision and implementation. This was an inside missionary policy and strategy of the mission and its connection with the sending mission agency. The area of translating the articulated mission agenda was with the people. Local people at the mission centre were the immediate and closest contacts and interaction in their daily dealings with the missionaries. What stood out prominently in this contact was a dialogue, a communication, listening and talking. In short, it was a spoken language that matter them most.

The missionaries began their activities by learning the local language spoken at the mission centre. The choice of Sohra dialect for the Khasi-Jaintia people, A'we for the Garos, Lushai for the Mizos and Mongsen for the Aos was not determined by their superiority or colonial dictation but precisely simply their being the local spoken dialects at the mission centres and residences of the missionaries. It is illogical to have a mission centre say at Cherrapunji but learnt a Pnar dialect or Bengali language. Any missionary who does so would subsequently experience confusion and failure.

After learning the local dialect, the next job that the missionaries did was to make it a universal standard language for the tribe that shared common origin. Most missionaries were expert linguists. They could pick up the local language in just few months. They also could determine whether the other sub-ethnic dialectical groups belong to the same linguistic family or not. For instance, the Jaintia people of Meghalaya should have been recognized differently from the Khasis but Rev. Thomas Jones included them within the larger Khasi linguistic family.[5] This decision was crucial and decisive and led to solidifying the fragmented Khasi-Jaintia tribe.

The adopted standard language was implemented and made compulsory in publication of text books, educational institutions, Church services, Sunday Schools, committee meetings, recording of minutes and proceedings and addresses in public gatherings or in issuing of official documents. In this manner, people were drawn to learning the same language and communicating with people from different dialectical groups without difficulty. People regarded this

---

[5] The British policy for the administration of the Khasi-Jaintia hills was threefold, viz., 'consolidate, divide and rule'. After consolidating the fragmented Khasi-Jaintia, the British divided the region into princely states and British areas or non-state. The British officer resident at Cherrapunji, Capt. Lewin, who most apparently wanted to promote this policy through the Welsh Mission, took Rev. Thomas Jones I to Jaintia hills so that similar policy could be applied in the missionary outreach among the Pnars in Jaintia hills. In this connection Rev. Thomas Jones was not convinced and advanced his missiological policy of confirming the Pnars as integral part of the inclusive Khasi linguistic family. For his mission to Jaintia hills under colonial guidance, see Jones, G. Angell, *op. cit.*, 11.

new development not as an imposition by force but a natural integrative growth and endowed them with a sense of ownership and belonging.

The introduction of an adopted universalized language went out side by side with the teaching of English language. Though most of the missionaries did not seem to have taught Hindi in educational institutions, that is, in the early years, but the introduction of English had enabled the people to function within the new imposed British administration. Learning the English language had contributed to sharing the same national consciousness and exposing to the outside world.

2. Promotion and Development of Indigenous Literatures: With an exception of the Assamese, Meitei of Manipur, Monpas, Wanchos of Arunachal Pradesh and Bengalis of Barak valley and Sylhet, others like the hill people, Boros, Rabhas, Hajongs and others of the plain areas were people without written scripts. There are no sufficient words to explain the problems that these people had faced without the written alphabet. Their stories, songs and family histories were passed on from generations to generations through words of mouth. These unwritten remembered accounts, in most cases, in due course tended to become corrupted, misinterpreted or misrepresented.

As days passed by, the importance of a written culture began to gain preeminence at various levels. The drawbacks were far beyond recovery. Tribal remembered myths about the possession of written alphabets but accidentally lost became means for ideological defense in response to the challenging dominance of neighbouring living written cultures but in the long run just placed the people in the most disadvantageous position.

History is proof that most hill people like the Khasis of Meghalaya had tried to acquire written alphabets either in Persian or Bengali or both in order to put on record important documents.[6] In this venture, there had never been any tutorial initiative from the neighbouring communities. Some Khasi intellectuals from Shella and other bordering areas with Bangladesh had learnt writing the Bengali alphabet through their self-study. U Ram Singh of Korkata and his family were well versed in Bengali language and literature.

The affinity and interest that the Shella Khasis had shown to Bengali language and literature were such that they had adopted even in study and learning at the Lba High School. Though some teachers at the School were Bengalis but the initiative to use Bengali as medium of Bengali literature had come from the indigenous leaders.

The Serampore Mission through Rev. K. C. Pal and others though had adopted the Shella dialect yet had introduced the Bengali alphabet in their evangelization. The first ever translated New Testament in Khasi was done through use of the Bengali alphabet. U Jeebon Roy and his friends from the Seng Khasi were serious in promoting Bengali language, learning of Bengali alphabet

---

[6] Cf. Bareh, H. **A Short History of Khasi Literature** (1979).

and reading of Bengali literature[7] but lack of support from most Khasis and even from Bengali intellectuals snarled all their efforts to a complete halt.[8]

In such slow and less effective efforts, came Christian missionaries of different Protestant mission societies both from England and the US. These missionaries have come with a specific Christian mission objective. Language and literature were regarded as significant means for evangelization. One should realize that Christianity was a religion of language and literature. Language brought people to a collective oneness and enabled the missionaries and Christian workers to share the message of faith to the people. Provision of literature was aimed at disseminating Christian belief and practices through the production of translated Bibles, Christian catechism and other evangelistic literatures. Though these objectives were religious, they however had the effect of shaping tribal people's destiny.

The missionaries who had decided to adopt a particular dialect for the entire homogenous group would then go for the introduction of alphabet. In this case, they have opted for Latin alphabet. It was the Serampore missionaries who introduced Bengali alphabet for their literary mission works among the Khasis but the closing down of their missionary operations in 1838 put off their fruitful efforts. The decision in favour of using Latin letters was done because of their simple and unsophisticated nature, fitting with the phonetic pronunciation of tribal words and less but complete in numbers. Besides that, Latin alphabet was the alphabet of the missionaries and they had no idea of Bengali alphabet or alphabets of Sanskritic origin. Insofar as tribal people did neither speak nor write the Bengali language and so the missionaries, then the learning process of the unfamiliar literature would take time and mental concentration and so that would prove unsuitable for the missionaries as their objectives of achieving speedy progress and immediate results should come by even through whatever resources available in hand. They were never against using neighbours' alphabet or language.

Though Roman alphabet was the alphabet of the British masters, these officers were against the policy of the missionaries of introducing the Roman script to the tribes. Their policy was both administrative and economic. Learning of Bengali alphabet and language would render convenient administration because most administrative staff in the region were Bengali babus from Sylhet or Kolkata. Keeping in mind of economic profit in border bazaars, both from the side of the tribal and Bengali traders, the British masters saw tribal economic prosperity through their knowledge of Bengali language and script.

Though the missionaries understood their strategic mission operation in the promotion of tribal language and literature but the way that this dimension had

[7] See "Ki Khasi ki dei ba'n pule Bangla" **U Khasi Mynta** (Lber 1, 1899), p. 1.

[8] Seng Khasi leaders became strong supporters of the introduced Roman alphabet. Cf. U Kynpham Singh, ed., **Ka Jingsdang Ka Jingspel bad Jingthoh ia ka Ktien Khasi da ki Dak Roman** (1969).

been successful was because of a well design, systematic and integrative approach and implementation. We have seen that the first thing that the missionaries had done was through the introduction of written alphabet. The Seng Khasi movement though had worked against Christian evangelistic venture, had however come out strongly in support of the missionaries' literary programme. It was they who corrected the flaws in missionaries spelling of Khasi words and they have also brought out relevant letters to make the introduced table of alphabet in full form.

The missionary residence became the first nursery institution in teaching the alphabet to the local people. This process went out simultaneously with the translation of the Bible, Christian teachings and preparation of primers. Application of these primary publications was made compulsory in schools, Sunday schools and church services. Later, books on grammar, dictionaries and others were published. These publications though were mostly Biblical and religious were significant literary writings and formed the basic foundation for the Khasi prose literature.

Learning these stories and prose literature had not just provided information of other people and their histories but helped creating interests in writing similar accounts of the local people and communities. Most missionaries like John Roberts, Lorrain & Savidge, Edward Clark, Harding and others have included local accounts, stories and poems in their publications. These missionaries and local converts have also written about India, Mahatma Gandhi and other topics of national interests.

Production of modern poetry was also a boon to the development of tribal literatures. Missionaries did not aim at promoting this aspect but just produced hymn books for singing in Church services. There were collections of translated Western hymns and tunes. Hugh Roberts brought out the Khasi hymn book as early as 1870. Though these hymns were published with a religious motive they nevertheless had the effect of creating a modern form of poetry in tribal literary history. It was from this background that had shaped tribal modern poets, like U Morkha Joseph Chyne,[9] U Soso Tham[10] and others.

Christianity was also a pioneer in journalism. **U Nongkit Khubor** (1889) was the first journal in Khasi language. It was a monthly magazine. In this area too, these pioneer Christian journals were responsible for the subsequent rise of popular magazines, ecclesiastical and academic journals. These publications became significant data and sources of information about tribal people's history and culture. Daily newspapers have also come up in a regular way and have contributed to raising the literary standard of the hill people. The impact of monthly magazines and daily newspaper was on the people at large. While books were either read only in schools, church's Sunday schools or by a negligible

[9] Chyne's poetry entiled **Ka Ryngkap** is regarded as the first Khasi modern poetry.

[10] Tham's **Ki Sngi Barim U Hynniewtrep** is historic and monumental. Prof. R. R. Thomas called it 'the Classic.'

individual readership, people from all walks of life including those in rural areas read daily newspapers. These papers enabled people to know not just about their own people and state but about the country as a whole and then have a sense of belonging, brotherliness and shared common vision. This was made manifest at the time when the country is in danger or threat from neighbouring nations.

Another contribution was in creating a sense of national awareness and consciousness. People did no longer see outside states like Delhi, Kerala or Rajasthan as different or distant but greatly part of one nation. They are now conscious of their dependence and inter-dependence. They also understand their inter-relation, co-operation and participation in collective national growth and development. The role that monthly journals and daily newspapers have played in this respect is encouraging. Christianity was also a factor for further development of literary thinking and criticism.

The literary world would not remain complete without the presence of typing machines and printing presses. Christian missionaries who have come for evangelistic works and involved in publication of gospel materials have brought typewriters and established printers in their mission stations. The investment that they have put in was enormous but they have done so for the sake of evangelization. Their objective was to spread the Christian message but the impact that it had brought was more social than evangelistic, that is, production of literatures through print media helped much in creating literary interests and building literate communities.

Christian investment in tribal literary world was stretched far to the establishment of publishing houses, book services and research centres. Most Christian churches, especially the Presbyterian, the Catholic and the Baptist churches put up their major concentration in publishing of books, booklets and monthly magazines. While most of these publishing houses cater to the needs of their respective members, they also cover most of social and national aspects. Closely related to the presence of publishing houses, there are also good numbers of book shops, which serve as literary circulation centres.

From these book services, books are distributed to different areas across the state for public sale or use in schools or church. This aspect had the consequence of providing continuity and strengthening to the promotion and development of tribal literatures. In the absence of strong people readership as among the Khasis and Garos, the setting up of Christian book shops mostly resulted in economic loss but since they are part of literary building measures, the challenge has never cowed down churches' literary mission.

Research centres and association of tribal authors have also participated in building communities and the nation alike. Most churches, both Protestant and Catholic, have carried out research projects and centre side by side their theological institutions. More important of such are the Sacred Heart Theological College, Shillong, Don Bosco Indigenous Centre, Shillong, Tribal Research Centre and

Women Studies at Eastern Theological College, Jorhat, Calvin Study Centre at Aizawl Theological College, Aizawl and many others. These centres have brought out books both in English and respective tribal languages.

3. Education as Effective Means for National Integrative Building: Most people in India and across the world have some form of educational system. Hill people of Northeast India though did not have a written culture, have significant education that have connection with morality, agriculture, farming, kinship code, economy and religion. These were wide ranging aspects but the place of study was at home. Those who engaged in providing direction and teaching were a mother, a father, uncles and elder brothers. The role of a mother was mainly in instructing children in good manners, kinship relations, in performing domestic duties, marketing for home needs and protection. She was also the harbinger of generating a spirit of love, compassion and responsibility.

The area of authority was reserved with uncles. It was they who exercised power in advice, guiding, moulding of nephews and nieces. Their instructions determined the future of their nephews and nieces alike while religious and ethical instructions took place in homes, agriculture and farming were mostly practiced in the field. Teaching on agriculture did not end up in tilling the ground, fallowing the field and sowing the seeds but mainly on seasonal change based on the rotation of the moon, raining and sunshine as well.

The processes of selling the agricultural products were also carried out practically. A child began to know the time of reaping, collecting and markets where to dispose off the agricultural goods. These practical developments helped build the children to know the course of dealing and to stand on their own feet. The kind of instructions both theoretical and practical, led to self-reliance and self-support. Such natural tutorial courses were part of people's daily life and informal growth.

The first formal education was started among the hill people in Shella in the early 19th century. It was at Lba High School. Started by village elders of Shella, the school used both Bengali and Shella as the medium of instruction, Bengali script and devoted to reading ancient Indian Vedic writings and texts. Some Bengali teachers were also appointed. Noted intellectuals like Rev. J. J. M. Nichols-Roy and others had studied in the school. This was the first formal educational school that was started long before the introduction of missionary schools. However, following the massive destruction of the great earthquake in 1897, the prestigious High school could no longer survive but remained nostalgically in human memory in Shella. The significance of the school was its exposure to the national course of school curriculum and introduced text books of Sanskritic origins. The other danger was that with the presence of teachers from Bangladesh (former East Pakistasn) then students could have been drawn to the larger Bangla national influence that eventually resulted in severing links with Indian national unity and integrity!

The Serampore Mission through Rev. Alexander Lish who established a mission station at Cherrapunji in 1832 had set up elementary schools at Mawsmai, Mawmluh and Sohra. Though the effort came to an abrupt ending in 1838, yet Lish's students, U Jungkha and U Duwan Rai were outstanding students who were instrumental in helping Rev. Thomas Jones of the Welsh Mission in 1841. In one sense, these students provided some form of continuity of the Serampore educational heritage but deeply immersed in the Welsh Mission educational system.

Western Christian Missions that had come and worked permanently included the American Baptist Mission (1836); the Welsh Calvinistic Methodist Foreign Mission (1841); the Church of England (1871); the Catholic Mission (1890) and others in the early 20th century. These missions understood the importance of education as one of the effective means for evangelization of the people in the region. Education would enable the converts to read and study the Bible, Christian Scriptures and to sing Christian hymns. There was at least no secular motive in their educational mission but the gradual impact of this educational venture was such that most hill tribal illiterate societies were becoming literate and able to work, function and adjust to the newly developed British set up.

These missionaries had to involve with isolated ethnic groups who most of them knew nothing about learning in schools. The entire hill tribal world was full with illiteracy, poverty, superstition, backwardness and ill-health because of mal-nutrition. In order to achieve their evangelistic objectives, the missionaries went ahead with the elementary education, first at the mission centre and then in different rural areas. These missionaries, who were serious in this missiological ministry, have invested their ideas, financial resources and manpower. As a result, in less than half a century of their mission they were successful in setting up a wide network of primary schools education in each geographical area of their involvement.

The evangelistic objective of educational mission remained evident in the missionaries' mode of operation. Starting of elementary schools in different rural areas went out side by side with starting of local congregations. A school building was used as a Sunday school and church services. Demands for qualified teachers became high and in order to secure trained teachers, missionaries introduced normal training of primary level teachers. They normally picked up candidates from their respective areas. After completion, they would go back to their villages and looked after church's school respectively. School teachers also took care of the church and served as evangelists. In this way, a church and education worked side by side in a simultaneous manner that one hardly found any space of demarcation.

Closely related to this mutual involvement was the raising of standard of Church's membership. The missionaries made reading and writing mandatory for native converts.[11] In other words, no new converts be entertained in the church unless he or she knew the art of reading books and writing as well. Protestant missionaries were never in a hurry to admit new converts. Their mission policies were study in schools first and then join the church later. This policy remained conspicuously implied in the juxtaposition of a church and school education.

Primary schools though were meant for evangelization and had served so but they became effective means for bringing homogenous communities, to a sense of unity through use of the adopted standard language, the same alphabet and text books. The application of the adopted universal language of a given tribe had not destroyed the daily spoken dialects.

Educational institutions were also centres that provided information. Traditionally, hill people had little idea about places, people or histories of others. Through school education and interaction with people from different cultures and geographical backgrounds, hill people could realize and know about others. No doubt Christian missionaries have taught mostly Biblical texts to the students so that they could grow in the faith but the topical contents that included ancient civilization of the Mediterranean world, history of the Israelites, prophecy, Graeco-Roman world, Jesus Christ and His disciples and Christian ideology have open up the exclusive and isolated tribal worldview. Information about the world's geography and solar system in addition to a simple arithmetic have helped widened people's minds. Christian teachings though were spiritual and evangelistic and sometimes strictly exclusive, have however endowed people with a sense of inclusiveness and universality. A Christian church is a community of believers irrespective of caste, class, colour, creed, gender or physical structure. These new information created a new thinking and made the people developed a new understanding of humanity that was beyond their clan, village or dialectical frontiers.

It was not just about seas, oceans, snowy mountains and communication by ships and cars that natives come to know but they also came to know about the existence of animals other than those that they have seen in the hill regions in addition to knowledge of trees, fruits and vegetables. Learning of geography had enabled them not just to observe a map of the world but to practice drawing them.

The other contribution of school education was in the area of reasoning. Hill people were highly reasoned people who always sought for the cause of sickness or misfortune in families. Their migration from one place to another was also based on specific reasons. Their decision to settle on a particular place too

[11] The early Welsh missionaries imposed a condition that converts could be admitted into a Christian community only once they have learnt the art of reading and writing. However, following the arrival of other mission agencies like the Catholic Mission in 1890 who did not lay such academic condition in church membership, the Welsh Mission had eventually withdrawn it by the revival period 1905-1907.

went out after making some sound collective scrutiny. Traditional councils - clan, village, commune and state Durbars, were avenues for debates, discussions and resolutions. These debates though sometimes generated temper and emotion but they were always addresses to the voice of reason. Debates were also witnessed in engagements, marriages and during periods of bereavement.

However, what had weakened their traditional reasoning was the intrusion of superstitious belief system. Most hill people were superstitious and their cultures highly receptive to all forms of superstitious propaganda. Education, especially scientific explanations, has contributed much to tribal people's reasoning. It was through the role of modern science that had reversed people's perception that the earth was the centre of the universe.

Again, in the traditional tribal set up, it was physical strength or muscle power that secured attention and recognition. While this was no doubt essential and necessary to oversee law and order in a village in the ancient past, it was no longer counted under the new administrative dispensation. It was knowledge of arts, science or commerce, passed the examination and qualification that worked and it was no longer determined on the size of a physical body or possessing of heavy muscle or on sentimental claim of belonging to a ruling dynastic clan.

Some scholars of the recent past who have begun critical examination of mission schools have come up highly negative on their emphasis only on the primary level of education and charged them for giving an insufficient or half baked education. It was argued that the standard of tribal education was low. While such contention carried significant elements of truth but anyone who had taken up new ventures would understand the crux of the problem. There were other criticisms that have been leveled against missionary education. The criticism that was made was that the missionaries did not come for education but for evangelization. That the missionaries were selfish could at least be drawn from the area of higher education. That is, certain missionaries did not want to see that tribal people were more educated or intelligent. That was apparently the main reason that had prompted U Jeebon Roy, a self-made educationist, to start a Zilla High School in 1890s in Shillong. Some Bengali intellectuals have supported U Jeebon Roy's venture and involved in teaching. The British government took over the school and renamed it the Shillong Government High School and placed its administration under the supervision of the Welsh mission.

There was some fact on the assertion against the Welsh Mission that its missionaries concentrated only on the low level of education. One should however look at the Christian educational mission in broad perspectives. While the Welsh Mission could not raise their primary level of standard, it was Catholic missionaries who had taken up in right earnest, with the introduction of high schools and colleges in hill areas. In this connection, certain issues that have far significant holistic and national implications may well be stated as under:-

1). Education for all Manner of People and Alienated Sections in Society: The education that had been introduced was for all inhabitants without discrimination. Schools and Colleges in cities and towns took care of all children and admitted students from different cultural backgrounds or identities. There was no discrimination in teaching or evaluating. The only difference was that Christian institutions, i.e., in the early years used to impart Christian knowledge and introduced Biblical teachings in their regular courses. Some classes witnessed dedicated prayers before teaching.

The other credible aspect of educational mission was its effort to provide education to victims of injustice like girls, rural folks and the haves-not. Though there were tangible oversights on the part of Christian institutions for running against the secular fabric of humanity but one should see the other dimension, that is, although there was religious motive in educational mission but the fact that they have given priority and pre-eminence to women, rural population and the poor should in no way be placed on unmindful rejection. Though women enjoyed greater privileges in hill tribal societies, they were never given leading role in administration, legislation, election, judiciary or religion. Though some societies gave women rights to custodianship but the de facto deciding authority rested with uncles and elder brothers.

Rural areas and people suffered untold hardships and difficulties. Even in today's fast changing situations, hardly people preferred to go and work in villages. During the early missionary period, hill people's villages were doomed in darkness and backwardness. Their life was rife with drunkenness, gambling, expensive series of rituals, ill-health and superstition. The efforts that Christian missionaries have done in starting works in villages were efforts that must not be looking down. A church and a school in rural area could turn the atmosphere differently. As a reiteration, although the objective in these rural investments was missiological but the subsequent impact remained evident in reconstruction, development and modernization. These contributions in rural ministry did not raise the standard of living of these rural populations but helped build a strong and developing nation.

The other victim of injustice was to a large poor population. Christian institutions have also engaged in providing education to students who hailed from poor families or have become orphans. Some of them have benefited from these modest trials and training. The Catholic missionaries in particular, have invested immensely in this area and have take care of such children in orphanages for school education and technical training in tailoring, motoring, electrical, shoe making, book building and other trades.

2). Educational Institutions Provided Ways for National Integration: It was not just students who belonged to different socio-religious and cultural persuasions that were entertained and admitted in educational institutions but more importantly was the policy of employment. Most of these institutions, especially Catholic institutions witnessed inclusive attitude in employing teachers. A school or a college especially in cities and towns and even in villages would see ecumenical, inter-religious, cross linguistic and national involvement and co-operation. It was with this background that had shaped the destiny of the hill people and their participation in attending the alienated and marginalized sections in societies, rural development and reconstruction and in taking care of the poor, needy and orphans.

Their employment policy was non-discriminatory. Both men and women were given at least equal opportunities, although in the end, it was qualification, efficiency and intelligence that matter most. These cross cultural interactions; dialogue and work contributed to openness, exchange of ideas, mutual respect and bolstered inter-personal relationships, a sense of human consciousness and national unity.

As previously stated, the implicit objectives of Christian educational institutions, their role in shaping the destiny of hill tribal people and other people's groups could well be seen not just in fostering national awareness and co-operation but in nation building. It was these western missionaries who have come, lived and worked in almost inaccessible hill areas and even in less healthy plain environment. Christian role in catering to all kind of people, women, rural folks and orphans was a concrete example of national building processes and contributed to taking the nation forward.

3). Participation in Nation Building: The role of educational institutions in nation building was also significant and enormous. Building a nation does not confine to holding a high position in government offices, having a highest degree or material possessions but more significantly in attending to the lower and neglected people, the poor, slum dwellers, orphans, the blind, lame, deaf, the paralytic, the aged, tribal, dalits, other backward communities and economically sections in societies.

Nation building begins with people's attitude to humankind. Christianity started off its mission with a loving spirit of the tribes and citizens of this great nation. Their great concern was for spiritual, physical and material well being of people. The special compassion that they had demonstrated was mainly for the general welfare, health and liberation of the downtrodden people in the society.

The next step was a translation of the attitude through personal identification, participation and involvement by providing institutional means, like education. Their commitment and investment became evident in their services and sacrifices. These activities that subsequently brought about tremendous social transformation were in the process contributing to nation building for progress, development, self-reliance and forward movement.

Educational institutions made preparation of the hill people for successful functioning in a developing world of science, technology and modern administrative set up. Christian churches have also moved ahead with the fast changing development. Though state and central governments have taken up their major part in setting up educational institutions in the region, churches too, especially the Presbyterian Church in Meghalaya, the Catholic and other Christian groups have participated in building the nation through the setting up of Christian Universities like Martin Luther Christian University, William Carey Christian University both located in Meghalaya and Don Bosco University in Assam. These academic institutions aim at giving the best academic education to the people in this region and from across the nation. They prepare tribal people and others to be well equipped with changes in the next generation. These are, therefore, means for nation building with vision and action. In this respect, Christianity takes an active participatory role in building up a strong nation through education, research and training.

Looking back at the early period of mission educational service, several schools were attached with government educational supervision in Kolkata. Later, they were connected with the School Board of Assam and Gauhati University. Renowned political leaders and educationists like U Rai Bahadur D. Ropmay, Prof. R. R. Thomas and many others had chosen to take up their higher education in colleges in Kolkata. These attitudes too have connection with the educational system in West Bengal and higher studies in Kolkata have the effect of being part with the larger Hindustan and not with Pakistan. Though one may not like to give any worth recognition of such developments, but they were highly crucial and decisive that has far reaching national integrative consequences.

4. Role of Medical Mission in Nation Building:[12] I have mentioned above that Northeast India is home to numerous and different people. History is proof that there is a great divide and unfamiliarity among these people both before and now but in at least one area that they share in common is suffering. The role that Christian Missions had done through their medical mission among the suffering people in Northeast India had far national integrative and building implications.

1). Traditional People's Perception of Suffering and Medical Care: The word 'suffering' is used in this paper in a broad sense meaning physical sickness, disease and mental problem. The kind of suffering that normally passed by the region had been malaria, diarrhoea, smallpox, chicken pox, enteric fever, cough, ricket, mental agony and even cholera. Here in this section, an attempt will be made to find out people's perception of suffering and human being and also to investigate their traditional treatment.

First, **Perception of Human Suffering** : Most tribal people believed that diseases of various forms, like cholera pox, smallpox, black fever, measles, chicken pox and of that kind were caused not by germs but by some kind of divine

[12] Major part of this section was published in the ICSSR-NERC academic journal under the title "Christian Medical Mission in North-East India" in **Man and Society: A Journal of North-East Studies**, Vol. VII, Winter 2010, pp. 71–85. Reproduced with permission from the ICSSR – NERC, Shillong.

manifestation, displeasure to natural spirits or attack by demonic powers.[13] The Khasi-Jaintia people looked at "measles" as "god's illness". That is an illness of divine manifestation. A person who suffers from this disease is normally taken with great care. There was a belief that family quarrelling, cooking of meat or frying of fish during a person's sickness would further aggravate his suffering and might even turn out to be fatalistic.

Cholera, black fever or smallpox was mostly perceived as supernatural intervention that manifested in some impersonated forms.[14] The role of clan or village priests during the outbreak of such diseases was significant. Treatment was normally done through sacrifices, prayers and incantations. A priest, whose role was highly influential, would always proceed with time bargaining that also involved some material contribution or financial implication.

Hill people were peace loving and sociable. They were always ready to help other in time of crisis and shared one another's burden. However, when it came to accidental injuries or unnatural death then they were the ones who believed in placing oneself on the safe side. In other words, people were not willing to extend service by themselves because of fear of formidable subsequent attack by the same malevolent demon called **Ka Tyrut**. This kind of demon that prevailed on accidental death or major wounds with profuse blood coagulating from a victim would haunt those who came to rescue the unfortunate particular person. So, instead of doing a Samaritan service to such persons and become a target of similar attack in the future, people in their traditional belief thought it right not to help so far their safety.

A belief that unnatural death would transmit to those who extend helping hands is also applicable in cause of suicide or death due to undelivered of a baby. Members of the victim families, however, could not do the task of disowning. They had to come forward and carry out the duty of helping the unfortunate member. Again, in such a situation, traditional priest play a very important role. There is a religious treatment called **ka mait tyrut** (literal meaning cutting off a demon of unnatural death) to be performed for those who have helped the victim and for the victim's members of the family.[15]

Beside that, most Khasi-Jaintia people believed in the prevalence of family deities like **U Thlen** (a human fed family spirit or clan python), **Ka Taro** or **Ka Shwar** (family goddess) or **Ka Bih** (a goddess of poison).[16] Though these familial or clanish deities are different in keeping, forms and systems of feeding but they share three things in common, viz; these deities eat only human beings, they do

---

[13] See Morris, John Hughes **Christ's Ambassadors in Khasia** (1939), p. 12.

[14] Cf. **Census of India, 1891, Assam**, Vol. I, Report (1892), p. 260.

[15] Information about Khasi-Jaintia People's religion, see U Hipshon Roy, ed., **Khasi Heritage** (1979); U Sib Charan Roy, **Ka Niam Ki Khasi** (1919/1966); Rodborne, R.T. **Ka Niam jong U Khasi Pnar** (1984).

[16] See Marwein, P. T. **Meghalaya Handbook** (1987), pp. 55-57.

not eat non-Khasi-Pnars being and they promise generating wealth to the keepers. Those who keep or rear of these demons do not spare taking the life of a person even if he or she belongs to the same family or clan. These developments are indications of the absence of humanly concern or relational consciousness. They look up to gaining wealth even at the expense of taking someone's precious life.

Second, **Understanding of Human Life**: An explanation in the above section refers mostly to the situation among the Khasi-Jaintia people in their pre-modern history. This section will touch upon the understanding of human being among most of the hill people in the region save the Khasi-Jaintia people.

One common feature that was prevalent in several tribal groups in Arunachal Pradesh, Nagaland, Manipur, Assam, Mizoram and Garo hills was a head cutting culture.[17] These societies not only entertained this inhuman practice but encouraged by giving headhunters some recognized honours. Women too preferred to marry some one who had achieved such horrific honours. Human heads were regarded as trophies and a family gained more respect if it could display more human heads to the visitors. This practice was a clear explanation of people's insensitivity to the value of human being. While traditional culture looked at it with greater amount of cultural pride, it is by spiritual of collective human consciousness an inhuman, criminal and devilish act.

Third, **Perception and Medical Care in Ancient Northeast India**: We have so far mentioned about people's understanding of human suffering in ancient hill tribal societies. Given the difference that hill people have with the plains, it is appropriate to examine plains people's attitude to patients and their medical attention and healthcare with reference to the Assamese and Bengalis.[18]

Both Assamese and Bengali people were brothers who shared much religious persuasion in common. They belonged at least to the same Sanskritic root and belief system. Vedas being the sacred writings of the Hindu religions are in all probability their holy scriptures. It is in one of the four Vedas that one may find a description on various diseases, their prognosis and diagnosis, symptoms and prescription for treatment. What had been written, explained and directed for medical healing service should well be declared as the great volume in healthcare. Treatment in the form of ayurveda, yoga, meditation and dietary restriction and discipline that was administered from very ancient times was among the very best. The healing process was simple, natural, herbal and vegetative that hardly did it destroy human physical system. There was no side effect through this ayurvedic treatment.

However, this holy ancient ayurvedic treatment, which should have served humanity became confined to the sole custodian of Brahmins. They alone had the right to practice this Vedic medicinal system. The problem was no longer with the holy book but with human mind that happened to hold absolute right

[17] See Bowers, A. C. **Under Headhunter's Eyes** (1929).

[18] For some information see Dutta, P. N. **Glimpses into the History of Assam** (1986).

over its dispensation. Hence, while the medical science and process of treatment as prescribed in the holy scripture were by for the most effective means but the social stigma based on caste system had in most cases left the low caste and the poor outside the benefit of this healing technique.

Like most of the hill people, rural folk in the plain areas of Assam and Bengal looked at the outbreak of serious ailments as signs of divine displeasure and punishments. In other words, there was a religious perception of human suffering and treatment for healing too had significant religious implication. In such a situation, the role of priests was so important. They wielded influence not only in times of sickness but in death as well. Treatment of sick persons mostly did not reach the outcastes, the poor and villagers.

Again those who suffered much were women. As ayurvedic practitioners were mainly men so it was almost impossible to extend healing touch to women, especially in traditional Hindu conservative society and also with the possibility of women seclusion or **pyrdah** system.

2). Healthcare After the Arrival of the British Administration: There were at least four reasons why the British came to Northeast India. First, their coming was mainly at the request of the Assamese in order to force out the Burmese whose rule in the Assam plains had been terrible and exploitative. The Assamese and other people in the region suffered far beyond human expression because of the Burmese reign of terror. Those who have come and helped the British intervention against the Burmese alien were the Raja of Manipur and the Chief of Jaintia hills in addition to the Assamese force. The Burmese were defeated and following the signing of the treaty of Yandabo in 1826, the British came in to the region.[19]

Secondly, the British entered upon the hill areas because of frequent tribal raids on the plain areas and so the intention was to seal off those raiding expeditions. The third reason was to construct road communication between Sylhet and Assam via Khasi hills on the one hand and Jaintia area on the other hand.

Lastly, the British officials found out that hill areas were very healthy and so they built sanitariums or health resorts and administrative headquarters, like at Nongkhlaw first and Cherrapunji later as early as 1824.

The British brought officers, soldiers, engineers and labourers to the hill stations.[20] Now, it was they who introduced the western system of medicine. While these medical treatments through allopathic pills and suspensions were good for recovery from sicknesses but they were not meant for Northeast Indian masses. British medical mission and healthcare were brought in order to look after the welfare and wellbeing of British officers, soldiers, engineers and native labour

---

[19] See Chaube, S. **Hill Politics in North East India** (1973), pp. 4f.

[20] Cf. Downs, F. S. "Christianity as a Tribal Response to Change in North East India." **Missiology** VII. 4 (October 1980), 408-409.

corps in government establishments and services. They did not introduce or initiate better sanitation or health care to villagers so that outbreaks of contagious diseases could well be controlled and prevented. Apart from providing medical facilities to their own, basic health care or rural clinic was a non-existence and the complexity and vulnerability of disastrous ailments appeared to have remained outside the British government medical mission in the region.

3). Christianity and Medical Mission: First, **Christian Medical Mission**: Christian Missionaries have come to Northeast India for mission and evangelism but the impact in certain areas of their involvement like education, language and literature and medical services had been far beyond ecclesiastical boundaries. Christian missions' attitude towards the people in the region was not only for their spiritual and mental well being but also for their physical health. There were no partialities, caste system, social discrimination or alienation in the medical mission. Services were given to all those who came for medical help.

The first Christian medical mission in Northeast India was introduced at Mawphlang, Khasi hills by the Welsh Presbyterian Mission in 1879.[21] Rev. Dr. Griffith, MBCM, a Welsh medical missionary, who arrived Khasi hills in 1878 and posted to Mawphlang, started a dispensary for the benefit of the people not only at Mawphlang but from the surrounding areas. This unsung pioneer medical missionary who get the credit of being the first to begin the medical mission should have been given the honour as the "father of medical mission" in Khasi-Jaintia hills if not of the Northeast.

Then Dr. A. D. Hughes initiated medical service in Jaintia hills in 1887.[22] Following the arrival of Dr. H. G. Roberts, CIE, MD in 1913, the medical mission began to achieve significant recognition. After accepting service with the Government and served under its supervision for some years, Dr. Roberts started a mission hospital at Jaiaw, Shillong in 1922.[23] Its contribution to serving humanity was well acknowledged by government authorities and its reputation was also recognized in the entire sub-continent. The Jaintia medical clinic was in due course upgraded to a renowned, hospital in Jowai. Like in Khasi-Jaintia hills, the Welsh missionaries had also started medical services in Durtlang, Mizoram. Though the early years of health services were rife with problems and uncertainties, yet the Welsh mission in Mizoram could establish a permanent hospital as early as 1928.[24]

The American Baptist Mission too had not passed over the important contribution of the medical mission in their mission operation in Northeast India. Dr. Rivenburg was apparently the first American missionary in the region who

[21] Natarajan, N. **The Missionary among the Khasis** (1977), p. 68.

[22] Cf Ropmay, D. "Ka Medical Mission" in **Ka Centenary History ka Balang Presbyterian ha Ri Khasi Jaintia naduh, 1841–1940** (1975), pp. 177-178.

[23] *Ibid.*, pp. 178-79.

[24] Lloyd, J. Meirion **History of the Church in Mizoram** (1991), p. 272f.

had started the medical mission in Kohima in 1894. Later it was followed by Dr. Bailey at Impur in 1910.[25] These initiatives led to the establishment of hospitals in Impur and Aizuto in Nagaland. Its mission work in Garo hills also witnessed the starting of medical service under Dr. & Mrs. Greenfield Crozier in Tura in 1900.

The Catholic church though had begun the missionary work in Khasi hills in 1890, could not devote much because of British internment of German missionaries during the first world war. It was only after the arrival of the Salesians of Don Bosco in 1922 that the mission of the church in the region could enter upon a period of stability. Orphanages and medical services were started as early as 1912 at Raliang, Jaintia hills and Shillong. The Church was serious in areas of medical services and health care. As of the recent report, the Catholic Church could provide a wide medical network in the region - 10 hospitals, 128 dispensaries, 5 homes for the aged and 2 lepers' colonies.[26]

Some churches like the Church of North India, Assembly Church of Jesus Christ and para - church organizations have come up with some efforts in rural clinics. Though their attempts were minimal but the fact that they have been able to start with spoke volume than without doing anything.

Second, **Service to Humanity**: Christian medical service is service to all those who are in real needs. The most common diseases in the region were malaria, diarrhoea, dysentery and high fever. Deadly diseases like tuberculosis, leprosy and polio were also prevalent. Those who were victims of such sicknesses had to pass through physical, mental and social turmoil. Medical care and treatment of these patients have brought about not just physical relief and wholeness but social liberation. Though Christian doctors have rendered satisfactorily ministries in their respective areas but the role of Dr. R. A. Hughes of the Welsh Mission hospital in Shillong in the mid twentieth century was worth mentioning.[27] His fatherly, friendly and pastoral heart in medical profession had sent messages of confidence and trust to patients and their attendants. He was a gifted medical practitioner and a renowned surgeon. Many precious patients have been healed through Dr. Hughes's healing touch.

The role of Christian nurses was also of high importance.[28] In a situation that looked down on services to patients in clinics and hospitals, the arrival of female missionary nurses to the region and their but in the night had turned people's mind upside down. Many Christian nurses have served in government hospitals also.[29]

---

[25] Philip, P. T. **The Growth of Baptist Churches in Nagaland** (1983), p. 189.

[26] Varghese, P. D. "The Church's Involvement in the Healing Ministry in North East India" in S. Karotemprel, ed., **The Catholic Church in North East India, 1890–1990** (1993), p. 356.

[27] See Rees, D. Ben Vehicles of Grace & Hope (2002), pp. 66-67.

[28] Cf. Mylliemngap, H. **Ki Missionary na Ri Wales sha Ri Khasi Jaintia** (1990), pp. 182-83.

[29] Varghese, P. D. *Op. cit.*, pp. 355-58.

Christian missionaries took care of the orphans and the aged. Orphanages were instituted in several places.[30] These orphanages gave training in tailoring, gardening and handicrafts. Though this kind of work was a burden but Christian Missions have never decided to close down. They continued to run these orphanages with perseverance in the best interest of the unfortunate children.

Care of the aged was also another significant attempt in medical healthcare. Though most churches of Protestant traditions have not given serious attention to this ministry, the Catholic missionaries have already started mercy homes for people in their old age.[31] Their compassionate ministry among the neglected aged in the region have filled up the gap and contributed to the fullness of Christian service.

Besides that, Catholic missionaries have devoted to medical and Pastoral care of the lepers.[32] Many of those who were attacked by leprosy especially in plain areas had to pass through social rejection, ostracization and expulsion. Missionaries who were endowed with a compassionate heart were not happy to see these rejected human beings. The blessed missionary of charity of St. Mother Teresa the great had done a tremendous service to the lepers not only in Ri-Bhoi district of Meghalaya but in other areas in the region.

Last but not the least, there was a collective consciousness on sanitation and hygiene. Medical mission contributed to making the people aware of the importance of cleanliness. People in towns and villages began to value the task of keeping one's surroundings and areas clean. So, drainage system was constructed, dustbins in proper place and maintaining safe drinking water. Septic tanks were also introduced. Though these instructions and advice did not become a reality all at once but have made people to realize these new hygienic structure and also able to translate them over a period of time to action.

4). Impact of Medical Mission on Traditional People's Worldview: The impact of medical mission and healthcare on the people both in hills areas and plains was tremendous and may be mentioned and described as follows:

First, **Reducing in Mortality Rate**: The presence of clinics, dispensaries in rural areas and hospitals in towns had been of great help to the patients. Diseases like diarrhoea, dysentery, malaria, polio, tuberculosis, smallpox and cholera that had normally taken away numerous, precious lives had through the introduction of a wide network medical services, vaccination and allopathic medicines brought down mortality rate. In at least one instance in what is known as Ri-Bhoi district of Meghalaya, Dr. R. A. Hughes reported that infant mortality rate and even adult early death fell dramatically after the introduction of Western allopathic

[30] For instance **A. W. Thomas Orphanage**, Jaiaw, Shillong, **Bethany Society Orphanage**, Nongsder, Ri-Bhoi District and **NEIMA Orphanage**, Sahsniang, Jaintia hills District & others.

[31] For example The **Catholic Mercy Home** at Demthring, Shillong.

[32] **The Missionary of Charity** is doing selfless service among the lepers in Nongpoh, Ri Bhoi District.

medicines.[33] Many mother's lives have also been saved through hospitals or else most serious cases in the communities simply ended in death.

Second, **Impact on Traditional Worldview:** Christianity believes in Jesus Christ not only as a divine saviour but a great healer from physical and mental illness. He even heals those who are possessed with demons. While Christian missionaries still adhere to this belief, they nevertheless do not set aside the importance of rationality and science in Christianity and in their mission. Medical mission had the consequence of removing people's perception of sickness as signs of divine displeasure and punishment and superstitious beliefs and treatments alike. A belief that deities or natural spirits caused sickness to human being was in due course beginning to lose trust and the people began to look at the outbreak of sickness with a certain reasoning and scientific attitude. Another development was that they lost faith in the efficiency of sacrifices, medicine men and priests.

The other impact was on the rise of caste system in traditional priestly system of ayurvedic dispensing. Though one should not ignore the effectiveness of ayurvedic medicines but the stigma that made it reachable only on the high caste group is something that should be ignored. Christian medical missionaries, who by rendering services to people without any religious discrimination and by adopting the policy that service should be above self or social background, had at least turned around the traditional social mindset. Medical science went out side by side with a sympathetic and compassionate heart. Human persons are equal in God's sight and more important than caste system or religious rites.

Third, **Social Relationship:** We have seen that some tribal groups strongly believed in head cutting and the Khasi-Pnars did not help those who were victims of unnatural death, but the impact that Christianity had brought on these groups was that they began to look at them as fellow divine created beings who needed God's redemption. There was a sense of love on those who were once regarded covetous targets for human heads. Love went beyond one's clan or ethnic identities but on humankind in whom God's image was created. The Missionaries who have come all over to these isolated and inaccessible areas for the good news of salvation, have demonstrated to the people of the love that they have in God for salvation and healing. It was this new religious conviction that resulted in ending the practice of headhunting and fratricide.

Fourth, **A New Concept of Service:** The situation that used to render service only to the nearest ones was by the impact of Christian teachings and medical service, greatly affected. Medical institutions hardly denied attending, caring and extending medical treatment to wounded persons, patients and neurotic persons. There was a tremendous change in people's attitude towards fellow human beings. As it was a feeling among the Khasi-Jaintia people that service to the unnatural fatalities would invite haunting of a demonic **ka Tyrut**,

[33] Hughes, R. A. "Ka Mission Jingpynkhiah" in Ki Khubor jong ki Jingiaseng Jubilee 1841-1966 (1967).

medical service had completely ignored this traditional belief. It was no longer entertained in a Christian community.

Nursing service was a tangible symbolic expression of love. It involved caring, supervising, counseling and dispensing. Above all it demands self-sacrifice and commitment. Nursing service does no longer take note of human excreta, vomiting or foul smelling. It is a service that runs far beyond traditional worldview. It also involves cleaning patients' wound, puss or phlegm. It was a medical mission that had imparted such attitude and a new caring and healing service.

Christian missionaries have introduced this new system of health services with some farsighted vision. This attitude was evident in their training of native nurses and encouragement of indigenous people to undergo medical education and to provide continuous service to the people.

Fifth, **A Sense of Mission:** We have seen that in most tribal societies people who belonged to other communities were normally looked with a destructive objectives of chopping one's head for trophies. The impact of the new faith was such that they began to look at others no longer as targets for headhunting but as targeted areas for evangelizing. They went with God's spirit of love and preached the good news of repentance, faith in Jesus Christ and salvation. It was because of this impact that the Assamese evangelist Godhula went to preach the Gospel among the Aos in Mokokchung district. Then Ao evangelists moved to the neighbouring Sangtam tribe and other tribes for the faith in Jesus Christ.

Similar change took place among the Khasi-Jaintia people. U Larsingh Khongwir from Khasi area had gone to Jaintia hills for evangelization and those from Shella area sacrificed themselves for mission and evangelism among the rural folk in Maharam area and West Khasi hills. Mawïang Christians have moved further to south western corner among the Lyngngams for the Gospel of salvation.

This change in missiological paradigm did not take place only among different tribal groups. Indigenized Christian Churches have gone out to Assam, mainland India, Nepal, Andaman & Nicobar Island, Bangladesh, Sri Lanka and other countries for mission work. People's understanding and concern for human beings were no longer limited to a clan or a homogenous community but in the area of cultural universality, commonality and collectivity.

A Summary: In the context of static, superstitious and socio-exclusive perception of suffering and traditional herbal techniques of treatment, the introduction of modern medical service through clinics, dispensaries and hospitals has been a source of help to people irrespective of class, caste or linguistic backgrounds. The new medical mission has brought about tremendous change in physical and mental well being. More importantly, the change was also in people's traditional worldview and habitation in the community. However, in spite of the services that have been made for the people in the region for the past hundred and fifty years, the pertinent needs of the villagers, the marginalized and the downtrodden even in the urban areas stand before the present Christian

Churches in the region as challenges for a more effective mission in medical and health services.

5. Change in Traditional Belief in Devils and Evil Designs:[34] Though this section will examine the role of people's belief systems in devils and evil designs in the region, the study will be done in reference to the tribal groups in Meghalaya. As a repetition, the Khasi-Jaintia people and that of the Garo counterpart are unique communities in India and the world alike for their continuing adherence to the matrilineal system and isolation. Though they are different culturally but when it comes to the question of evil they tend to share much in similarity. Like the other neighbouring groups in the region, they are a kind of people full of devils and evil designs. The words "devil" and "evil" are used here in a more flexible manner. While devil is a word used for active demonic powers that mostly expressed in tangible forms, evil is more a concept or planned theoretical design. This exploration will be done on the assumption that devils and evil designs are indigenous friendly but disastrous and fatalistic to the tribal people and the society alike.

1). Devil, Evil Plans and the Rise of Ecological Destruction: Before narrating the origin of evil in the Khasi-Jaintia society, it will not be out of place to give a brief highlight on the traditional belief on the origin of the people.[35] The Khasi-Jaintia people are people of traditional stories, legends and folklore.[36] One of such was in connection with their origins. Tradition says that some groups of the Hynñiewtrep were once an integral part of the *Khathynriew* community in

---

[34] Originally published under a caption entitled "An Exploration of Dimensional Perspectives of Devils and Evil Designs among the Khasi-Jaintia People of Meghalaya" in **Construction of Evil in North East India: Myth, Narrative and Discourse**, Copyright 2012 © Prasenjit Biswas & C. Joshua Thomas. All rights reserved. Reproduced with the permission of the Copyright holders and the publishers, Sage Publications Pvt. Ltd., New Delhi. pp. 157-171.

[35] Cf. Lyngdoh, U Maurice G. **Ki Parom Barim u Khun Khasi Khara** (2007), pp.1-8. Some groups of the Hynniewtrep community could have come from the plains of Bangladesh, India or from elsewhere.

[36] For more information about folklore, myths and legends of the Khasi-Jaintia people, see Singh, U Rabon **Ka Jingiathuh Khana Puriskam** (1908/1987); Mrs. John Roberts, ed., **Jaintia Folklore and Legends and the History of the Khasi Religion : From the Papers of the Rev. John Roberts, D. D.** (Carnavon : c. 1915); Mrs. Rafy, **Khasi Folk Tales** (1920/1985); Bacchiarello, **J. Ki Dienjat jong ki Longshuwa** (1930/1990); Gosta, G. Ka **Riti jong ka Ri Laiphew Syiem** Vols. I & II (1937), Elias, H. **Ki Khanatang U Barim** (1937), Gatphoh, U Primrose **Ki Khanatang bad U Sier Lapalang** (1937);. Mawrie, H. O. **The Essence of the Khasi Religion** (1981); Nongbri, Dhonsing L. **Ka Kot Rimbah** (2001); Nongkynrih, Kynpham Sing **Around the Hearth: Khasi Legends** (2007); Paslein, P. P. **Jaintia Antiquity: Sabat Pnar** (2006); Mawrie, Barnes L. **Ka Iew Luri Lura** (2007); Lyngdoh, Dlosingh **Ki Pukri Pashat 'Waidong** (1991), Sawian, Bijoya **Khasi Myths, Legends & Folk Tales** (2006) and others. Some of such traditional stories were reflected in Khasi Poetry, Cf. Joseph, Morkha **Ka Ryngkap ne ki Poetry Khasi** (1967); Khongdup, U. Dewi Singh **Na Lum Khasi** (1968); Jyrwa, U. B. Chedrack **Na Nengpei ki Sur Myllung** (1971) & c.

heaven.[37] It was God who created them and they lived together with him. It was understood that the creation of the Hynñiewtrep was unique because of the gift of a free will.[38]

There were two habitations in the sky, one was called *hajrong* (above) and the other was *hatbian* (below).[39] The latter is identified as the earth. Though the *Khathynriewtrep* era was believed to have been a golden period but in exercise of a free will, the Hynñiewtrep desired to live on the earth below[40] and so sought for autonomy and independence. The God of the heavens conceded to the Hynñiewtrep's plea and provided a golden ladder that connected between the sky above and the earth below.[41] The connecting point of the golden staircase was identified as U Lum Sohpetbneng.[42] God granted independent existence to the Hynñiewtrep by sealing a cosmic covenant. The covenant was that the Hynñiewtrep below must live holy, righteous and obedient to God's laws and God will bless them.[43]

The sealed covenant became symbolic in the planting of the giant tree known as U Diengiei.[44] Following that, the Hynñiewtrep people lived in peace. However, in the midst of divine bliss, prosperity and ambience there came into the picture an enemy from the abysmal underneath[45] and tempted the Hynñiewtrep. He came out with envious and jealousy spirit. Fr. Elias described this being thus, "He was U Iakjakor of nine abysmal pit."[46] This was the beginning of a devil in the form of a stranger with an unbecoming face but his sweet sounding voice was enough to mesmerize U Hynñiewtrep till he became attentive, dumb and speechless.[47] His evil intention was multiple that remained implicated in destroying God-man covenant relationship, sowing the seed of enmity and injecting the idea that a sealed covenant Diengiei tree be cut off. Much to the heaven's surprise, U Hynñiewtrep simply accepted u Iakjakor's advice and carried out the task of felling down the giant covenanted Diengiei tree.[48]

---

[37] Kyndiah, B. "Ka Jaka Kyntang – Ka Bri Lajong Hi" in **Souvenir: Seng Khasi Shispah Snem, 1899-1999**, p. 74.

[38] Snaitang, O. L. "Evolution of the Khasi Language and Literature: A Study in Folkloristic and Historical Perspectives" in B. War ed., **Tribal Literature of North East India** (2009), p. 88.

[39] Cf. Rymbai, R. T. "Evolution of Modern Khasi Society" in U Hipshon Roy, ed., **Khasi Heritage** (1979), p. 56.

[40] Snaitang, O. L. *Op. cit.*, p. 87f.

[41] Cf. Kyndiah, B. *Op. cit.*, p. 74.

[42] Read Kharakor, S. "U Sohpetbneng" in **Souvenir: Seng Khasi**....., p. 80.

[43] Elias, H. **Ki Khanatang U Barim** (1937/1972), p. 3.

[44] *Ibid.*

[45] *Ibid.*, p. 3f.

[46] *Ibid.*, p. 4.

[47] *Ibid.*

[48] *Ibid.*, p. 5f.

The Khasi-Jaintia people did not believe that the devil was God's creation but was one of the members of the divine family but because of his rebellion he was rejected, condemned and sent out to the bottomless earth's underneath. Though he had an ugly face, two wings, dark skin and sparkle moving eyes he was nevertheless sociable with human beings through his soft spoken, reasonable, convincible and wealth promised words.[49] As mentioned above, the Iakjakor's mission was to bring chaos, disorder and a world without peace. The Hynñiewtrep's failure was his acceptance in letter and spirit of U Iakjakor's voice.[50] The community did not realize that the cutting down of the sealed divine symbolic tree was a violation of God's commandment and amounted to commiting a sin. Therefore, the Hynñiewtrep's action resulted in a one-sided breaking down of the divine covenant and the rise of the first committed sin[51] in the Hynñiewtrep's remembered memory.

2). Devils and Evil Design that Perpetuated Culture of Blood: The first devil, U Iakjakor, was a perpetuator for chaos, spiritual darkness and ecological destruction. He was intrumental for severing links between the Hynñiewtrep below and the divine above.[52] The committed act resulted in God's removal of the golden ladder.[53] The humankind, who did no longer see the connection between their existence and nature's essence, appeared to have lost the ecological conscience. There was no more a sense of guilt in felling down of trees. The first devilish episode was related to ecology.

The subsequent development in the rise of *u thlen, ka taro, ka shwar, ka sabuit ka sakai, ka siatban* and *ki nongaiksuid* become evident in the society among the Khasi-Jaintia people and had connection with violence, shedding of blood and homicide. A brief description of each of these satanic forces is not just necessary but important.

First, ***U Thlen and Human Blood:*** The literal meaning for "u thlen" is a python or a big snake.[54] Its expression in disguise is also connected in the symbolic form of a black cat or a living fish out of water.[55] Fr. Elias explained that U Thlen was the same devil as U Iakjakor, who had successfully carried out his evil designs on the innocent, simple and God - fearing Hynñiewtrep people.

A story about U Thlen was well connected with Ka 'Lawsuidnoh at Laitryngew, U Suidnoh, ka Pomdoloi cave, ka Daiñthlen, u Dkhar (a non-tribal) and a piece of u Thlen's flesh.[56] Ka 'Lawsuidnoh was a forest land fully covered with

---

[49] *Ibid.*

[50] *Ibid.*, p. 5.

[51] Mawrie, H.O. **The Essence of the Khasi Religion** (1981), p. 29.

[52] Elias, H. *Op. cit.*, pp. 6f.

[53] Rymbai, R. T. *Op. cit.*, p. 56.

[54] Cf. Elias, H. *Op. cit.*, p. 116.

[55] *Ibid.*, p. 123.

[56] *Ibid.*, p. 120.

thick natural vegetations, trees, grasses and ferns. It was a habitation of a natural deity named U Suidnoh.[57] People, both the Hynñiewtrep and ki Dkhar, dared not entering the designated 'Lawsuidnoh forest for fear of u Suidnoh.[58] Later, people began to worship him by offering sacrifices and prayers.[59] This was perhaps the beginning of worshipping a natural deity in the Khasi-Jaintia tradition.

The excommunicated demon who after wandering the earth below saw Ka 'Lawsuidnoh as the most convenient place to settle down, requested u Suidnoh's approved permission for staying underneath Ka 'Lawsuidnoh's surface.[60] Following his permission, U Iakjakor took possession of the undergrounds, stretched himself through the zig zag penetrable ground and turned into a python, u thlen.[61] While his head was at Ka 'Lawsuidnoh his tail reached up to Ka Pamdoloi[62] a place near Dainthlen at Cherrapunjee. He laid his head near in a deep trench by the side of people's pathway. There he began to eat human beings especially the unfortunate ones.[63]

Both the Hynñiewtrep and u Dkhar were not happy with the presence of u Thlen because his role of sucking passers - by had affected their movement and business.[64] They then began their ritual of offering sacrifices to U Suidnoh and requested him to help destroy u Thlen.[65] The natural god attended to people's prayers and requested and through his help U Thlen's life was eventually put to an end.[66]

Upon his death, all people gathered together at Pamdoloi and pulled out U Thlen's body at a place called later Ka Daiñthlen.[67] U Dkhar ate up the entire allotted portion.[68] The Hynniewtrep who could no longer consume the allotted meat portion began to burn the remaining flesh in a fire.[69] But before the burning process began, a woman who wanted to give u Thlen's meat for her son who was not present at that time, took off a piece of the meat and after reaching home placed in an empty dried fish basket that was hung around the hearth to the wall.[70] After that, the woman's memory of the meat slipped into oblivion.

[57] *Ibid.*, pp. 113-115.

[58] *Ibid.*

[59] *Ibid.*, p. 114.

[60] *Ibid.*, p. 115.

[61] *Ibid.*

[62] *Ibid.*, pp. 115-116.

[63] *Ibid.*, p. 115.

[64] *Ibid.*, pp. 116-117.

[65] *Ibid.*

[66] *Ibid.*

[67] *Ibid.*, p. 119.

[68] *Ibid.*, p. 120.

[69] *Ibid.*

[70] *Ibid.*, p. 120.

One day later, she heard a moving sound in the empty dried fish basket and she was surprised to see that a piece of meat that she kept in there had now turned into a living small make who began to converse with an eloquent dialogue convincing the woman for his life.[71] In the words of Fr. Elias, his prayer to the woman was, "Have mercy on me, keep, take care of and feed me, and I too, will bless you, I will give you wealth and riches, gold and silver, attire and ornaments; I will beautify your dwelling house, bless your activities, business, and you will reap the benefit of peaceful and prosperous life."[72] O! What a wise and reasonable counsel and promise.

Again, Fr. Elias reported thus, "The woman, when she heard about wealth riches, gold and silver, attire and ornaments, was extremely happy beyond human measure, stretched her hand on to the snake, wrapped him up under ka jaiñsem dhara (a precious silk woman dress) and placed him in a box."[73]

That was not the end of the *thlen* culture but the beginning of a clandestine monster in the community. In due course, u Thlen started demanding human blood from the family who kept him.[74] His promise of material gains would not happen unless he gets first what he wanted. He would not accept non-Khasi blood. He would also reject outright blood drained from a person who was already dead or from strangulating by force of a Khasi – Jaintia man or woman. It was only fresh blood drained through a person's nostrils that u Thlen would accept. This demand precipitated violence and perpetuated culture of blood at least in the community.

In order to get Khasi-Jaintia human blood for u Thlen, those who keep him mostly adopted two ways strategies. First, it is by way of ambushing a person in a secretive place away from public eyes and knowledge. This involves physical attack and leads to a victim's death.[75]

The second way is by cutting someone's hair or cloth and places it through a magical process of sacrifice and incantation.[76] Once this process becomes effective, the real person would become sick, then weak until his personality wanes and finally breathing his last.

U Thlen is a devil who utilizes his keepers so that he could eat to his desire the Khasi-Jaintia human beings. His promise for providing such food was for generating wealth, prosperity and happiness. Those who reared such demonic creature, believed in the culture of shedding human blood. It is rather unfortunate that for the sake of gaining material wealth and riches, their conscience allowed them to go to the extent of killing fellow Khasi-Jaintia precious beings.

---

[71] *Ibid.*, p. 121.

[72] *Ibid.* (Translation is mine).

[73] *Ibid.* (Translation is mine).

[74] *Ibid.*, p. 122.

[75] *Ibid.*, pp. 122-123.

[76] Mawrie, H.O. **The Khasi Milieu** (1987), p. 45.

Violence does not confine to the keepers of u Thlen. The Khasi-Jaintia community too who could not tolerate the prevalence of u Thlen culture among them and could not condone families who keep him, become furious and angry at such families. They too respect the *thlen's* keepers mostly with violent means.

Second, **Ka Taro, ka Shwar and other Demonic Forces and the Indigenous People's Suffering and Death**: While U Thlen deity was more popular among the Hynñiewtrep - Khasis, Ka Taro was most commonly evident among the Hynniewtrep-Pnars in the region.[77] The origin of this evil force is mysterious and obscure but could have likely emerged at the same time with the emergence of promised wealth generating monstrous deities. Like U Thlen, Ka Taro too is a family goddess that assures promise of bringing material riches, wealth, prosperity and splendour. Those who keep her as their household worshipping object maintain their own private and secretive ways of worshipping her in the form of offering sacrifices. The common knowledge in the community is that the deity desires some kind of ritual connected with Khasi-Jaintia people. Again, if the Taro keepers failed to offer the needed sacrifices then the deity would turn against them and would bring physical torment, ruin and even death to the members of ka Taro keeper's family.[78] This kind of deity too has far significant effect of fostering inhuman practice and violence in the society.

Ka Taro is inherently related to the material wealth and possessions of the keeper's family. This demonic force plays a role of bringing physical suffering and mental agony to those who borrow money or material articles from her keeper.[79] She would do similar action on those who have misused or squandered the keeper's earned property.[80] Another adverse way of bringing sickness, seizure or mental problem is through love. In this way, the Taro would pay a visit to the close and intimate friends of her keeper's family.[81] Even in close and friendly relationship, the Taro does not know how to bring happiness, trust and confidence. Her only way of social dealing is by bringing physical distress, mental disorder, demonic and pain that gradually lead to death.

Are such sufferings and ailments curable? In his explanation of the means of curing, H.O. Mawrie provides us with the following information:-

For cure of the affliction caused by this deity the victim must repay the debt owed to its keepers, or return the benefit derived from using the keeper's earnings. In the case of the keepers' friends suffering from Ka Taro's visit the affected persons family must visit the house and pick up a quarrel with its keepers, and, as a result of the quarrel the friendship must cease to be.

[77] *Ibid.*, p. 43. Also see Lamare, S. **Ki Tnat Ka Kolshor** (2007), p. 50.

[78] Mawrie, H.O. *Op. cit.*, p. 43.

[79] *Ibid.*

[80] *Ibid.*

[81] *Ibid.*

...if the borrower has cash in hand the entire amount borrowed should be paid back, if no ready cash is available the borrower has to submit himself to Ka Taro in prayer with a promise that the loan taken will be paid and as a token of this promise he must throw out from his house a coin or two after the prayer.[82]

Like Ka Taro, Ka Shwar[83] too is another feminine deity in the Khasi-Jaintia society. Its origin is mostly contemporaneous with Ka Taro and other devils. This is another wealth generating goddess and that is the reason why certain families choose to keep her as their household deity. In order to generate riches, wealth and prosperity, Ka Shwar believes in a merciless spirit on the indigenous human beings and promotes violence. It is also a deity connected with the keeper's material wealth. Ka Shwar always attacks a victim by twisting his or her neck.[84] It is said that when this satanic force twists a victim's neck for two times instantly then the result is mostly seen in death.[85]

Ka Bih[86] is a different household tormenting goddess but belongs to the same family of wealth generating deities or deities of riches. It is a poison deity. Those who keep this family goddess are connected with their trade mostly though selling tea, snacks and other eatables. The impact of ka Bih elements is twofold. First, it causes slow and gradual pain on a person and makes a person sickly and weak. The other impact is deadly, that is its attack on a victim would subsequently result in instant fatality.

Kaba ai ksuid (literal meaning that which is given with the devil) was also another demonic and monstrous force in the community. This institution believed in a demon who demanded indigenous human beings. There was no human sacrifice as such in it but a diviner who subsequently became u nongaiksuid (a giver of devil) always involved in performing sacrificial practices in some unseen places and involving certain magical prayers. Any unfortunate person who became victim of this cyclical magic and witchcraft would become demon possessed. He or she would pass through mental disorder, scream aloud and could even divulge the very person u nongaiksuid, his evil intention and even the ritualistic processes involved. This was another community's self-fatalistic practice.

3). Evils and Demonic Forces that Cause Sickness: Ka Sabuit ka Sakai[87] (a deity that causes stomach ache) has also emerged and developed among the Khasi-Jaintia people. The role of this demonic force is in connection with causing intense stomach or intestinal pain resulting in physical seizure and serious illness. Jealousy, spirit of envy and self-centredness are among the elements mostly involved with this family deity. Such satanic ailments could be cured of through

---

[82] *Ibid.*

[83] Shabong, P. R. **Harud ka Ding Ba Rhem** (2007), pp. 39-41.

[84] H.O. Mawrie, *Op. cit.*, p. 45.

[85] *Ibid.*

[86] *Ibid.*, p. 45.

[87] *Ibid.*, p. 44.

rubbing of lime on a betel leaf with words of chasing out the demon and burn in the fire or through burning of dried reddish chilies and also with words of rebuking the monster.[88]

Like ka Subuit ka Sakai, another kind of demon that engaged in causing pain on a Khasi-Jaintia person is ka Lasam.[89] This kind of evil is kept by certain families and is connected with mere jealousy, envy or inhuman spirit. Based on this attitude, Ka Lasam brings some kind of rash followed by severe itching and literally connected with what is known as urticaria or nettle-rash.

Ka 'Lei Khuri[90] is a family protecting deity that lives on three supporting stones of the hearth. Its duty is to bring stomach pain on those who involved in stealing or quarrelling with its keepers. Thieves will also become victims of chronic intestinal ailment through the hand of this protecting goddess.

Ka Siatban practice, most common in the distant past, was a kind of demonic revenge on those who have done wrong. Its duty was to cause physical torture, pain, fear and terror by sending a portion of fresh cow's flesh to stick to a victim's body. There was no material gain in it but just a matter of tit for tat or revenge on one who had caused unnecessary displeasure on a Siatban's keeper.

While these evils have connection with causing pain and suffering on fellow Khasi-Jaintia persons, there are also family deities that cause suffering on both human beings and domestic animals. Ka Raliang[91] family goddess is an example of such demonic forces in the society. Ka Raliang brings physical misery in whatever occasions like cursing or praising. This household deity is also transferable. There is a belief that if ka Raliang attacks a person for the third time, the victim would soon realize that he has possessed the deity and would carry out her business on others alike.[92]

4). Demonic Evils that Destroyed Human Compassion and Humanitarian Service: There are at least two evil spirits prominent in traditional society which made the Khasi-Jaintia unwilling to render Good Samaritan service, viz., *Ka Tyrut* and *Ka Iap khet.*

First, **Ka Tyrut:**[93] Ka Tyrut meaning demon of unnatural death. An evil spirit connected with this incident is always viewed with caution and seriousness. The belief was that any help or service to the victim would bring similar fate to a helper. If for any reason the incident warrant service, it can be extended after performing cock sacrifices. In most cases, people leave the victim alone or in other words they put themselves on the safe side by not helping at all.

---

[88] *Ibid.*

[89] *Ibid.*, p. 42.

[90] *Ibid.*, pp. 42-43.

[91] *Ibid.*, p. 43.

[92] *Ibid.*

[93] Sylvanus Lamare, *Op. cit.*, p. 51.

Second, **Ka Iap Khet:** The literal meaning of *Ka Iap Khet* is pre-matured death. For instance, a pregnant woman who died during delivery is mostly viewed as an attack of ka Tyrut deity. In such cases, though some members of the community could come for help but young people prefer to stay away from helping the victim's family.

5). Impact of These Demonic Forces on the Khasi-Jaintia Society: What impact do these evil spirits have on the Khasi-Jaintia community? On the basis of the description above, its impact may be seem in seven areas and may be described as follows:

First, **An Evil of Destruction:** One of the consequences that had impacted the people following the coming of the dragon that led to the felling down of a *diengiei* tree was the rise of a destructive spirit on the nature. An ecological conscience and sympathy had gravely been affected. In due course, people began to look at natural vegetations, stones, rivers, sands and others no longer as subjects for people's survival but objects for use.

It was this wanton and inhuman desire that made village, clan or raid councils to curb reckless cutting down of trees by declaring designated forest areas as sacred so that there is preservation of natural vegetations and prevention of people's freedom from destroying plants.[94] The felling down of the tree produced three results. First, the God of the heavens who was displeased at man's doing removed the golden connected ladder thereby severing physical contacts with the Hynniewtrep.[95] Secondly, there was a rift and enmity between humankind and tiger. A tiger that was wounded by man's trap was looking for revenge.[96] Thirdly, the action could well be regarded as the original sin.[97]

Second, **A Sense of Fear:** Another impact was on people's psyche. People begin to live always with a sense of fear of the evil spirits.[98] There developed some kind of a mental slavery. People became slave to the presence of *menshohnoh, nongaiksuid, nongaibih, nongaitaro, nongaishwar, nongaisabuit,* etc. The fear does not take control of people's movements from one place to another but even in their staying at home lest these evil perpetrators might come at night. The fear psychosis controls even in the day time even among the crowds lest whatever they do or speak may bring displeasure to Ka Taro or ka Shwar. A sense of fear touches a person's consciousness even in the area of buying of eatables. The Khasi-Jaintia people were people with fear psychosis.

Third, **Loss of Human Concern:** Evil in the Khasi-Jaintia society had brought about a matter of little concern for fellow human beings. People were identified by a political jurisdiction, dialect or clan. In their contacts once a person

---

[94] Cf. **Ka Meiramew bad u Hynñiewtrep** (1994), pp. 6ff.

[95] Cf. Maurice G. Lyngdoh, *Op. cit.*, pp. 2-7.

[96] H. Elias, *Op. cit.*, p. 7.

[97] *Ibid.*

[98] Fear is common in most tribal religions.

is identified, and then a suspicious spirit is applied. Some would be suspected as *menshohnoh*, others as *ki nongritaro*.

Both *ki menshohnoh* and *ki nongritaro* though are different but on one thing they agree and that is to take the very being and life of fellow Khasi-Jaintia people. The rise of such evils perpetrates violence and culture of blood. However, such spirit of killing does not prevail on the entire Khasi-Jaintia people but on those who keep such demonic beings.[99] As a reiteration, keepers of demons do so just for the sake of becoming prosperous and rich. Hence, evil practices were endowed with far materialistic returns.

The community as a whole does not condone evil institutions and killing of human beings. In this connection, there is a self-conscious perception that violence respects violence. If the village durbar finds evidence that a family belongs to ki menshohnoh or ki nongritaro etc. and carries acts of killing people then most actions of the durbar resulted in the extermination of the family by burning them alive along with their houses and belongings.

There was no human concern and help to an ill-fated person who was injured by accident or passed through unnatural death either in the garden or on the pathway. People fear of the evil ka Tyrut who by dint of displeasure might cause similar fate on those who extend good Samaritan service.[100] In a similar way, most people do not help those whose member faces premature death. Besides that, some families condone evil practices just for the sake of fulfilling their intended wish of bringing revenge on others.

Fourth, **Superstitious Belief System:** The presence of demonic and evil spirits also contributed to the rise of superstitions belief.[101] The struggle of this system is between life and death. People were conscious of early death, suffering and poverty. Some of bad lucks were attributed to the clandestine work and operation of evil spirits. There was no reason in it. Any question as why it is so, the simple answer is always attributed to the elders, parents or uncles. In most cases, superstition came into the belief systems of the Hynniewtrep from outside influences.

Superstitious belief had the tendency of personifying any strange happenings. Cholera, small pox or chicken pox was never believed to have been caused by germs but by impersonated beings sent by angry spirits. Looking at the crossing of a black cat as a black omen was most apparently a non-indigenous origin. However, in the midst of the growing rise of devils and demonic environment, the Hynniewtrep society tended to have become a productive ground for all sorts of superstitious belief systems.

---

[99] Clans who keep the deities maintain strict confidential and secretive and so they are few and far between.

[100] H.O. Mawrie, *Op. cit.*, p. 48.

[101] Nalini Natarajan, **The Missionary Among the Khasis** (1977), p. 27.

Fifth, **Materialistic Gains at the Cost of Human Beings:** The rise and growth of devil and demonic forces in the community was precisely for the sole objective of getting personal materialistic gains.[102] It appears that the Hynniewtrep who had possessed the free will did no longer learn to acknowledge its divine origin or god's gift but took it completely as his own possession. His settlement on earth below away from the divine above made him receptive to all materialistic related demons. Then, he became greedy, egoistic and avarice.

The kind of getting wealth and becoming riches did not go the common way of working in the fields, selling products in markets or through setting up shops and stores but through clandestine operations of killing only Khasi-Jaintia persons. Devils and evil designs bring wealth, riches and prosperity to those who keep them only at the cost of exterminating indigenous human beings.

Sixth, **Hynniewtrep People's Character:** In one sense, the Hynniewtrep people were uniquely created and blessed. However, an examination of his character in the context of his nexus with devils and demonic plans unveils some form of character that becomes evidently clear in approachability and accessibility,[103] easily convinced community[104] and unmindful acceptance of anything for self-benefit and that at the expense of a fellow neighbour's suffering and death.[105] U Iakjakor or U Thlen did not have human face neither was he beautiful or handsome but his appearance was ugly, dark and monstrous but could get access to the uniquely created and blessed people. History is proof that a combination of an individualistic character and materialism always makes the Hynniewtrep people not only accessible and approachable but divisive and rubber stamp type of people.

The first demonic episode that led to the felling down of the covenanted Diengiei tree witnessed a collective decision. Words of admonition that came from the mouth of U Iakjakor were taken up at the people's durbar and the resolution that ended up in the cutting down was passed by the community's council. It appeared to me that there was so much of people's emotion in it rather reason and religiosity than spirituality. A stranger's eloquent poisonous message proved to him a successful achievement.

The second incident that took place between a woman and a small snake was more individualistic. The woman finally agreed to keep the demonic python merely at the promising words of generating material gains in wealth, gold and silver, dresses and ornaments and in getting beautiful residential buildings. These

[102] Sohblei Sngi Lyngdoh "Ki Riti Khyndew u Hynñiewtrep ha ka Them Ri Bhoi" in **Ka Meiramew bad U Hynñiewtrep** (1994), "Ban kamai ia ka longspah bad ban bam ia ka longbriew". p. 13.

[103] H. Elias, *Op. cit.*, p. 5.

[104] *Ibid.*

[105] H.O. Mawrie, *Op. cit.*, pp. 42-48.

gains would come after the keepers provide the monster with blood from the Khasi-Jaintia persons alone including her loved and dear ones.

This experience and other experiences with devils and evil designs are glaring examples of the Hynniewtrep people's character and that they are a kind of people who entertain and receive wealth related demons. More importantly was their character that for the sake of getting material benefits for themselves, they did not have conscience to protect and give shelter these blood sucked monsters even at the cost of merciless killing of their own people or disposing off people's natural resources.

Seventh, **Relationship with U Dkhar:**[106] Ancient happenings like the python incident, the story of losing the written script and other stories always indicated the closer cooperative relationship with u Dkhar, i.e., plain people. In such incidents, u Dkhar proved himself successful. First, when an allotted portion of U Thlen's meat was given to him as a community, he did his duty to clean up the entire part by eating the allotted portion there and then without leaving any sparks of left over. Secondly, while swimming the flooded water, he tied the written script by a turban on his head and retained it till date. His successful achievements had the consequence of the community's progress. In respect of the Hynniewtrep community, the above mentioned stories of devils and evil designs were indications that the threat to their existence that came from within tended to have been more vulnerable and dangerous as from without.

A Summary: This brief study has attempted to bring out the origin of devil and evil designs among the community since the primordial period in antiquity. The first development was in injecting ecological destructive spirit. We have also mentioned that the rise of U Thlen, Ka Taro, Ka Shwar and other related satanic forces had the consequence of fostering violence and perpetuating culture of bloodshed. The other type of devils and evil plans in the emergence of deities of unnatural death resulted in losing a compassionate heart and humanitarian spirit of service in the ancient society. Some devils were interested and responsible for bringing sickness to the neighbours, especially the children. The impact of these forces on the community was evident in the rise of uncared spirit on natural plants, development of psychological phobia, the emergence of violence and shedding of indigenous human blood, superstitious belief system, individualistic interests and material gains at the cost of destroying precious human lives, inhuman character of certain families or clans in the society and u Dkhar's participation in the history of the Hynniewtrep people right in the ancient past historic happenings. The community will run the risk of survival and sustainability if the influence of materialistic gains at the cost of the community's continuity and identity continues to dominate political, social, religious, industrial or academic schemes and spheres.

---

[106] Most folklore mentioned of the interaction between U Khasi and U Dkhar. It is wrong to say that their closer relationship is of recent development.

6. Promotion of Youth Culture:[107] Northeast India is a region of young people whose training opportunities began mostly where they turned out middle age. Memories were still afresh that most students from rural areas started joining schools only when they were already advanced in years. Normally, the future of a community or a nation depends on shaping children and young people right from the early stage. Most youths in the distant past, who in the absence of training institutions used to indulge in raiding, drinking or entering into early marriage. Young people were backbones of the society and nation alike.

Christian missions have taken up native children and young people seriously. Both churches of Protestant tradition and Catholic Mission have shown commitment to raising up tribal people right from their early ages and put up significant investment with whatever resources they could manage and worked themselves. The Catholic missionaries who belonged to the Salesians of Don Bosco (SDB) have come with a mission of translating their founder's vision, St. John Bosco, for caring, educating and leading young people for personality development, self-dependent, effective instrument for others' growth and people's well being.[108]

In what ways did Christian Missions carry out their vision? Missionaries, who have come to Northeast India at the invitation or protection of the British colonial rule, have come with an attitude of helping the weak and fragile native people. The first thing that they did after establishing educational schools was to admit children and young people and taught them the art of writing, reading and learning lessons. There was no discrimination in admission. Both boys and girls were treated equally in schools. The main objective of introducing higher and college education was to provide opportunities to local and native young students for advanced studies and the door was open to all irrespective of nationalities, ethnic, linguistic backgrounds or religion.

Taking care in schools and colleges was also supplemented by providing hostel facilities for rural students. Care of the inmates under the supervision of assigned authority took young people to an entirely different atmosphere and environment that touched upon academic, spiritual and inter-personal relationships. Staying together with fellow students from different places and states helped create a new sense of unity and national feeling. Hostels provided ample opportunities for dialogue, exchange of ideas and cultural interaction. Besides that, inmates learnt the discipline, value of time, regular working schedules, a corporate life, personal study and cleanliness.

---

[107] U Don Bosco was a brother and friend of young people. It was his vision and mission that had inspired the Salesians for their missionary activities among the youth in Northeast India. See Bacchiarello, J. **Ki Khanatang jong U Don Bosco** (1983).

[108] Karotemprel, S. "Youth in Transition in Northeast India and Salesian Involvement" in **Indian Missiological Review** (September-December 1990), pp. 201-216.

Long before the arrival of Christian institutions, there were traditional bachelors' dormitories in most villages especially among the Nagas, Mizos, Kukis, Hmars and others but following the advent of Christianity and introduction of modern education, the traditional institutions were in the process dwindled and ceased to exist. Educational schools, colleges and Boarding homes appeared to have replaced morung and zawlbulk.

Secondly, the training that was given to tribal youths was broad based that enabled securing employment opportunities as teachers in village schools, church workers, and employment in government offices. Some students have gone outside the region for higher studies. Christian churches also helped some of trained tribal priests to work outside in the plain areas and took them abroad also. So, it was education and boarding houses that provided the needed training and made young people equipped for service, outside exposure and cross cultural contact.

The introduction of technical training schools, agricultural resource centre and other practical institutes has been a boon to the isolated young people. Training was comprehensive and multi-dimensional touching upon shoe making, carpentry and furniture, tailoring, agriculture, motoring, electrical, book binding, printing technology, typing, electronic and computer education.

The third related implementation was in the area of physical education and sports. Churches took initiative for establishing playgrounds and introduced various sport activities like football, volleyball, basketball and indoor games like table tennis, badminton, corrom board, chess and others. Along with these went instruction on physical training and exercise. Before the government initiated opening schools in villages and in towns, it was Christian churches that built playgrounds for children, young people and sport persons side by side of the school buildings.

Fourthly, the creation of youth services in almost every local church and their connection with higher levels like districts, Presbyteries, Synods or Assembly has contributed to building sound spiritual life and strengthened their ethnic, regional and national consciousness. Through these ecclesiastical channels, young people could learn together the art of singing, composing of songs, and learning playing musical instruments and presenting choirs in public gatherings.

These activities helped build young people's spirituality, human relations and social etiquette.[109] They also brought social awareness for a better living that would prevent them from indulging in drinking liquor, gambling, unrest or loose married character at least.

[109] See Marbaniang, Nazarene V. "Youth Participation in Socio-Political Awareness in the North-east" in S. K. Chatterjee, ed., **Society and Culture in North-East India: A Christian Perspective** (1996), pp. 36-40.

7. The Church Organization and Its Impact on Tribal Life:[110] Tribal societies were rural based and isolated. Geographical nature with hills, deep gorges, rivers, thick forests, wild animals and fear of natural spirits could have reduced tribal societies to village and limited level of their identity. The kind of political administrative system that was prevailing in their life was highly democratic. The political hierarchy began from a clan council, village, raid (commune) to the highest state durbar. There was popular people's participation in this political structure. The main drawback was that it functioned only within the sub-ethnic group but excluded other groups although they would belong to the same community.

Christianity that came to the people in the region was successful in converting them to the new faith. Missionaries and native workers were responsible for planting local churches and spreading the faith. The church that was introduced is a community of believers transcended traditional clan, village or state councils. Its nature is inclusive and entertains converts from different sub-ethnic groups, clans, dialectical backgrounds in addition to men, women, children and people of all manner and walks of life. Despite the primary objective of the church that was religious and evangelistic, but its application and effectiveness went out collectively and crossed over limited tribal interests. The introduction of a hierarchical church structure that included these planted local churches under appropriate ecclesiastical line of authority had broken down traditional self contained institutions and helped creating an inclusive and larger fellowship. These hierarchical administrative organizations provided the elective members the opportunities for participation in the decision making processes, debate, discussion, worship and resolutions in the larger interests of members and in strengthening the Church.

The Catholic Church's organization laid mostly on the leadership of priests but its administrative catholicity is well designed that connected its life on a participatory nature right from the top level down to the grassroots level of a local church. The structure was inclusive and provided a connection that allowed missionaries, priests, lay people not only at the regional level but also at the level of the entire sub-continent.

The two larger Protestant churches in Northeast India are the Baptist and the Presbyterian Churches. These churches run their affairs on the collective democratic principle. Churches of Baptist tradition are now under a single comprehensive body known as the Council of Baptist Churches in North East India (CBCNEI).[111] Its headquarter is located in Guwahati. This organization is well represented by members from different communities and states and serves as a model of modern democratic institution. There is a clear involvement in

---

[110] Snaitang, O. L. **Christianity and Social Change in Northeast India** (1993), p. 168ff.

[111] For some information about the CBCNEI, Cf. Sangma, L. J. et al., eds., **Community of God's People in North East India: The 150th Anniversary of CBCNEI, 1836–1986** (1996).

this comprehensive body from the local church, convention, regional association up to the highest council. There is no space for single tribe domination in this highest body but poses itself as a national body.

The Presbyterian Church of India is another example of a well organized democratic Christian movement. Its administration is designed in such a way as it effectively functions through appropriate line of authority from a village church, a Pastorate, a district, a Presbytery, a Synod and up to the supreme highest body, the Assembly. There are orderliness, discipline, equality, rationality and emotion in the Presbyterian system. Like the Baptist Council, there is equal representation and active people's participation in the Presbyterian Church of India. People from different states, ethnic groups and linguistic backgrounds except women could involve in decision making bodies.

These ecclesiastical structures of the Catholic Church and churches of Protestant origins are structures that transcended clan, ethnic or linguistic barriers and although are related to religious affairs, are however institutions that carried significant integrative, national, inter-people and cross cultural relations.

8. Attitude and Comprehensive Participation of Christianity in Building a Modern India: Christian missionaries came and worked among the secluded and isolated people who in their period of history have settled and lived in the hills, mountains and even in certain plain areas. These people concentrated homogenously in respective geographical areas. Though the British classed them on the scheduled tribal list, they were however not tribal in a sense of being low, outcaste, oppressed or marginalized but of being in minority. Lack of road transportation, communication and less business minded were at least the main reasons for keeping these tribal communities illiterate, backward and poor. They were also people without written alphabet or script.

Apart from that the hill people had advanced idea of political, social life, agriculture and folk medicine. As already stated before, the democratic durbar political system that the hill people maintained was well in an advanced stage that could be compared at least to the modern day parliamentary system. There was collective participation in decision for people and unity, general welfare and well being. Their main difference with today's system democratic could be seen in two areas, viz., whereas today's democratic political system functioned on party structure, traditional policy was partyless. Secondly, in a multi-party political democracy, the leadership rested on majority vote but in the traditional system, most decisions were carried out on the basis of consensus.

Caste system, purdah, female infanticide, dowry, devadasi or untouchability was not prevalent in hill tribal societies. There was mutual social and inter-personal respect and relationship. No doubt certain social ills had entered into most hill people's practices that tended to shatter the egalitarian nature of tribal social life, like headhunting, slavery (bawi), alcoholism or human sacrifice to a clandestine python deity but these had not overshadowed people's freedom of movement, work culture, openness, dialogue and vision.

Tribal people's main economy was agriculture. This occupation provided a two way benefit to the people like making themselves-sufficient in home needs throughout the year and dispose of local products in markets. Before the introduction of money transaction, the people engaged in exchange of commodities or the barter economic system. This system balanced the different agricultural products of the people both from the upland cold region and the southern slope warm and hot climate. Like business transaction in markets so also it was in agricultural fields, both men and women did the job without any sense of inferiority. Men and women work with a sense of responsibility, co-operation and sharing.

The other development was in the area of health care. Hill people and those in the plain areas could also develop folk medicines and engaged in caring through massaging, prayers and sacrifices.

These were traditional institutional developments that had built the people. Hill people were also maintaining closer contacts and co-operation with people of Sanskritic traditions, like the Banglas, Assamese and others. Christian missionaries who have come and worked with hill people have not brought down these traditional existing values. Given the fact that most of these dimensions have been mentioned and described above, what we want to address is more on the attitude of Christianity to the nation and its overall participation in showing loyalty and building these people and Christian activities were in turn contributing elements to the entire nation.

Christian missionaries though have come for evangelization, have neither shown negative attitude to the nation nor taught anti-national subjects. The fact that they have not included Vedic texts and other Sanskritic literatures, one should not jump to the conclusion by saying that they were anti-national. Some reasons why such native subjects were not included were because these were not available in English translation in the early 19th century and since these texts were exclusive monopoly of Brahmins, their introduction to non-Brahmin students would generate backlash-and that neither the missionaries nor British administration would want.

The missionaries' positive attitude towards the nation was evident in their personal identification and involvement with the native people, activities in adopting local languages and promoting tribal literatures, providing health care and nursing, starting of schools, taking care of orphans and the aged, giving training for indigenous leadership. The enemies of the nation were illiteracy, poverty, social discrimination, ill health, economic backwardness, headhunting, human sacrifice to a python, superstition, witchcraft, sorcery, black magic, tribal warfare-all these were prominent in the region and fighting against these evils was an integral and vital mission in building the nation. Involving in such sacrificial activities was slow and unpopular but Christian missions and Churches have committed and seriously invested in the programmes. These are significant national building measures and integrative means.

Prominent missionaries and native Christians who have contributed to people's political consciousness included Rev. J. C. Evans, Rev. T. B. Philip, Rev. J. J. M. Nichols-Roy,[112] Fr. H. Elias[113] and others. Rev. J. C. Evans took active part in the Governor's Legislative Council and Rev. T. B. Philips was a missionary who gave befitting admiration of Mahatma Gandhi. The missionaries who have worked in Northeast India have come from a conviction and standing rule of separation of the church from politics and government. The rule that was operative then in their home boards, was also applied in Northeast India.

Their non-involvement in politics did not mean anti-national. Though they did not directly teach the native Christians on the question of politics, but their activities were clear indications of supporting Indian national movement and unity. While a description on this aspect might be interesting but suffice it to mention just two illustrations. First, educational system in the region was affiliated with the educational offices in West Bengal, Kolkata and Calcutta University. Second, before the formation of the Assam Christian Council in 1937, Christian missions and churches in North East India were part of Bengal Christian Council, Kolkata.

Christian churches that have established themselves in Northeast India, have never worked against the larger national interests. Though Rev. M. Scott, a missionary in Nagaland, was outspoken and tried to demonstrate Naga's distinctive identity and their political self-determination but that was more of his personal opinion. It was neither an official policy of the Baptist church nor a statement representative of the church as a whole. Again, some Christians in Nagaland under the leadership of A. Z. Phizo appeared to have followed the understanding that Nagaland was not part of India. These Christian secessionists were also not officially representative Christians and it is wrong to pass on any general remarks against the church in Nagaland. As a matter of fact, majority of Naga Christians and church leaders though remained in silence but were loyal to India and Indian leadership. Many of them have actively participated in the general elections, sent representatives to the Lok Sabha and the Rajya Sabha, joined civil services, police force and more importantly worked in National Defence.

Besides that, following the declaration of Independence in 1947 and well up to the recent times, certain independent movements have come up in Nagaland. These movements came out openly fighting for independence and fought against Indian national army. The jungle warfare that had blown up into unimaginable

[112] Read Snaitang, O. L. ed., **Memoirs of Life and Political Writings of the Hon'ble Rev. J. J. M. Nichols-Roy** (1997).

[113] Fr. Elias' love and concern for the unity and integrity of the nation is well reflected in his publications where he gave importance to the country, national anthem, national leaders and others. See Elias, H. **Na Mihngi – Sepngi** (1973).

proportion had claimed numerous precious lives. Most leaders who knew that majority of people in Nagaland were Christians, that leaders of these movements were also members of the Christian Church and the slogan that these outfits had put up was "Nagaland for Christ" were convinced that these were no other than the sanction of the Church.

Though these developments could have lent credence to the church's role and encouragement in these secessionist movements but the sudden conclusion that Christianity was behind these was unreasonable, unfounded, generalistic and very unfortunate. Those who have attributed the rise of independent or insurgent movements to Christianity have done so at the cost of those loyal citizens to India. These were Christians who lived in silence, who did not dare to express their views openly lest their existence would gravely be at stake but patiently supported the nation through their persistent participation in running school education, medical service, production of books and strengthening local Christian communities. Administration of church offices, holding of regional or state level conventions and councils, several ecclesiastical departments like women department, youth affairs, Sunday school committee, missionary movement and other departments functioned without opposition to the nation, India. Authors who have written on areas with majority of Christian population should restraint from making provocative conclusions. Therefore, churches and majority of Naga Christians and church leaders not only in Nagaland but in Northeast India were citizens whose loyalty to India should in no way be questioned.

There are also those who did not remain silent but actively involved in public spheres and in support of the nation. As before 1947 and till the present, most regional and national political leaders and bureaucrats are people whose standing religious membership are in churches of several traditions. Some of such were (L) Rev. J. J. M. Nichols-Roy of Khasi-Jaintia hills, (l) Shri Larsingh Khyriem of Jaintia hills, (L) Rev. Longri Ao of Nagaland, (L) Capt. W. A. Sangma of Garo hills, (L) Rev. Zairema of Mizoram, (L) Shri B. B. Lyngdoh of Meghalaya and other present leaders included Shri S. C. Jamir of Nagaland, Shri R. Keishing of Manipur, Shri Lalthanhaula of Mizoram, Shri Purno A. Sangma of Meghalaya, Shri P. R. Kyndiah, and many others. Christian leaders in the pre-independent India took part in the freedom movement and in the person of (L) Rev. J. J. M. Nichols-Roy, one found significant role in integration of the hill areas with India.[114]

To repeat on what had already been started earlier, the role of Christianity in national integration was encouraging. Christianity is not a religion of one group of people or a clan. It is an inclusive, universal and a global religion. Its nature is in fact a model of people's affiliation and movement. Those who belong to any clan,

---

[114] See Rani, Merostar "Christianity and National Integration in Northeast India: A Study of the Role and Contribution of Rev. J. J. M. Nichols-Roy" in Snaitang, O. L. & Merostar Rani, eds., **Christianity and National Integration** (2009), pp. 209-216.

cultural background, colour, creed or physical condition could become member of the Christian church. It is also cross-cultural and trans-national in character. Main churches in Dimapur, Imphal, Jorhat, Shillong, Aizawl, Guwahati, Dibrugarh, Diphu, Tura and elsewhere have Sunday services not only in local languages, English but in Hindi too. Christianity, therefore, demonstrates itself as a significant model of national unity.

India is a unique country because its unity is well built up in diversity. It is these diversities that contributed to making India beautiful. The contribution that Christianity has made to the nation became tangible to the establishing of permanent channels through native solidifying languages, literatures, education, medical health services, humanitarian works and social activities, research institutions, publications and establishment of archives, museum, career guidance, youth and personality development, education of women, rural reconstruction, agriculture and provision for outside academic exposure. These activities help both in bringing the nation to a sense of belonging, in ushering it to function effectively and making the people fully equipped in facing challenges.

Christian institutions are also areas that gave employment to people from all walks of life. Some training schools that trained men and women in different trades have also contributed to self-reliance and private business. Nursing schools have also a great part in health ministry and in securing employment opportunities.

People take active and enthusiastic part in state and national elections. Churches though do not involve in politics but make official advice that voters should not waste their voting rights on notified election dates and some church leaders even condemned those who tended to pass over this electoral reality as uneducated or uncivilized.

Some school or college textbooks in vernacular or English that were written by Christian writers or priests and published by churches would see that topics of national importance including accounts of freedom fighters, map of the country, national flag, and national anthem were included for teaching and study.

Christian role and participation in relief and rehabilitation among all manner of people in the region are important and have helped caring and assisting unfortunate victims of natural disasters. India in general and Northeast India in particular have experienced various natural calamities and how much those who have been affected by these happenings have faced physical and mental hardships. Floods in plain areas have not only claimed precious lives but have brought about sufferings. Homes were washed out, crops destroyed and many lived on shanty sheds on safer grounds. Earthquakes too have occasionally caused human misery through damages that brought upon people's settlement, occupation and economy. Churches have in most cases come up to the forefront in providing the needed help. Other ecumenical Christian organizations like the World Vision of India, Church Auxiliary Social Action, North East India Committee on Relief and Development (NEICORD), Evangelical Fellowship of India Committee on

Relief (EFICOR) and other agencies are organizations with humanitarian concerns and services. Their activities are mainly in providing relief to the victims through financial assistance, building of houses, providing drinking water, distribution of essential commodities, blankets and clothing materials. They also involved in giving scholarship to deserving students, installing of solar energy, conducting medical camps and holding of seminars on social issues.

Orphans and the aged were normally taken care of by their kiths and kins but the resulting impact of modernity and globalization had placed them in difficult situations. While governmental agencies and other humanitarian groups have come forward to help such unfortunate folks, the part that Christian churches have made in setting up orphanages and homes for the aged too was another contributing factor towards caring of the marginalized human beings and building the country.

Christian churches did not confine their social mission and compassionate ministry only to urban and town areas like in Kohima, Imphal, Aizawl, Guwahati, Shillong or Agartala but moved into the interior among the alienated rural people. They provided the needed help to the villages and organized basic Christian communities through primary education, worshipping centres and serenity and their children could see a glimmer of hope for their future.

The Indo-Bangla war in 1971 that led to the creation of Bangladesh, witnessed large influx of refugees into the region. Though their entry and settlement in the hill and plain areas caused heavy burden on the already overpopulated nation but several Christian agencies have gone and worked in refugee camps with food supplies, clothing materials, medicines and nursing care for their general welfare.

II. A Critical Assessment of Christian Presence and Role in Northeast India

We have made a survey of Christian Missions and churches in the region and described their historical origins, growth and development in the 19th and 20th centuries. We have seen their similarities and differences, conflicts and comity, rise and fall and people's responses to the new faith. Now, before we examine and evaluate the role of Christianity in national integration we will begin by looking into the drawbacks and negative aspects of Christian presence in the region. Such academic adventure would remain unacademic and incomplete unless the limitations and of Christianity are passed over. This study would try to remain objective and do justice to historical developments.

Further clarification is needed before this aspect is taken up in-depth. This assessment on the limitations of Christian work among the people in this part of the country is done not for the sake of criticism. It is also not done on the pretext of copying of what others have said so. There could have some overlapping in my assessment but the drawbacks are drawn from appropriate historical developments and might be explained as under:-

1. A Religion that was Divided: Despite the sacrifices and investment that Christian missionaries have done to the people, one major lacuna that had affected the region was that Christianity came with a divided face. **1). Denominationalism**. The region witnessed the arrival of Welsh Calvinistic Methodism, Baptist, Anglicanism and Catholicism in the 19th century; Pentecostalism, Adventism, Salvation Army, Charismatic groups in the 20th century. Each of these maintained strict administrative independence, different theological stance, connection with one's own mission agency at home.

These differences were so great that disunity went out side by side with a competitive spirit. Mission fields became open grounds for denominational competitive ministries in order to gain greater influence and numbers. Such spirit gave rise to attacks and counter attacks leaving an unchristian mentality. These developments were indications that their preaching of God's Kingdom was in reality an attempt to take converts to a denominational kingdom.

2). Different Cultures and Nationalities: The difference was further compounded by the cultures and nationalities that the missionaries came from. While Welsh missionaries hailed from Wales in the U. K, Baptist missionaries came from the U. S., the U. K. and New Zealand, most Catholic missionaries were Germans, Italians or Belgians and also from South India. Most of them had come from bitter conflicts and religious wars in the 16th and 17th centuries and had brought these unnecessary evils to the mission fields in Northeast India.

In this backdrop, there were cases of sheep stealing, schism and the rise of splinter and independent movements. These differences tended to bring division in families, clans, villages and in the community. Ecclesiastical differences, denominational mud slinging, casting personal aspersion and disunity found receptivity, productivity and support in the already fragmented tribal societies. Christian missionaries did not regard disunity to be a sin rather provided avenues for encouragement and approval in the interest of a denomination.

Applying of different approaches also bolstered ecclesiastical disunity. Though a detail explanation of this aspect is important but suffice it to mention that while Welsh missionaries rejected elements of traditional religion, missionaries of the Catholic Church did not oppose rather inculturated them in their rituals and teaching.

The difference was so deeply entrenched that some denomination did not acknowledge other as Christian and publicly circulated the idea that a particular head or global Christian body represents that of an antichrist. Smaller groups were nicknamed as sectarian, proud or heretics.

3). Differences in Life Style: Differences were also observed in life-style. Some churches did not object members in a Christian community to continue use of tobacco, smoking or eating of areca nuts. Other churches did not admit converts to full membership unless they have given up smoking, drinking or eating betel nuts. Other Christian groups still prohibited using of any intoxicants including drinking tea or coffee.

The impact began to become evident in literature. Catholic writers and Protestant writers in Khasi literature at least though use the same Khasi language but began to differ in areas of spelling. For instance, while Catholic writers would spell *jymphong* for dress, Protestant insisted on *jingphong*, Paulus for Paul etc.. Ending of words were used differently like *ieid* (Catholic), *ieit* (Presbyterian) *ieij* (Church of God).

These churches shared much in common in their faith in God's creation, Trinity, Jesus Christ the Saviour, the Pentecost and the Second coming. But differences in rituals are deeper than commonality. The Catholic Church has seven sacraments, the Presbyterian and the Baptist Churches two and the Church of God three. Though the Presbyterian and the Baptist Churches have two, they differed in baptism, infant and adult baptism. These differences were enough to set aside their ecumenical desire for Church union. A divided Christianity has further widened the solidified tribal societies.

2. Intrusion of Western Culture and Life Style: Christianity came along with certain elements of Western culture. This was evident in dress and life style. As of now, traditional dress of tribal men had disappeared almost totally. Changing of dress though would have raised the standard of living but the pride of having dressed almost like the white missionaries more often than not paved way to looking down at the poor, the rural folks and manual labourers. A class consciousness began to find a space in hill tribal societies.

The other area was Christian tribal adoption of Western hymns and musical instruments. These were regularly applied in services, schools and public gatherings. Hymns were translated ones and even indigenous composed songs and tunes followed almost the same Western pattern. Adoption of piano, organ, guitar, synthetic drum, violin in church services and public performances has given a Western outlook in the community.

Western form became tangible clear in wedding ceremony. In hill tribal societies, bride and groom put up colourful Western attires and hardly one could observe local elements. Use of wedding veil, crown, cosmetic, bow and neck ties, suits and boots etc, though had raised the social standard had however been elements even at the cost of traditional pattern.

Church buildings were also built almost exactly like buildings in Europe. These no doubt gave a new look to the isolated jungle society but the displacement of whatever should have been indigenous, left these elements westernized.

Western names have also attracted tribal people and in some cases new Western named clans have come up.

3. Tribal People and Native Church Workers: Missionaries though had shown tremendous love and concern for the tribal people but their underrated reports of the people to their constituent sending mission agencies did not sound appreciable because perhaps their objective was to gain increasing sympathy and support. Their reported messages of the people as primitive, backward, idolaters, naked or drunkards appeared to have smeared with excessive exaggeration. Such reports were indications of imperialistic conquering spirit and superiority complex.

In certain cases, native Christian workers were regarded low. There was lukewarm support and encouragement of tribal candidates for theological studies. Those who have completed and joined the ministry were given ministerial assignment over a vast stretch of scattered rural congregations.

4. Hindi and English: Christian missionaries were pioneers in starting modern educational institutions in the region. Their aim was to introduce the best education among the people. Certain schools and colleges like the St. Edmund's, the St. Anthony's, the St. Mary's, the St. Peter's, Synod School, Synod College, Holy Cross and numerous institutions in towns and villages have in most cases achieved their intended objectives. Since the missionaries have come from Europe or North America, their outlook was always beyond the regional or even the national level. One of the means to take the people to that level was to insist on English as the medium of instruction. This attempt has enabled the people not only in the Northeast but in India to communicate with each other at ease. But the communication was applicable only at the academic higher level. Given the influence and impact of Hindi as a national language, Christian run educational institutions should imbibe strong feeling and adaptation of Hindi as the medium of instruction and communication so that the people from this part of the country could function effectively at the grass root levels and even otherwise.

Chapter 8

General Conclusion

A study on "Christianity and National Integration in Northeast India" has now come to its end. This Chapter will bring out a summary of what had already been described in the previous Chapters of this investigation. It is informative and also more reflective in the summation.

By studying the subject from historical perspectives, the investigation began with the examination of the people's traditional historical setting. This is the first perspective in the process of this academic study. Its main heading has been titles as 'Northeast India in the traditional historical perspectives.' Given the vastness of this period, the study has tried to touch upon four areas, viz., geographical identity; people's composition, people's social structure, languages, experiences in polity and religion. Land was an important component in the life and existence of the people in the region. Geography indicates that Northeast India is gradually an integral part of India. While that historical fact can in no way be questioned, what had been explored in this section was that the physical features like the presence of mountains, hills, rivers, dense forests and the absence of communication networks have in the process not facilitated easy contact. This dimension was so significant because the impact that it had on the people was such that they tended to see the world just around their own self-contained enclosure.

A description on people's composition in the region though is not in detail yet is more informative. It stated the presence of numerous people's groups and communities in each state. These groups maintained their own distinctive identities. Besides that, the chapter looked at the prevailing social system and addressed most specifically on the evils of caste system, headhunting, human sacrifice and social victims of injustices. These social elements had gravely affected the harmonious social system and shattered national unity and integrity.

Another area that it had studied was on languages. Most communities in hill areas have several unintelligible dialects and without any written script. These linguistic differences caused a great rift even in a given homogenous society and gradually affected their progress and liberation. The other area that had been examined was on the question of polity and religion. These components though were so significant in each local situation but taking them together in the community, they were not unifying elements.

The second significant major change that had greatly affected the people in Northeast India was the role of the British administration. The Northeast was mostly the last territory in the country that the British colonial power had extended it political control and rule. Given the mountainous conditions of the hill areas and the less benefit from ruling the region, the British appeared to have remained reluctant at least in the beginning to bring the hill areas and even the plains of Assam, within the colonial political enclosure. From an in-depth evaluation, it appeared that there were four main reasons why the British extended its policy into this region. First, it was local chiefs from the plains who had invited the British to help them in fighting the Burmese whose rule for over six hundred years had brought discontentment and fear. Second, they also saw the profit of annexing the hill areas so that construction of road transportation between the plains of Assam and Sylhet could be done so that the distance could be shortened. Third, annexing the hill areas was in the eyes of the British officials an urgent necessity in order to control and curb the terrific frequent raids from the hill people. Lastly, the British preferred to take control of the hill areas because they found the areas best suited for their health. This vision led to the establishment of Military Cantonments and Sanatoria.

The impact that it made upon the people and the territory was mainly through the imposition of a new political rule that brought the entire region under a single administration. Along with that, they brought laws and jurisprudence, a written culture, new economy through the medium of money and through Christian missions. The political process of consolidating the once fragmented Northeast India was in one way the best political policy and the British should deserve the credit of bringing about a great political breakthrough and that for setting up a sense of unity. However, the subsequent application of the 'divide and rule' policy in the midst of political consolidation was nothing but a protective political mechanisms. Though the divided sections, especially in the hill areas, still remained under the single alien administration but the administrative policies became more vulnerable and damaging after the country had achieved independence in 1947. It has been noted that the imposition of the British system in the region through the English medium of communication, through ration shops and use of money besides the encouragement of Christian mission activities and in the process greatly affected the life and thought pattern of the people. Therefore, British colonialism was the primary agency in bringing about major change among the people in the region.

The third perspective that this study has given serious attention was in regard to the coming and role of Christianity. This was another major development in the history of Northeast India. Given the intrusion of several Christian Missions and churches, this survey tried to put the account in historical developments under three main sections. First, it brought out the early Christian contacts beginning from 1627 till 1838. Catholic priests who happened to visit Assam in 1627 did not intend to start missionary work in the region but they were on their way to Tibet. Catholic settlements at Rangamati - Hossompur, Bondashil - Baniyachong and Mariamnagar – Kashipur were Portuguese and Indo-Portuguese soldiers under Mughal armies. They were mercenaries and not missionaries and so their concern with the Church was only in terms of their membership. The Serampore Mission that had started work among the Khasis in Khasi hills too though had shown signs of progress but was by 1838 completely closed down.

The next historical development of Christianity was by the arrival of Christian Missions in the nineteenth century. They were no longer temporary but permanent missions that played a significant role in shaping the destiny of most people in the region. They were the American Baptist Mission (1836); the Welsh Calvinistic Methodists' Foreign Mission (1841); the Anglican Church or the Church of England (1876), the Catholic Mission (1890) and the Baptist Missionary Society (1894). As already stated, it was these mission agencies that made their presence permanent, stable, growing and influential in the society at large. Their contributions were mainly in the standardization of a single dialect for the homogenous community, introduction of written alphabet and development of indigenous literatures, setting up of a wide network of educational institutions, healthcare and medical services, rural construction, church planting, raising of native leaderships, ecclesiastical polity and organization, theological belief and practices. These institutional means though were meant for evangelization but had in the process becoming contributing factors in making the people to become effectively functional and adjustable in the newly British introduced situation.

Another Christian development that was treated was on the rise of Christian indigenous movement. These Christian groups that have come up highly in the twentieth century were splinter, independent, Pentecostal and charismatic. In short, they were divided groups. These indigenous Churches have at least become productive in Mizoram, Manipur, Nagaland and Meghalaya. While Christianity was initially responsible for creating a sense of unity in tribal societies but with the arrival of several Christian Missions and the emergence of independent groups became significant force for the development of a new tribalism. Given the fluid cultural context of the people in the region, Christian division found receptive and productive in and among the people in tribal areas.

After examining the Northeast India subject in three dimensional perspectives, the focus on the role of Christianity in national integration and nation building is treated in Chapter Seven. It evaluated on the attitude of these Christian Missions towards the nation and their role in respective areas of missionary involvement. This Chapter looks at the overall role and ministry of Christianity in national integration and nation building in two contrasting examinations, viz., positive and negative contentions. The positive contribution of Christianity was assessed areas of creating a common intelligible language, promotion of indigenous literatures through use of the Roman or Latin alphabet, education, medical and humanitarian activities, influence on the traditional belief in devils and evil designs, promotion of young people, Church structure that brought the divided tribes to a common sense of solidarity and other constructive channels in building the modern country.

This kind of study will fail to do justice to the academic discipline if it does not do justice in bringing out the negative aspects of Christian presence in the region. While one can identify several areas that Christianity had brought negative impact on the people but the most glaring developments that did not give credit to Christian integrity have been mentioned and described in areas that Christianity came to Northeast India and in India in general as a major divided religion. This was true not just between the Catholics and the Protestants but among the different denominations in Protestant family. The imposition of a western culture among the people that became tangibly evident in dress, music, life style, use of English as a preference to local languages and the passing attention to traditional cultural elements did not contribute to the culture of the people. In certain cases, Western missionaries tended to overlooked native intellectuals. The important integrative link of Hindi as a national language had in most cases been passed over at least in the past.

In the light of these descriptions and explanations, one is convinced that the introduction of new dispensations among the people in the region had brought about an awareness, consciousness and knowledge of the value of human persons. Most of their role and activities were related to his/her dignity, freedom and liberation. Land was also regarded indispensible in the people's continued existence with honour and liberty, survival and sustainability. They have also laid a strong foundation for writing of people's history, documents and promotion of indigenous literature, preserving such important data so that the future generations would see more light than darkness. While these new elements have contributed to people's thinking vision and thinking they have also endowed the indigenous people with a dynamic spirit and a spirit of moving forward. Though looking at the past is important and necessary so that the foundation would not rest on hearsay and hype but what is more important and extremely necessary is a forward looking and movement alike with knowledge, understanding and consciousness of human values of growth, development and socio-economic and political liberation. The rise of insurgency in most of the states with majority of Christian population in the recent past had suddenly cast negative aspersion on Christianity but never once was it emerged and moved with official ecclesiastical support and backing. Though one could not ignore the material investment by the new dispensations but a long term immaterial investment in education and learning that witnessed in the evolution of wisdom, intelligence, knowledge and academic endowment among the tribal people are the most prized possessions, assets and treasury of academic and intellectual merits that none would dare jump to the conclusion of condemnation except in the area of emotional revivalism, fanaticism and extreme fundamentalism.

Bibliography

Unpublished Documents

"Ain Bri Khyndew ha ki Hima Khasi, Ka-Kumba la pass da ka Khasi National Durbar kaba la long naduh ka 6th haduh ka 8th November 1929" (1956).

Beckers, G., S. J., "Evolution and Growth of the Catholic Church in North East India" (24/1/1987).

"Constitution of North East India Christian Council" (Revised in the Assam Christian Council of 4th May, 1961).

Doulatram, Jairamdos (Governor of Assam) "Ka jingkren ha kaba plie ia ka jingialang jong ki member ba la jied jong ki Hima Khasi, ha Shillong, April 29th 1949."

Doulatram, Jairamda Khasi, U. "Ka Election da u Paidbah bad ka jingthung. S'iem", **U Nongialam Katholik,** 2 (Rymphang 1902), pp. 1-20.

Khasi J. Dkr U, "Ki Khasi Hyndai", Supplement Jong **U Nongialam Katholik,** 13 (Naiwing 1902), pp. 164-165.

Government of West Bengal, General Department (Date of previous order B. File October 1868) Nos. 106 and 107 (Date of order 28th November 1868).

Kottupallil, George "Roman Catholic Historiography in North-East India" (1986).

Menamparampil, Thomas "The Church in North-East India: A Study 1974" (A private circulation 1974).

Nichols-Roy, J. J. M. "Ka Jingkren ha u paidbah ka Ri Khasi-Jaintia, ha ka 8 tarik 1948".

Nichols-Roy, J. J. M. "Speech Regarding the Cabinet Mission Declaration, Shillong 1946".

Nichols-Roy, J. J. M. "Speech at the Inaugural Meeting of the District Council of the United Khasi and Jaintia Hills on 27. 6. 1952".

Nichols-Roy, J. J. M. "Letter to the Chairman, British Parliamentary Delegation". Dated Shillong the 30th January, 1946.

Nichols-Roy, J. J. M. "A Memorandum Regarding the Hill Districts of Assam: Their future in the New Constitution of India" (Submitted to the sub-committee of the Constituent Assembly for the Excluded and Partially Excluded and Tribal Areas of Assam, 1946).

Nichols-Roy, J. J. M. "Memorandum of Personal Views Supporting the Demand for a Separate Hills State" (c. 1954).

Proceedings Jong Ka Khasi National Durbar, Ki (Dorbar Hima Khasi) Kaba Lai Kaba la long ha Shillong naduh 25 tarik haduh 26 tarik U March, 1925 (Shillong: 1925).

Proceeding Jong Ka Khasi National Durbar, Ki Kaba Saw Kaba la long ha Shillong naduh 30 tarik September haduh 2 tarik October 1925 (Shillong: 1925).

Proceedings Jong Ka Khasi National Durbar, Ki Kaba la long ha Shillong naduh 13 tarik haduh 15 tarik U October 1926 (Shillong: 1927).

Proceedings of the Third Session of the Assam Christian Council held at Shillong, Assam, March 29th-31st 1940.

Proceedings of the Assam Christian Council, 1947 (1948).

Proceedings of the Lieutenant Governor of Bengal, Political Department, 31st March 1859, Pro. Nos. 3-5.

Proceedings of the Lieutenant Governor of Bengal, General Department (Misc.), 2nd June 1859. Pro. No. 17-1.

Proceedings of the Lieutenant Governor of Bengal, General Education Department, Nov. 1862, Pro. Nos. 43-45.

Proceedings of the Lieutenant Governor of Bengal, Education Department, October 1863, Pro. Nos. 17-19.

Proceedings of the Lieutenant Governor of Bengal, General Department, Dec. 1863, Pro. No. 54.

Proceedings of the Lieutenant Governor of Bengal, General Department, Nov. 1864. Pro. Nos. 20-25.

Proceedings of the Lieutenant Governor of Bengal, General Department, Nov. 1864. Pro. Nos. 20-23.

Proceedings of the Lieutenant Governor of Bengal, (Misc.) Dec. 1864, Pro. Nos. 5-62.

Official Addresses, Treaties, Souvenirs and Other Sources

Addresses Presented to His Excellency the Right Hon'ble lord Curzon of Kedleston and His Excellency's thereto on the occasion of his visit to Assam, March 1900 (Shillong, Assam Secretariat Printing Office, 1900).

Aitchison, C. U. **A Collection of Treaties Engagements and Sanads relating to India and Neighbouring Countries,** Vol. I (Calcutta, Office to the Superintendent of Government Printing India, 1892).

Allen, B. C. **Gazetteer of the Khasi and Jaintia Hills, Garo Hills Lushai Hills** (Originally published 1905, reprinted Delhi, Gian Publications, 1980).

Allen, B. C. Gait, E. A. Allen, C. G. H. Howard H. F., **Gazetteer of Bengal and North East India** (1905/1979).

Assembly of the Presbyterian Church in North East India, Golden Jubilee Souvenir, 1926-1976 (Shillong, Central Ward, 1976).

Balang Presbyterian Lyngkyrdem, 1933-1983, Ka: Ka History Jong Ka (Lyngkyrdem, Presbyterian Church, 1983).

Catholic Directory of India, The. 1916, 1921, 1931, 1935, 1941, 1959, 1964, 1969, 1972, 1977, 1980, 1990.

Census of India, 1872 (Calcutta, 1872).

Census of India, 1881: Report on the Census of Assam for 1881(Calcutta, 1883).

Census of India, 1891: Assam, Vol. I, Report, and Vol. II, Tables (Shillong, 1892).

Census of India, 1901, Vol. III Assam, Part I, Report (Shillong, 1912).

Census of India, 1921, Vol. III, Assam, Part I, Report (Shillong, 1923).

Census of India, 1931, Vol. III, Assam, Part I, Report (Shillong, 1932).

Census of India, 1941, Vol. IX. Assam-Tables (Delhi, 1942).

Census of India, 1951, Vol. XII, Assam, Manipur and Tripura Part I A Report and Part II A (Shillong, 1954).

Census of India, 1961, Paper No. 1 of 1962.

Census of India, 1971, Paper No. 2 of 1962.

Census of India, 1981, Series I, India, Paper 4 of 1984.

Centenary of the Catholic Church in North East India 1890-1990: A Souvenir.

Constituent Assembly Debates, Official Report, Vols I, IX (Reprinted, New Delhi, Lok Sabha Secretariat, n.d.).

Hunter W. W., **A Statistical Account of Assam,** Vol. 2 (First published 1879, reprinted, Delhi, B. R. Publishing Corporation, 1975).

Ka Jingdap 50 Snem Ka Pateng Khristan, 1937-1987, (Shillong, KJP Synod, 1987).

Ka Jingiaseng Samla Jong Ka KJP Synod, (Souvenir 1951-1976).

Ka Pateng Khristan Jubilee, 1966.

Ka War Shella Socio-Cultural Organization: Souvenir 1987.

Kharshiing, Hipshon Roy ed., **Ki Symboh Pyrkhat Na Ka Seng Kut Snem, 1899-1988,** (Mawkhar, Seng Khasi-Seng Kmie, 1988).

Khasi-Jaintia Presbyterian Synod Reports, (1953-1990).

Ki Jingrwai Seng Khasi, (First Published 1921, reprinted, Shillong, Seng Khasi, 1980).

Mills, A. J. M**. Report on the Khasi and Jaintia Hills** 1853 (Shillong, 1901).

North and North-Eastern Frontier Tribes of India (Reprinted, 1983). Originally published 1907 as Vol. IV of "Frontier and Overseas Expeditions from India".

Notes on Some Industries of Assam from 1884 to 1895 (Shillong, Assam Secretariat Printing Office, 1896).

Pemberton R. **Report on the Eastern Frontier of British India** (1835/1966).

Periodical Accounts of the Serampore Mission, No. 1 From January 1827 to January 1828.

Periodical Accounts of the Serampore Mission, No XXXII (February 1830).

Periodical Accounts of the Serampore Mission, 3 D series, No. LXVIII (January 1833).

Periodical Accounts of the Serampore Mission, 3 D Series, No. CXI (September 1836).

Periodical Accounts of the Serampore Mission, 3 D Series, No. CXIV (December 1836).

Physical and Political Geography of the Province of Assam (Shillong, Assam Secretariat Printing Office, 1896).

Presbyterian Church of India Platinum Jubilee Souvenir (1926-2001).

Proceedings of the North East India History Association, First Session, Shillong, 1980; Second session, Dibrugarh 1981, Third Session, Imphal, 1982, Sixth Session, Agartala, 1985, Seventh Session, Pasighat, 1986, Eight Session, 1988.

Provincial Gazetteer of Assam, (Originally published 1906, reprinted, Delhi, Cultural Publishing House, 1983).

Rama Krishna Cherra Golden Jubilee Souvenir, 1922-1982.

Rama Krishna Shillong Golden Jubilee Souvenir, 1937-1987.

Report on the Administration of Assam (Shillong, Assam Government Press, 1890).

Report on the Administration of Eastern Bengal and Assam, 1908-1909 (Shillong, 1910).

Report on the Administration of Assam (Calcutta, Foreign Department Press, 1890).

Report on the Administration of the Khasi and Jaintia Hills 1890 (Calcutta, Foreign Department Press, 1890).

Report on the Administration of the Province of Assam for the year 1893-94 (Shillong, 1895).

Report on Special Enquiry into the Excise on Country Spirits in Assam, (Shillong, Assam Secretariat Printing Office, 1890).

Report on Vital Statistics of the Province of Assam 1874 (Shillong, Assam Secretariat Press, 1876).

Roberts, John tr. **Ka Histori, Ka Jinglong, Ki-Rukom Pynbeit Synran, Bad Ka Jingphla, Ka Jingngeit Jong Ki Welsh Presbyterian Kumba la Pynthikna ia Ki ha ki Assembly ha Aberystwith bad Bala ha Ka snem 1823** (Cherra, Welsh Mission, 1927).

Ryntathiang, P. **Assembly Church of Jesus Christ (F. G.) Meghalaya, India, Golden Jubilee, 1930-1980.**

Sesquicentennial Jubilee of the Presbyterian Mission, 1841-1991: A Souvenir, K.J.P. Synod, 1991.

Shillong Centenary Celebration, 1874-1974 (Shillong, 1976).

Singh, Hajom Kissore Ed, **Ki Sarvis bad Ki Jingrwai Na Ka bynta Ka Jingmane lang ne marwei,** (Shillong, Khasi Hills Unitarian Union, 1907).

St. Mary's College Shillong, Golden Jubilee, 1937-87.

The Assam School Manual, (Shillong, Assam Secretariat Printing Office, 1905).

The Constitution and Bye-Laws of the Church of God-Ecclesia, (1979).

The Imperial Gazetteer of India: The Indian Empire, Vol. 1 Descriptive (Oxford, At the Clarendon Press, 1907).

The Imperial Gazetteer of India: The Indian Empire, Vol. II Historical (Oxford, At the Clarendon Press, 1908).

The Imperial Gazetteer of India: The Indian Empire, Vol. IV Administrations (Oxford, At the Clarendon Press, 1907).

The Imperial Gazetteer of India: Vol. VIII Karens to Madnagarh, Second Edition (London, Truebner & Co. 1886).

You're Kingdom Come (Pastoral Reflection for the centenary year 1990): Joint pastoral Letter of the Regional Bishops Council of North East India.

Books

A Common Perspective for North-East India (Calcutta, 1967).

Acharyya, N. N. **A Brief History of Assam: From Earliest Time to the Year 1983** (New Delhi: Omsons Publications, 1987).

Aerath, C. & G. Menachery, eds., **Christian Contribution to Nation Building: A Third Millennium Enquiry** (Cochin: Documentary Committee of CBCI-KCBC, 2004).

Agrawal, A. K. **North East India: An Economic Perspective** (Allahabad: Chugh Publication, 1985).

Ahluwalia, B. K. and Ahluwalia, S. Ed, **Social and Economics Development in North East India** (Delhi: Gyan Publishing House, 1986).

Allen, B. C. **Naga Hills and Manipur** (Delhi: Gyan Publisher, 1981).

Aluckal, J. **Pioneer Diocesan Priests of Northeast India,** Vol. I (Shillong: Fr. Jacob Aluckal, 2005).

Ao, A. B. **History of Christianity in Nagaland: A Source Material** (Mokokchung: Shalom Ministry, 1998).

Ao, Alem **Tsungmerology: Ao Naga Christian Theology** (Mokokchung: Clark Theological College, 1994).

Arles, S. & I. Ben Wati, eds., **Pilgrimage 2100: A Self Reflection on Indian Evangelicalism** (Bangalore: Centre for Contemporary Christianity, 1995).

Bacchiarello, J. **Ki Khanatang Jong U Don Bosco** (Shillong: Don Bosco Book Depot, 1983).

Bareh, Hamlet **The History and Culture of the Khasi People** (Shillong, 1967), Revised and Enlarged Edition 1985.

Bareh, Hamlet **A Short History of Khasi Literature**, (Shillong: At Ri Khasi Press, 1979).

Bareh, Hamlet **The Language and Literature of Meghalaya** (Shimla: Indian Institute of Advanced Study, 1977).

Bareh, Hamlet. **U Tirot Singh** (New Delhi: Publication Division, Ministry of Information and Broadcasting, Government of India, 1984).

Barkataki, Meena S. **British Administration in North East India, 1826-74** (Delhi: Mittal Publications, 1985).

Barooah, Nirode K. **David Scott in North East India, 1802-1831: A Study in British Paternalism** (New Delhi: Munshiram Manoharlal, 1970).

Barpujari, H. K., S. K. Barpujari, A. C. Bhuyan, eds., **Political History of Assam, 1825-1919,** Vol. I (Dispur: Government of Assam 1977).

Barpujari, H. K. **Problem of the Hill Tribes North East Frontier, 1822-42** (1970), **Problem of the Hill Tribes North East Frontier, 1843-72** (1970).

Bars, E. **Khasi-English Dictionary** (Shillong: Don Bosco, 1973).

Basic Statistics of North Eastern Region (Shillong: NEC, 1987).

Basu, K. **The Sovereignty of God and Christian Nationalism** (Delhi: ISPCK, 2003).

Beck, J. R. **Dorothy Carey: The Tragic and Untold Story of Mrs. William Carey** (Michigan: Baker Book House, 1992).

Becker, Christopher, **History of the Catholic Missions in North East India**, Trans, and ed., by G. Stadler and S. Karotemprel (Calcutta: Firma KLM Private Ltd, 1980) German Original Published 1923, revised 1927.

Becker, Christopher, **History of the Catholic Missions in North East India**, Trans, and ed., by F. Leicht and S. Karotemprel (Shillong: Vendrame Institute, 1989).

Berry, R. S. **Ka Jingsneng Tymmen Shaphang Ka Akor Khasi** *I & II* (Shillong: 1902, 1903).

Bhattacharjee, J. B. "The Messenger of Khasi Heritage", in U Hipshon Roy, ed., **Khasi Heritage: A Collection of Essays on Religion and Culture** (Shillong: Seng Khasi, 1979).

Bhattacharjee, J. B. ed., **Social Tension in North East India** (Shillong, 1982).

Bhattacharjee, K. K. **North East India: Political and Administrative History** (New Delhi: Cosmo Publications, 1983).

Bhuyan, A. C. & S. De, eds., **Political History of Assam, 1920-1939**, Vol. 2 (Dispur: Govt. of Assam, 1970).

Bhuyan, A. C. & S. De, eds., **Political History of Assam, 1940-47**, Vol. 3 (Dispur: Govt. of Assam, 1980).

Bhuyan, B. C. **The Tribal Women** (New Delhi: Omsons Publications, (1993).

Bose, M. L. **History of Arunachal Pradesh** (New Delhi: Concept Publishing Company, 1997).

Bottomore, T. B. **Sociology: A Guide to Problem and Literature**, New edition, (Bombay: Blakie & Son-India, Ltd., 1975).

Burman, B. K. Roy **Indigenous and Tribal Peoples: Gathering Mist and New Horizon** (New Delhi: Mittal Publications, 1994).

Cantlie, Keith **Notes on Khasi Law** (Aberdeen: Henry Munro Ltd., 1934).

Celebration of 150th Death Anniversary of U. Tirot Singh Syiem of Nongkhlaw: An Illustrious Khasi Hero and Personage (Shillong: The Khasi Cultural Society, 1984).

Chakhcsang Baptist Church Council: Golden Jubilee Souvenir, 1950-2000.

Chakravorty, B. C. **British Relations with the Hill Tribes of Assam since 1858** (1981).

Chatterjee, S. P. **Le Plateau De Meghalaya (Garo-Khasi-Jaintia)** iEtude Geographique d'une region nauralle de L Inde. (Paris: Les Presses Modernes, 1936).

Chatterji, S. K. ed., **Society and Culture in North-East India: A Christian Perspective** (Delhi: ISPCK, 1996).

Chattopadhyaya, S. K. **The Jaintias** (New Delhi: Cosmo Publications, 1988).

Chattopadhyaya, S. K. ed., **Tribal Institutions of Meghalaya** (Gauhati: Spectrum Publications, 1985).

Chaube, Shibanikimkar **Hill Politics in North-East India** (Calcutta: Orient Longman, 1973).

Choudhury, J. N. **The Khasi Canvas: A Cultural and Political History** (Shillong: Shrimati Jaya Choudhury, Quinton Road, 1978).

Choudhury, P. **The Antiquity of Khasi-Jaintia People** (Calcutta: Self Employment Bureau Publication, 1981).

Chudgar, P. L. **Indian Princes under British Protection** (Chandigargh: Sameer Prakashan, 1976).

Community of God's People in North East India: The 150th Anniversary of CBCNEI, 1836-1986 (Guwahati: CBCNEI, 1986).

Compendium: The Baptist Church of Mizoram, 1903-2003 (Lunglei: The Baptist Church of Mizoram, 2003).

Costa, G. **Ka Riti Jong Ka Ri Laiphew Syiem**, Bynta-I (Shillong: St. Anthony's, 1936).

Costa, G. **Ka Riti Jong Ka Ri Laiphew Syiem**, Bynta-II (Shillong: St. Anthony's, 1937).

Dalton, E. T. **Descriptive Ethnology of Bengal** (Originally Published 1872, reprinted, Calcutta, 1973).

Darliensung, **The Hmars** (Imphal: The Author, 1987).

Das, B. M. **Variation in Physical Characteristics in the Khasi Population of North East India** (New Delhi: D. K. Publishers Distributors, 1978).

Das, Gurudas **Tribes of Arunachal Pradesh in Transition** (New Delhi: Vikas Publishing House Pvt. Ltd., 1995).

Das, Somen. ed., **Christian Faith and Multiform Culture in India** (Bangalore: UTC, 1987).

Debbarma, D**. Treatise on Traditional Social Institutions of the Tripuri Community** (Agartala: Directorate of Research, 1983).

Debbarma, S. **Origin and Growth of Christianity in Tripura with Special Reference to the New Zealand Baptist Missionary Society, 1938-1988** (New Delhi: Indus Publishing Co., 1996).

Dena, Lal **British Policy towards Manipur, 1891-1919** (Churachandpur: L & R Printing Press, 1984).

Dev, Bimal & D. K. Lahiri, **Manipur Culture and Politics** (Delhi: Mittal Publications, 1985).

Dev Varman, S. B. K. **The Tribes of Tripura: A Dissertation** (Agartala: Directorate of Research, 1986).

Deogaonlar, S. G. ed., **Problems of Development of Tribal Areas** (Delhi, Leeladevi Publications, 1980).

Dihingia, Hameshwar **Assam's Struggles against British Rule, 1820-1863** (New Delhi: Asian Publication Service, 1980).

Donrai, U. **Ka History Shaphang Ka Jing-Wallam Nyngkong eh ia ka Niam Khristan ha Kane Ka ri Khasi Jaintia Da Ka Welsh Calvinistic Methodist Mission** (First Published 1914, revised and reprinted by O. D. Laitphlang, 1956).

Downs, Frederick S. **The Mighty Works of God: A Brief History of the Council of Baptist Churches in North East India: The Mission Period, 1836-1950** (Gauhati: Christian Literature Centre, 1971).

Downs, Frederick S. **Church Union: Theological and Non-Theological Factors** (Shillong: North East India Christian Council, 1965).

Downs, Frederick S. **Christianity in North East India: Historical Perspectives** (Delhi: ISPCK, 1983).

Downs, Frederick S. "Christianity and Cultural Change in North East India", in Somen Das, ed., **Christian Faith and Multiform culture in India** (Bangalore: UTC, 1987).

Downs, F. S. **The Christian Impact on the Status of Women in North East India** (Shillong: NEHU Publications, 1996).

Downs, F. S. **History of Christianity in India: North East India in the Nineteenth and Twentieth Centuries,** Vol. V, Part 5 (Bangalore: The Church History Association of India, 1996).

Dube, S. C. ed., **Tribal Heritage of India, Vol. 1, Ethnicity, Identity and Interaction** (1977).

Durrany, K. S. **The Women's Movement in Religious Communities in India** (Delhi: ISPCK, 2002).

Dutta, B. Ray, **Assam Secretariat 1874-1947: An Administrative History of North-East India** (Calcutta: K. P. Bagchi & Company, 1978).

Dutta, K. N. **Landmarks of the Freedom Struggle in Assam** (Gauhati: Lawyer Book Stall, 1969).

Dutta, P. C. **Arunachal Pradesh: An Overview** (Itanagar: Directorate of Research, 1993).

Dutta, P. N. **Impact of the West on Khasis and Jaintias** (New Delhi: 1982).

Dutta, P. S. ed., **Electoral Politics in North East India** (New Delhi: Omsons Publications, 1986).

Elias, H. **Ki Khanatang U Barim** (Shillong: St. Anthony's, 1972).

Elwin, Verrier, **A Philosophy for NEFA** (Shillong: North East Frontier Agency, 2nd revised ed, 1959).

Elwin, Verrier **India's North – East Frontier in the Nineteenth Century** (Madras: Oxford University Press, 1959).

Evans, S, "Ka Jingpyniaid Balang", in D. Ropmay, ed., **Ka Centenary History Ka Balang Presbyterian Ha Ri Khasi Jaintia Naduh 1841 Haduh 1940** (Shillong: KJP Synod, 1975).

Fernandes, W., G. Bharali and V. Kezo, **The UN Indigenous Decade in Northeast India** (Guwahati: NESRC, 2008).

Fernandes, W., M. Pereira, V. Khatso, **Tribal Customary Laws in Northeast India: Gender and Class Implications** (Guwahati: NESRC, 2008).

Fernando, L. & G. Gispert-Sauch, **Christianity in India: Two Thousand Years of Faith** (New Delhi: Viking by Penguin Books India, 2004).

Ferrando, Stefano Nell' **India Nord-Est** (Roma, 1975).

Gait, Edward. **A History of Assam** (Originally published 1905, reprinted, Gauhati, 1981).

George, K. M. **Christianity in India through the Centuries** (Hyderabad: Authentic, 2007).

Ghosh, S. K, and P. Chopra, **Echoes from North-Eastern India** (New Delhi: S. Chand & Company Ltd., 1980).

Giri, Helen **U Khasi ha Ka Por U Phareng** (Shillong: NEHU Publications, n. d. c2001).

Gohain, B. C. **Human Sacrifice, and Head-hunting in North-Eastern India** (Gauhati: Lawyers Book Stall, 1977).

Gopalakrishnan, R. **Arunachal Pradesh: Land & People** (New Delhi: Omsons Publications, 1994).

Goswami, B. B. ed., **Cultural Profile of Shillong** (Calcutta: Anthropological Survey of India, 1979).

Goswami, P. **Essays on the Folklore and Culture of North Eastern India** (Gauhati: Spectrum Publications, 1983).

Goswami, S. **Aspects of Revenue Administration in Assam, 1826-1874** (Delhi: Mittal Publications, 1989).

Grewal, Dalvinder S. **Tribes of Arunachal Pradesh,** Vol. II (Delhi: South Asia Publications, 1997).

Griffiths, B. **Khasis and the Welsh Legacy** (Cymru: Basil Griffiths, 2007).

Gupta, Pranab Kumar Das **Life and Culture of Matrilineal Tribe of Meghalaya** (New Delhi: Inter-India Publications, 1984).

Gurdon, Major P. R. T. **The Khasis** (First published 1907, reprinted Delhi: Cosmo Publications, 1975).

Handa, R. L. **History of Freedom Struggles in Princely States** (New Delhi: Central News Agency, 1968).

Hansaria, B. L. **Sixth Schedule to the Constitution of India: A Study** (Gauhati: Ashok Publishing House, 1983).

Hedlund, R. E. **Quest for Identity: India's Churches of Indigenous Origin** (Delhi: ISPCK, 2000).

Hefley, James & Marti **God's Tribesman: The Rochunga Pudaite Story** (Wheaton: Victor Books, 1974/1976).

Hnuni, R. L. ed., **Transforming Theology for Empowering Women** (Jorhat: Women's Studies, 1999).

Hodson, T. C. **The Naga Tribes of Manipur** (Delhi: B. R. Publishing Corporation, 1982).

Hodson, T. C. **The Meitheis** (Delhi: B. R. Publishing Corporation, 1982).

Hrangkhuma, F. ed., **Christianity in India: Search for Liberation and Identity** (Delhi: ISPCK, 2000).

Hrangkhuma, F. ed., **Tribes in Transition: Indian Christians Reflection on the Original Inhabitants of the Land** (Bangalore: SAIACS, 1996).

Hughes, R. A. "Ka Mission Jingpynkhiah" in **Ki Khubor Jong Ki Jingiaseng Jubilee** (Shillong: KJP Synod, 1967).

Imchem, N. ed., **Women's Issues in the 21st Century** (Jorhat: Women's Study Centre, 2001).

Imchen, N. ed., **Tribal Women and Globalization** (Jorhat: Women Studies Centre, 2008).

Jaitdkhar, Sib Charan Roy. **Ka Niam Ki-Khasi, Ka Niam Tip-Blei, Tip-Briew, Ka Tien-Hok, Tien-Blei Don-Sot, Don-Kular** (Originally published 1919, reprinted, Shillong: Ri Khasi Press, 1966).

Jajo, C. **Christian Life in a Tribal Context in Manipur** (Ukhrul: Ukhrul District, 1990).

Jamatia, N. **Rev. B. K. Smith: A Man of Vision for Tripura** (Agartala: Naphurai Jamatia, 1998).

Jeyaseelan, L. **Impact of the Missionary Movement in Manipur** (New Delhi: Scholar Publishing House, 1996).

John, C. J. & K. V. Varghese, **Vision to Mission: Fifteen Pioneer Christian Educators** (Thiruvalla: Christava Sahitya Samithi, 2000).

John, E. C. & S. Prabhakar eds., **Christian Identity and Cultural Nationalism: Challenges and Opportunities** (Bangalore: SATHRI, 2006).

Johnstone, J. **Manipur and the Naga Hills** (Delhi: Cultural Publishing House, 1983).

Jones, G. Angel. **Ka History Ka Balang, 1841-1966** (Shillong: KJP Synod, 1966).

Jyrwa, J. Fortis. **The Wondrous Works of God: A Study of the Growth and Development of the Khasi-Jaintia Presbyterian Church in the 20th Century** (Shillong: Mrs. M. B. Jyrwa, Lawjynriew, Nongthymmai, 1980).

Jyrwa, J. F. ed., **Reports of the Foreign Mission of the Presbyterian Church of Wales on Khasi-Jaintia Hills 1864 to 1899** (Shillong: Christian Communications Department, 1998).

Ka History Jong Ka Balang Presbyterian Riatsamthiah, 1960-1985. (Shillong, 1985).

Ka History Lyngkot ki Pastor Ba La Khladnoh Jong Ka Balang Presbyterian ha Ri Khasi-Jaintia (Shillong: Christian Communications Department, 1999).

Ka Jingiateh-Jutang Ka Hima Mylliem, (Shillong, 1938).

Ka Jingialang Kynmaw ia U Babu Jeebon Roy ha ka 20th July 1932, (Shillong, 1933).

Ka Jingialang Kynmaw ia U Sib Charan Roy Jait Dkhar *ha* ka 28th April 1952, (Shillong, 1953).

Ka Kot Maham Shaphang Ka Jingsniew Ka Kiad, Ka Aphin Bad Kiwei Kiwei, (Shillong: The Women's Christian Temperance Union, 1929).

Kamkhenthang, H. **The Paite: A Transborder Tribe of India & Burma** (Delhi: Mittal Publications, 1988).

Kanti, R. D. **Manipur Tribal Scene: Studies in Society and Change** (New Delhi: Inter-India Publications, 1985).

Karotemprel, S. **The Catholic Church in Northeast India, 1890-1990** (Shillong: Vendrame Institute, 1993).

Karotemprel, S. & B. D. Roy, eds., **Tea Garden Labourers of North East India** (Shillong: Vendrame Institute, 1990).

Karotemprel, Sebastian **Albizuri among the Lyngams: A Brief History of the Catholic Mission among the Lyngams of North East India** (Shillong: Vendrame Missiological Institute, 1985).

Keitzar, R. **In Search of a Relevant Gospel Message** (Guwahati: Christian Literature Centre, 1995).

Keitzar, R. ed., **Asian Theology at the Frontiers** (Jorhat: Eastern Theological College, 1993).

Khasi-Jaintia Presbyterian Synod Mihngi: Ki Report bad ki Kam Synod (19-22 March, 2009).

Kharakor, Sr. Philomena **Ka Khasi Kolshor Kumba Ka Paw Ha Ka Khasi Literashor, 1930-1940** (Shillong, 1989).

Kharkongor, I. **Ka History Jong Ka Balang Laban** (Shillong, 1980).

Khasi Ha La Ka Rukom Bad Kiwei de Ki Jingthoh, U. (Shillong: Seng Khasi, 1976).

Khongphai, A. S. **Principles of Khasi Law** (Shillong, 1974).

Khongsit, S. **Ka History jong ka Balang Mawklot** (Shillong: Ka Balang Mawklot, 1985).

Ki Khubor Jong Ki Jingiaseng Jubilee, 1842-1966 (Shillong, 1967).

Kipgen, M. **Christianity and Mizo Culture** (Jorhat: Mizo Theological Association, 1996).

Ki Report bad ki Kam Jong Ka Jingiaseng Kynthei Ri Bhoi Presbyterian Synod Kaba Khatwei (12-15 March, 2009).

Kirti, M. Singh **Religion and Culture of Manipur** (Delhi: Manas Publications, 1988).

Kottupallil, George **History of the Catholic Mission in Central Bengal, 1855-1886** (Shillong: Vendrame Institute, 1988).

Kshiarngap, Rev. S. G. **Ka Miss A. W. Thomas: Ka Nongprat Shrah ha Ryngibah** (Thangsning: IRL Warbah Three Sisters & Family, 2009).

Kuppuswamy, B., **Social Change in India** (New Delhi: Vikas Publishing House Pvt. Ltd. 1989).

Kuriakose, M. K. ed., **History of Christianity in India: Source Materials** (Madras: C.L.S., 1982).

Lahiri, R. M., **The Annexation of Assam, 1824-1854** (Calcutta: Firma KLM, 1975).

Lakiang, U. H. B. **Ka Shnong Jatinga Shnong Baphylla** (Shillong: Author, 2005).

Lalmuankima, C. **In His Service: History and Missionary Work of Lairam Baptist Church** (Lawngtlai: Publication Board of the LBC, 1997).

Laloo, Donbok T. **Ka Rongbiria U Hynniewtrep** (Shillong, 1974).

Lalsawma, **Revivals: The Mizo Way** (Aizawl: Author, 1994).

Lasetso, R. ed., **Garnering Tribal Resources for Doing Tribal Christian Theology** (Jorhat: ETC Programme Coordination, 2008).

Lavan, S. **Unitarians and India: A Study in Encounter and Response** (1977).

Lloyd, J. M. History of the Church in Mizoram: Harvest in the Hills (Aizawl: Synod Publication Board, 1991).

Long, Rev. J. L. **Analysis of the Rajmala or Chronicles of Tripura** (Agartala: Tripura State Tribal Cultural Research Institute, First published 1850/ reprinted 1995).

Longchar, A. Wati **The Traditional Worldview and Modernity** (Jorhat: ETC, 1995).

Longchar, A. W. & Y. Vashum, eds., **The Tribal Worldview and Ecology** (Jorhat: Tribal Study Centre, 1998).

Longkumer, C. S. **Nagaland Missionary Movement: Celebrating 25 Years of Ministry, 1970-1994** (1994).

Longkumer, L. ed., **No More Sorrow in God's Garden of Justice: Tribal Women Doing Theology** (Jorhat: Women Study Department, 2007).

Longkumer, L. **Christian Education for Adults in Tribal Context** (Jorhat: Author, 1998).

Lotsuro, Angeline **The Nagas: A Missionary Challenge** (Shillong: VIP, 2000).

Lyngdoh, J. D. S., **I Thymmei Ka Long-Briew** (Mawmluh, 1979).

Lyngdoh, Mon and Passah, John **Ka History Lyngkot Ka Christ National Church Khasi and Jaintia Hills** (Shillong, 1933).

Lyngdoh, Maurice G. **Life and Works of Dr. Homiwell Lyngdoh** (Shillong, 1980).

Lyngdoh, R.S. **Ka Histori Ka Thoh Ka Tar**, Bynta I (Shillong, 1988).

Lyngdoh, S. Sngi. **Ki Riti-Khyndew ba la buh u Longshuwa-Manshuwa Jong Ka Ri Bhoi** (1965).

Mackenzie, Alexander **The North East Frontier of India (Originally published 1884, in a title History of the Relations of the Government with the**

Hill Tribes of the North-East Frontier of Bengal, reprinted, Delhi: Mittal Publication, 1979).

Majaw, S. S. **U Kpa ka Thoh ka Tar Khasi** (Shillong: S. S. Majaw, 1992).

Majumdar, D. N. and B. Datta Ray, **Tribal Occupational Mobility** (Calcutta: Research India Publications, 1984).

Mali, D. D. **An Introduction to the Economy of Meghalaya** (Shillong: Retina's Mascot, 1978).

Maliekal, George **History of the Catholic Church among the Khasis** (Shillong: DBIC, 2005).

Malngiang, Pascal. **Ki Nongmait Shrah: Ki Missionary Salvadorian** 1890-1914 (Shillong: Don Bosco Publication, 1983).

Malngiang, Pascal **U Apostol Ki Khasi-Pnar: Ka Jingim Jong U Phadar Vendra 1893-1957** (Shillong: Archbishop's House, 1985).

Marbaniang, Iscot **Assam in Nutshell** (Shillong: Chapala Book Stall 1970).

Marwein, I. Drickarton **Ka History Ka Balang ha Ri Bhoi, 1875-1984** (Umsning, 1984).

Marwein, Phrangbonsen Trevor **Meghalaya Hand Book** (Shillong: Warphlang Garikhana Road, 1981).

Massey, J. ed., **Contextual Theological Education** (Delhi: ISPCK, 1993).

Matthew, T. **Tribal Economy of North Eastern Region** (Gauhati: Spectrum Publications, 1980).

Mathur, P. R. G. **Khasi of Meghalaya: A Study in Tribalism and Religion** (New Delhi: Cosmo Publications, 1979).

Mathur, P. R. G."Khasi Solidarity Movements", in K.S. Singh, ed., **Tribal Movements in India**. Vol. I (New Delhi: Manohar Publications, 1982).

Mattumana, M. **Christianity in Assam and Inter-Faith Dialogue** (Indore: Satprakashan Sanchar Kendra, 1984).

Mawrie, H. Onderson, **Ka Pyrkhat U Khasi** (Nongkrem, 1973).

Mawrie, H. Onderson **The Essence of the Khasi Religion** (Shillong: Seng Khasi, 1981).

Mawrie, H. Onderson **The Khasi Milieu** (New Delhi: Concept Publishing Company, 1981).

Mawthoh, P. R. **Balei U Khasi um roi-spah**? (Shillong, 1967).

M'Cosh, John **Topography of Assam** (First published 1837, reprinted Delhi: Sanskaran Prakashak, 1975).

Mibang, T. **Social Change in Arunachal Pradesh: The Minyongs, 1947-1987** (New Delhi: Omsons Publications, 1994).

Miri, Mrinal ed., **Linguistic Situation in North-East India** (Shillong: North-East India Council for Social Science Research, 1982).

Miri, Sujata ed., **Religion and Society of North–East India** (New Delhi: Vikas Publishing House Pvt. Ltd. 1980).

Morris, John Hughes **The History of the Welsh Calvinistic Methodists Foreign Mission: To the End of the Year 1904** (Carnavon: The C.M. Book Room, 1910).

Morris, John Hughes **The Story of Our Foreign Mission** (Liverpool: Hugh Evans & Sons Ltd., 1930).

Morris, John Hughes **Christ's Ambassadors in Khasia: William Lewis, Jerman Jones** (Liverpool: Foreign Mission of the Presbyterian Church of Wales, 1939).

Mukhim, Rose Mary **Ki Mraw Ka Jingngeitbieit** (Shillong, 1982).

Murch, J. DeForest **Christians Only: A History of the Restoration Movement** (Cincinnati: Standard Publishing, 1962).

Murry, E. **Tribal Spirituality Reconsidered: A Psychological Study of Religion** (Delhi: ISPCK, 1995).

Nakane, Chie **Garo and Khasi: A Comparative Study in Matrilineal Systems** (Paris: Norton & Co., 1967).

Nath, N. C. tr., **Sri Rajmala,** Vol. I to IV (Agartala: Tribal Research Institute, 1999).

NBCC Women Department 25th Anniversary: A Brief History.

Natarajan, Nalini **The Missionary among the Khasis** (New Delhi: Sterling Publishers Private Limited., 1977).

Nengzakhup, S. **Amazing Mizo Missions: The Presbyterian Church of Mizoram** (Bangalore: SAIACS, 2000).

Ngapkynta, H. B. **William Carey in a New Perspective** (Guwahati: Spectrum Publications, 2004).

Ngapkynta, H. B. **The Church of England Now The Church of North India in Bengal, Assam & Meghalaya** (Shillong: Ri Khasi Book Agency, 2009).

Nichols-Roy, J. J. M. **U Blei Bad Ka Spah** (Shillong: Shillong Printing Works, 1926).

Nongbri, B. L. ed., **Theological Education in North East India: Problems and Prospects** (Shillong: JRTS, 2008).

Nonglait, U Homiwell Lyngdoh **Ka Pomblang Nongkrem bad ka Thang Syiem Sohra** (Shillong, 1928).

Nonglait, U Homiwell Lyngdoh **Ki Syiem Khasi Bad Synteng** (Originally published 1938, reprinted, Shillong, 1964).

Nonglait, U Homiwell Lyngdoh **Ka Niam Khasi**, (Originally published 1937, reprinted, Shillong, 1970).

Nongrum, U Kitbor W. **Ki Nongthoh Kot Khasi**, Ka Bynta I (Shillong, 1982).

Nongrum, U Kitbor W. **Ki Nongthoh Kot Khasi**, Ka Bynta II (Shillong, 1982).

Nongsiej, T. **Ka Kam U Blei Ha Ka Mawphlang-Khadsawphra Presbytery 1896-1949** (Nongsawlia: Cherra Theol. College, 1984).

Nuh, V. K. **Nagaland Church and Politics** (Kohima: Author, 1986).

Nungshitula, **The Naga Images of the Human Being** (Jorhat: Tribal Study Centre, 2001).

Ondromoney, U. **Ka Geography Khasi**, Part I, Second edition (Calcutta, Baptist Mission Press, 1927).

Osik, N. N. **A Brief History of Arunachal Pradesh** (New Delhi: Omsons Publications, 1996).

Pakem, B. ed., **Shillong, 1971-1981** (Calcutta, Research India Publications, 1984).

Pakem, B. ed., **Insurgency in North East India** (New Delhi: Omsons Publications, 1997).

Pakhuongte, R. **The Power of the Gospel among the Hmar Tribe** (Shillong: EFCI, 1983).

Parrot, S. N. **The Religion of Manipur** (Calcutta: Firma KLM Private Ltd., 1980).

Pathrapankal, J. ed., **Service and Salvation: Nagpur Theological Conference on Evangelization** (Bangalore: Theological Publications in India, 1973).

Patrick, G. **The Role of Oral Traditions in Theology** (Shillong: DBIC, 1999).

Paviotti, O. **The Work of His Hands: The Story of the Archdiocese of Shillong-Guahati, 1934-1984**, (Shillong: Archbishop's House, 1987).

Pianazzi, Archimedes **Dare and Hope: Life of the Salesian Missionary Bishop Archbishop Louis Mathias S. D. B**. 1887-1965. trans. by Hugh Meghinchy (Madras: Salesian Publications, 1979). Latin original entitled *Ardisci e spera: Vita el Vescovo missionario Luigi Mathias* 1887-1965, Published 1976.

Prabhananda, Swami **U Nongprat Lynti ha Ri Lum Khasi** (Cherrapunji: Ramakrishna Mission, 1974).

Pryse W. **Introduction to the Khasia Language** (Calcutta, 1855).

Pugh, B. M., **The Story of a Tribal: An Autobiography** (Bombay: Orient Longman Ltd., 1976).

Pugh, F. M. **Ka History Jong Ka Assam** (Shillong, 1963, reprinted 1975).

Puthenpurakal, J. **Bishop Orestes Marengo, SDB: North East India's Unparalleled Missionary** (Shillong: VIP, 2000).

Rafy, Mrs. **Khasi Folk Tales** (Originally published 1920, reprinted Guahati: Spectrum Publications, 1985).

Rao, O. M. **Some Concerns of the Indian Church** (Guwahati: Christian Literature Centre, n. d.).

Rao, V. M. **Tribal Women of Arunachal Pradesh** (New Delhi: Mittal Publications, 2003).

Rao, V. Venkata, **A Century of Tribal Politics in North East India, 1874-1974** (New Delhi: S. Chand & Company Ltd., 1976)

Rao, V. Venkata, Barrister Pakem and Niru Hazarika, **A Century of Government and Politics in North-East India, Vol. 2. Meghalaya 1874 to 1983** (New Delhi: S. Chand & Company Ltd., 1984).

Ray, B. D. & S. P. Agrawal eds., **Reorganization of North-East India Since 1947** (New Delhi: Concept Publishing Co., 1996).

Reid, J. K. S. **Presbyterians and Unity** (London: A. R. Mowbray & Co. Ltd., 1962).

Ri Bhoi Presbyterian Synod: Ki Report bad Ki Kam (12-15 March, 2009).

Roberts, Mrs. John ed., **Jaintia Folklore and Legends and the History of the Khasi Religion: From the Papers of the Rev. John Roberts D. D.** (Carnavon, n.d.).

Roberts, J. H. **Ka Shang Khmih-Pyrthei la Ka Ri Khasi: Ka Diari Naduh Ka Sngi U Blei, Nai Nohprah 14 tarik 1884 Haduh Ka Sngi Saitjain, Nai Kylla Lyngkot 17 tarik 1885**, tr. F. M. Pugh (Shillong, 1964).

Robinson, William **A Descriptive Account of Assam** (Originally published 1841, reprinted Delhi, Sanskaran Prakashak 1975).

Rodborne, Trevore, **Ka Niam Jong U Khasi-Pnar** (Shillong, 1946).

Rongpi, S. **Principles of Effective Church Administration: A Study of the Karbi Baptist Churches in Karbi Anglong** (Jorhat: Tribal Study Centre, 2005).

Ropmay. D. ed., **Ka Centenary History Ka Balang Presbyterian Ha Ri Khasi-Jaintia Naduh 1841 Haduh 1940** (Shillong: KJP Synod, 1975).

Roy, Jyotirmoy **History of Manipur** (Imphal: Eastlight, 1958).

Rymbai, R. T. "Some Aspects of the religion of the Khasi-Pnars" in U Hipshon Roy, ed., **Khasi Heritage: A Collection of Essays on Religion and Culture** (Shillong: Seng Khasi, 1979).

Rymbai, R. T. **Ban Pynieng La Ka Rasong bad Kiwei de ki Ese** (Shillong, 1982).

Rymbai, R. T**. Ka Shadsuk Mynsiem** (Shillong: Seng Khasi, n.d.).

Rynjah, Tngensi **Ka History Ka Ri Khasi-Jaintia: Ki Por Barim Bajah** (Shillong, 1983).

Roy, U Hipshon ed., **Where lies the soul of our race**? (Shillong: Seng Khasi, 1982).

Roy, U Hipshon ed., **Khasi Heritage: A Collection of Essays on Khasi Religion and Culture** (Shillong: Seng Khasi, 1979).

Roy, U Jeebon, **Ka Kot Pule Khasi Nyngkong** (Shillong, 1899).

Roy, U Jeebon, **Ka Kitab Ba Batai Pynshynna Shaphang Uwei U Blei** (Shillong, 1901).

Roy, U Jeebon, **Ka Niam Jong Ki Khasi** (Shillong: The Ri Khasi Press, 1887).

Saikia, Dwika **Development of Elementary Education in Khasi and Jaintia Hills** (Shillong: B. R. Saikia Prakashan, 1984).

Saika, J. P. ed., **The Land of Seven Sisters** (Guahati: DIPR, Assam, 1976).

Samaddar, H. R. **All One-in-Christ Church Fellowship: Bridal, Apostolic and Prophetic** (Debagram: A Fellowship Publication, 1982).

Sandys, comp., **History of Tripura** (Agartala: Tripura State Tribal Cultural Research Institute, First published 1915/reprinted 1997).

Sangma, M. S. & D. R. Syiemlieh, eds., **Essays on Christianity in North–East India** (New Delhi: Indus Publishing Co., 1994).

Sarkar, R. L. **Christian Tea Garden Workers of Tribal Origin: A Social, Economic and Political Study** (Delhi: ISPCK, 1998).

Sen, Sipra **Tribes and Castes of Manipur** (New Delhi: Mittal Publications, 1982).

Sen, Soumen **Social and State Formation in Khasi-Jaintia Hills: A Study of Folklore** (Delhi: B.R. Publishing Corporation, 1985).

Sen, S. ed., **Women in Meghalaya** (Delhi: Dasa Publishing House, 1992).

Shadap, Namita Catherine-Sen **The Origin and Early History of Khasi-Synteng People** (Calcutta: Firma KLM Private Ltd., 1981).

Shimray, S. ed., **Tribal Theology: A Reader** (Jorhat: Tribal Study Centre, 2003).

Shispah Sanphew Snem Mynshwa: U Tirot Singh Bad Ka Mynnor ba iphuh iphieng (Shillong: Khasi Cultural Society, 1984).

Shourie, A. **Missionaries in India: Continuities, Changes, Dilemmas** (New Delhi: ASA Publications, 1994).

Shukhla, Bhanu Pratap **What Ails India's North-East** (New Delhi: Suruchi Sahitya, 1980).

Shullai, L. G. **Ki Hima Khasi** (Shillong, 1975).

Singh, Ch. P. ed., **Tribalism and the Tragedy of the Commons: Land, Identity & Development-The Manipur Experience** (New Delhi: Akansha Publishing House, 2009).

Singh, J. P. **Urban Land Use Planning in Hill Areas: A Case Study of Shillong** (Delhi, Inter-India Publication, 1970).

Singh, K. M. **History of Christian Missions in Manipur and other Neighbouring States** (New Delhi: Mittal Publications, 1982).

Singh, K. Suresh ed., **Tribal Situation in India, (1972), Singh, K. Suresh ed., Tribal Movements in India,** Vol. I (1982).

Singh, Kynpham **Ka Jingsdang ka Jingspel bad Jingthoh ia ka Ktien Khasi da ki Dak Roman** (Shillong: Author, 1969).

Singh, Kynpham **Ka Jingim U Babu Jeebon Roy: The Father of Modern Khasis** (Shillong, 1972).

Singh, Kynpham **A Collection of Writings About Khasi Hills and A Collection of Poems** (Shillong, 1979).

Singh, Ollin **Ka Jingiathuh Lyngkot Shaphang Ka Jingsdang bad jingroi Ka Kam U Blei hapoh Ka Thain Ri War Khadar Blang naduh ka snem 1870 haduh ka snem 1970** (1975).

Singh, R. P. **Geography of Manipur** (New Delhi: National Book Trust, 1982).

Singh, U Rabon **Ka Kitab Niam Khein Ki Khasi** (Probably written 1900, reprinted Shillong: 1972).

Singh, Yogendra **Modernization of Indian Tradition: A Systemic Study of Social Change** (Jaipur: Rawat Publication, 1986).

Smith, A. S. **The Serampore Mission Enterprise** (Bangalore: Centre for Contemporary Christianity, 2006).

Snaitang, O. L. **U Rev. J. J. M. Nichols-Roy, Ka Balang U Blei Bad Ka Jingiatylli Khristan** (Shillong, 1983).

Snaitang, O. L. **Tylli La Ia Saphret Te: ka History jong ki Balang Khristan ha Meghalaya naduh 1813 haduh Mynta** (Shillong: Dr. O. L. Snaitang, 2006).

Snaitang, O. L. **Rev. J. J. M. Nichols-Roy and National Integration** (Shillong: El Sawkmie Group of Publication, 2009).

Snaitang, O. L. ed., **Churches of Indigenous Origins in Northeast India** (Delhi: ISPCK, 2000).

Snaitang, O. L. & Merostar Rani, eds., **Christianity and National Integration in India** (New Delhi: Akansha Publishing House, 2009).

Souvenir of Lairam Baptist Church, 1894-1994 (Lawngtlai: LBC, 1994).

Srinivas, M. N. **Social Change in Modern India** (Bombay: Allied Publishers, 1966).

Stephens, C. L. **Khasi Primer** (Khadsawphra, 1895).

Subba, T. B., J. Puthenpurakal, S. J. Puykunnel, eds., **Christianity and Change in Northeast India** (New Delhi: Concept Publishing Co., 2009).

Sumi, Akheto **Perspectives: Current Issues in Theological Thought** (Mokokchung: CTC, 2002).

Syiemlieh, David R. **British Administration in Meghalaya: Policy and Pattern** (New Delhi: Heritage Publishers, 1989).

Tariang, J. E. **Ka Histori Ka Ri Khasi-Jaintia** (Shillong: Mrs. B. W. Tariang, 2005).

Tariang, J. E. **Bormanik Syiem: The Last of the Syiems of Shyllong** (Shillong: J. N. Bawri, 1994).

Taylor, R. W. ed., **Society and Religion** (Madras: CLS, 1976).

Tewari, R. P. **Development and Problems of Education in North East** India (Shillong: Akashi Book Depot, 1989).

Thakur, P. **India's North East: A Multi-Faceted View** (Tinsukia: Prakash Publishing House, 1982).

Tham, Soso **Ki Sngi Barim U Hynniew Trep** (Originally published 1936, reprinted, Shillong, 1976).

Thanzauva, K. **Towards a Tribal Theology: The Mizo Perspective** (Jorhat: Mizo Theological Association, 1989).

Thanzauva, K. ed., **Reports of the Foreign Mission of the Presbyterian Church of Wales on Mizoram, 1894-1957** (Aizawl: The Synod Literature & Publication Board, 1997).

The Amazing Guidance of God: Manipur South Christian Diamond Jubilee Souvenir, 1910-1985 (Churachandpur: Independent Church of India, 1985).

The Khasi Primer: Ka Kitab Nyngkong Ban Hikai Pule ia ka Ktien Khasi (1916).

Thomas, M. M. and R. W. Taylor, eds., **Tribal Awakening** (Bangalore: Christian Institute for the Study of Religion and Society, 1965).

Tirkey, C. A. B. **Religion-Primal Religions** (Delhi: ISPCK, 2005).

Tombi, N. Singh **Manipur and the Mainstream** (Delhi: Rajesh Printing Press, 1975).

Vanlalchhuanawma, **Christianity and Subaltern Culture: Revival Movement as a Cultural Response to Westernization in Mizoram** (Delhi: ISPCK, 2007).

Vanlalchhuanawma, ed., **Mizoram Presbyterian Church: A History of Departments** (Aizawl: Aizawl Theological College, 2007).

Vanlalchhunga, **Marvellous Mission: The role of the Welsh Presbyterian Mission in the Transformation of Socio-Cultural Life in North East India** (Aizawl: Shalom Publications, 2008).

Vincent, Kaushal. **Socio-Economic Study of Bhoilymbong: A Village in Meghalaya** (Bangalore: Christian Institute for the Study of Religion and Society, 1978).

Warbah, W. **Ka Histori Ka Balang Smit, 1927-1977** (Smit, 1978).

Wendel, F. **Calvin: The Origins and Development of His Religious Thought** (London: Collins, 1965, reprinted 1974).

Zaltmann, Gerald and Robert Duncan, **Strategies for Planned Change** (New York: A Wilay-Interscience Publication, 1977).

Zeliang, E. **A History of the Manipur Baptist Convention** (Imphal: The MBC, 2005).

Zeliang, E. Comp., **History of Christianity in Manipur: Source Materials** (Guwahati: CLC, 2005).

Zimba, D. T. **Geographical Identity of Meghalaya** 4th ed. (Shillong: P. Zimba, Shillong 1, 1989).

Articles in Ecclesiastical and Non – Ecclesiastical Journals

Alter, James P. "Liberty, Equality, Fraternity: Themes in Anglo-Saxon Protestant Missions in the Church in North India, 1800-1914", **Indian Church History Review**, VIII.1 (June 1974).

Alukal, Jacob "Marriage among the Khasis", **Indian Missiological Review**, 2.1 (January 1980), pp. 41-50.

Berry, R. S. "Ka Jingsneng Tymmen Akor Babha", **U Khasi Mynta**, 9 (Nai Rymphang 1897), pp. 3-4.

Bornadi, Paul, "In Assam during holiday-time", **The Salesian Bulletin**, XV. 4. (September-October 1923), pp. 149-152.

Bornadi, Paul, "Heathen Worship amongst the Khasi Hills of Assam", **The Salesian Bulletin**, XVII. 5 (September-October 1925), pp. 146-49.

Bonheim, C. ed., **Ka Iing Khristan**, 1.2 (Risau, 1906).

Cajee, T. ed., **Ka Syngkhong Jingtip** (Iaiong 1937 to Iaiong 1938).

Deponte, John S. C. "Missionary Episode: An Orphan to adopt", **The Salesian Bulletin**, XV.3 (May-June 1923), pp. 1-3.

Diengdoh, Hormu Rai "Ka jingiapoi Kurim bad Ka Jingiaiohtnga", **Ka Juk**, 1-9 (September 1933), pp. 8-12.

Diengdoh, Hormu Rai ed., **U Khasi Mynta**, (Lber 1896 to Kyllalyngkot 1905).

Dkhar, Khasi J. "Opening Speech", **U Nongialam Katholik**, 6 (Jyllieu 1903), pp. 94-97.

Don Bosco in India 1.1 (December 1930) to 111.12 (December 1933).

Downs, Frederick S "New Perspectives on the Missionary Role in the Nineteenth Century Language Agitation in Assam", **Indian Church History Review**, XXX. 1 (June 1986), pp. 3-29.

Downs, Frederick S. "Rangamati: A Christian Community in North East India during the Seventeenth and Eighteenth Centuries", **Indian Church History Review**, XII. 2 (December 1978), pp. 88-89.

Downs, Frederick S. "Tribal Ecumenism in North East India: The Christian Role in Solidarity Movements", **ETC Journal** 2.2 (January-May 1989), pp. 4-66.

Downs, Frederick S. "The Church of Christ in North East India", **National Christian Council Review**, LXXXV.9 (September 1965), pp. 377-82.

Downs, Frederick S. "Faith and Life-Style: How Christianity was understood by 19th Century Converts in North East India", **Bangalore Theological Forum**, XIV.1 (January-June 1982), pp. 20-43.

Downs, Frederick S. "Early Christian Contacts with North East India", **Indian Church History Review**, V. 1 (June 1971), pp. 69-77.

Duncan, S.J. ed., **Ka Syngkhong Jingtip** 1.1 (Rymphang 1958).

Evans, E. "The Century of the Welsh Mission in Assam", **National Christian Council Review**, LX1.3, (March 1941), pp. 124-131.

Fernando, Fr. "Flowering Christianity in the Salesian Mission Assam", **The Salesian Bulletin,** XVIII-4 (July-August 1926), pp.115-117.

Ganguly, Tapash "Arise; Awake! The Call has been given out for 100 years now", **The Week**, 5.11 (March 1-7, 1987).

"Haba Ka Jingialong Shi-Kha-Shi-man ka la Poi Shaba eh", **Ka Juk**, 2.10 & 11 (October and November 1934), pp. 4-6.

Hauber, Don "Life in Assam", **The Salesian Bulletin**, XV.2 (March-April 1923), pp. 46-47.

Hodson, T.C "Notes on the Marriage of Cousins in India" **Man in India**, V. 324 (September & December 1925), p. 163ff.

"Ia Kiei Yn Khot Ki Khasi?" **Ka Pyrta U Riewlum**, (2 June 1959), p. 1.

"Jah Burom, Ka" **U Lurshai**, (May 1910), p. 2.

"Jingdih Kiad, Ka" **U Khasi Mynta**, 1 (Lber 7, 1866), p. 3.

"Jingiadei Ki Sorkar bad Ki Syiem Khasi Ki Kular-rim, Ka" **U Nongphira**, 17 (Nai Jymmang 1904), pp. 65-66.

Jingialap-Gospel Bakhadduh, Ka Bulletin No. 6/1 (1989).

"Jumai ha ka 12 tarik u Nai Jylliew 1897, U" **U Khasi Mynta**, 14 (Nailur, 1, 1897).

"Ka Jingkhot U Blei Ia I Rev. J.J.M. Nichols-Roy ban trei ha ka lyngkha jong U," **Ka Jingshai ka Gospel** (December 1959).

"Ka Jinglong jaidbynriew Khun Khasi Shi byllien, Kaba Kylluid jingmut ban mane mashin, ban nguh dem, ban ngeit ban leh," **Ka Iing Khristan**, XII. 1 (Kylla Lyngkot 1926), pp. 4-6.

"Ka Jingiapthem ha Mawkhar," **U Khasi Mynta**, 2 (Jymmang 1, 1896), pp. 4-5.

"Ka Jingkren Paidbah Shaphang La Ka-Niam," **U Nongpynim**, 2 (Nai Iaiong, 1928), pp. 1-9.

"Ka Jingkyrsiew bad Plie Lynti ia ka Jingmut Ki Para Khasi," **U Khasi Mynta**, 43 (Lyber 1900). pp. 4-5.

"Ka Jingphla U Sachindra Nath Dkhar," **Ka Jingshai Ka Gospel**, XXXII. 6 (June 1936), p. 6.

"Ka Dorbar ka Dorsha Jong Ki Khasi Hyndai," **U Nongialam Katholik**, 1 (Kyllalyngkot 1903), pp. 29-32.

"Ka Jingiasyrdoh lang Ki Hima Khasi (Federation of Khasi Native States)," **U Lurshai,** XIX. 9 (September 1929), pp. 1-2.

"Ka Jing Shong Kurim Khristan ba Nyngkong ha ri Khasi Synteng," **U Lurshai,** XV. 3 (March 1925), p. 4.

"Ka Kot Jingrwai Thymmai Ki Khristan Khasi," **U Khasi Mynta**, *36* (Nailar 1, 1899, pp. 3-4.

"Ka Kajia Ialeh Ilekshon Member Jong Ka Assam Council," **Nongpynim**, 15 (Nai Jyllieu 1929), pp. 16-17.

"Ka Ministry Assam," **U Lurshai**, (January 1940).

"Ka Niam Khasi," **U Khasi Mynta**, 1 (Kylla Lyngkot 1, 1898), pp. 1-2.

"Ka Niam Khasi-2," **U Khasi Mynta**, 19 (Rymphang 1, 1898), pp. 1-2.

Ka Pateng Khristan, (1897-1903), (1937-1991).

"Ka Synjuk Khasi-Synteng (Khasi-Synteng United Guild)," **U Nongphira**, 63 (Lber 1907), pp. 10-11.

"Ka Welsh Mission ha ri Khasi," **U Nongialam Khristan**, XXIV. 2 (December, 1925), p. 177ff.

Karotemprel, Sebastian "The Catholic School and a Growing Church", **Indian Missiological Review**, 2.3 (July 1980), p. 241f.

Karotemprel, Sebastian "Salesian Contribution to Evangelization in North East India : An Evaluation", **Indian Missiological Review**, (January 1984), pp. 5-19.

"Ki Khasi ki dei ban Pule Bangla," **U Khasi Mynta**, 31 (Lber 1, 1899), p. 1.

"Ki Khasi mynhynndai bad ki Khasi mynta", **U Nongialam Katholik**, 9 (Nailur 1902), pp. 107-109.

"Ki Khasi Hyndai", **U Nongialam Katholik**, 1 (Kyllalyngkot, 1903), pp. 3-15.

"Ki Khristan bad Ka Ain Shongkurim", **U Lurshai**, (January 1920), p. 2.

"Ki Khubor Mynsiem", **U Nongpynim**, 53 (Jymmang 1906), pp. 169-70.

Khasiphilos, "Shaphang Ki Jingkhaii Ka Ri Khasi", **U Khasi Mynta**, 9 (Nai Rymphang 1. 1897), pp. 4-5.

Kottupallil, George "Don Bosco, Don Rua and India", **Indian Missiological Review**, *10. 1* (January 1988), 53-63, 99.

Kottupallil, George "Roman Catholics and Shillong 1871-1890", **Indian Church History Review**, XXIII. 1 (June 1989), pp. 72-3.

Laitphlang, W. R. "Ka Niam ha U Khasi", **Seng Khasi**, 5. 19 (December 1981), pp. 4-10.

"La leh bein ia ki Khasi: Ia Ka Shnong Nongwah la Kwah ban Pyniasoh bad Ka District Khasi Jaintia Hills", **Ka Pyrta U Riewlum**, (10 June, 1959), p. 1.

Lish, A. B. "A Brief Account of the Khasis", **The Calcutta Christian Observer**, VII (January to December 1838), pp. 129-143.

Lyngdoh, M. "Ka jingkhein Jaid ki Khasi bad Ki Synteng sha ki Kynthei" **U Lurshai**, (May 1912), pp. 1-3.

Mac Donald "Ka Nongtymmen bad ka Nongkhynraw", **U Lurshai**, (January 1921), pp. 3-4.

Mac Donald "Ka Nongtymmen bad ka Nongkhynraw", **U Lurshai**, (February 1921), pp. 3-4.

Mathias, Mgr. Louis "Assam", **The Salesian Bulletin**, XIV. 5 (September-October 1922), pp. 147-150.

Mathias, Mgr. Louis “The Perfecture Apotolic of Assam”, **The Salesian Bulletin**, XV. 6 (November-December 1923), pp. 174-176.

Mawroh, J., “Ka Rukom Ka Jinghiar Pateng Ka Niam Khasi”, **U Lurshai**, (January 1921), pp. 2-3.

Menamparambil, Bishop Thomas “The Role of Youth in Salesian Missionary Methods”, **Indian Missiological Review**, (January 1984), pp. 59-67.

Missionary Herald, CC XXIV (June 1838).

Muenzloher, A. ed., **Ka Iing Khristan**, 1.11 (Naitung 1908).

Nichols-Roy, J. J. M. “Ka Ain Pyrshah ia kaba Dih Sigret”, **Ka Jingshai Ka Gospel**, XXI, 10 (October 1925).

Nichols-Roy, J. J. M. “Ki Syiem Khasi”, **Ka Jingshai Ka Gospel**, XIX, 6 (June 1923), p. 4.

Nichols-Roy, J. J. M. “Ki Kynthei Assam Bad Shillong Kin ioh vote”, **Ka Jingshai Ka Gospel,** XX, 12 (December 1924), p. 12.

Nichols-Roy, J. J. M. “Ka Jingsngewthuh bakla jong ki briew ba ka niam kam dei ban ia khleh bad ka kam synshar-1”, **Ka Jingshai Ka Gospel**, XLVIII, 10 (October & November 1952), pp. 1-3.

Nichols-Roy, J. J. M. “Ka Jingsngewthuh bakla shaphang ka jingpyniakhleh ia ka Niam Bad ka Politics”, **Ka Jingshai Ka Gospel**, XLVIII/XLIX, 12 & 1 (December 1952 and January 1953), pp. 1-6.

Nongpyrta Shua Ka Jingwan U Khrist, U Special Jubilee Issue (XXI, 9 & 10, !980).

“Notes on Assam”, **The Salesian Bulletin**, XIV. 5 (September & October 1922), pp. 147-150.

Pugh. B. “U Khasi Lawei”, **U Lurshai**, XIX. 3 (March 1829), pp. 3-4.

Puthenpurackal, J. “Missionary Methods of the Protestants”. **Indian Missiological Review,** (January 1984), pp. 3-49.

Roberts, J. and J. C. Evans, eds., **U Nongialam Khristan**, 1.1 (July 1902).

Roy, Sib Charan “Ka Niam Khein-kur Khein-kha Ki Khasi”, **U Nongpynim**, 4 (Nai Jylliew 192), p. 1f.

Roy, Sib Charan ed., **U Nongphira** (Nai Kyllalyngkot 1904 to Jylliew & Naitung 1915).

“Seng Khasi, Ka” **U Khasi Mynta**, 53 (Kyllalyngkot 1, 1901). pp. 4-5.

Sinha, A. P. “Khasi Language and the Changing Society”. **Khasi Studies**, 11.3 (October-December 1988), pp. 44-47.

“Skul ha ri Khasi bad Synteng, Ki” **U Khasi Mynta**, 10 (Nai Lber 1, 1897), pp. 3-4.

Snaitang, O. L. “Christianity and Cultural Change among the Khasis” **Indian Church History Review,** XXIII. 1 (June 1989).

“Social Creed”, **U Lurshai**, (August 1910), p. 2.

Solomon, J. "Ka Jingroi Jong Ka Ri Khasi", **U Khasi Mynta**, (Lber 7, 1896), pp. 1-2.

Stroscio, R. "A History of Salesian Missionary Activity in Eastern India", **Indian Missiological Review**, (January 1984), pp. 1-37.

"Table of Kindred and Affinity, A" **Ka Juk**, 2.10 & 11 (October and November 1934), pp. 4-6.

"The Advancement of the Khasis and their Future Prospects," **U Khasi Mynta**, *9* (Nai Rymphang 1897), pp. 1-2.

Thekkedathu, Joseph "Missionary Methods of the Salvatorians", **Indian Missiological Review**, (January 1984), pp. 50-5.

"U Minister Thymmai Jong Ka Assam," **Ka Jingshai Ka Gospel**, XXIII. 2 (February 1928).

U Khasi, "Ka Election da u Paidbah bad ka jingthung. S'iem", **U Nongialam Katholik,** 2 (Rymphang 1902), pp. 1-20.

U Khasi J. Dkr "Ki Khasi Hyndai", Supplement Jong **U Nongialam Katholik**, 13 (Naiwing 1902), pp. 164-165.